Datsun Cherry Owners Workshop Manual

by J H Haynes
Member of the Guild of Motoring Writers
and H S H Phelps

Models covered:

Datsun Cherry 100A Saloon   988 cc
Datsun Cherry 100A Estate   988 cc
Datsun Cherry 120A Coupe   1171 cc

Does not cover the Datsun F11

ISBN 0 85696 195 7

ABCDE
F

Printed in England   *(195 - 4N5)*

Haynes Publishing Group
Sparkford Nr Yeovil
Somerset BA22 7JJ England

Haynes Publications, Inc
861 Lawrence Drive
Newbury Park
California 91320 USA

Acknowledgements

Thanks are due to the Nissan Motor Company Limited of Japan for the supply of technical information and certain illustrations. Castrol Limited provided lubrication data, and the Champion Sparking Plug Company provided the spark plug photographs.

Lastly, thanks to all of those people at Sparkford who helped in the production of this manual.

About this manual

Its aim

The aim of this book is to help you get the best value from your car. It can do so in two ways. First it can help you decide what work must be done, even should you choose to get it done by a garage, the routine maintenance and the diagnosis and course of action when random faults occur. But it is hoped that you will also use the second and fuller purpose by tackling the work yourself. This can give you the satisfaction of doing the job yourself. On the simpler jobs it may even be quicker than booking the car into a garage and going there twice, to leave and collect it. Perhaps most important, much money can be saved by avoiding the costs a garage must charge to cover their labour and overheads.

The book has drawings and descriptions to show the function of the various components so that their layout can be understood. Then the tasks are described and photographed in a step-by-step sequence so that even a novice can cope with complicated work. Such a person is the very one to buy a car needing repair yet be unable to afford garage costs.

The jobs are described assuming only normal spanners are available, and not special tools. But a reasonable outfit of tools will be a worthwhile investment. Many special workshop tools produced by the makers merely speed the work, and in these cases guidance is given as to how to do the job without them, the oft quoted example being the use of a large hose clip to compress the piston rings for insertion in the cylinder. But on a very few occasions the special tool is essential to prevent damage to components, then their use is described. Though it might be possible to borrow the tool such work may have to be entrusted to the official agent.

To avoid labour costs a garage will often give a cheaper repair by fitting a reconditioned assembly. The home mechanic can be helped by this book to diagnose the fault and make a repair using only a minor spare part.

The manufacturer's official workshop manuals are written for their trained staff, and so assume special knowledge; therefore detail is left out. This book is written for the owner, and so goes into detail.

Using the manual

The manual is divided into twelve Chapters. Each Chapter is divided into numbered Sections which are headed in **bold** type between horizontal lines. Each Section consists of serially numbered paragraphs.

There are two types of illustration: (1) Figures which are numbered according to Chapter and sequence of occurrence in that Chapter. (2) Photographs which have a reference number on their caption. All photographs apply to the Chapter in which they occur so that the reference figure pinpoints the pertinent Section and paragraph number.

Procedures, once described in the text, are not normally repeated. If it is necessary to refer to another Chapter the reference will be given in Chapter number, Section number and where necessary, paragraph number. Cross references given without use of the word 'Chapter' apply to Section and/or paragraphs in the same Chapter (eg; 'see Section 8' means 'in this Chapter').

When the left or right side of the car is mentioned it is as if one is seated in the driver's seat looking forward.

Whilst every care is taken to ensure that the information in this manual is correct no liability can be accepted by the authors or publishers for loss, damage or injury caused by any errors in, or omissions from, the information given.

Introduction to the Datsun Cherry

The Datsun 100A and 120A models are the first radical departure from the previous conventional approach by this large Japanese company.

The transverse-engine front-drive layout was adopted to achieve as much internal space as possible. The designers have obviously succeeded extremely well, since inch-for-inch, the Cherry compares more readily with an 1100 or Escort than a standard 'Mini' car.

The engine is an adapted version of the 988 cc unit used in the Datsun 1000 with the compression ratio raised to 9.0 to 1. Although the engine and transmission are an integral unit, the gearbox and final drive share a separate casing and oil supply.

The 120A Coupe version is a rather more 'up-market' version of the 100A, with more power, a five-bearing crankshaft engine and a very distinctive body style.

Suffice it to say, that at the time of writing this manual, the Datsun Cherry is one of the fastest selling cars imported into the UK.

Contents

Datsun Cherry 100A Estate

Datsun Cherry 120A Coupe

Safety first!

Professional motor mechanics are trained in safe working procedures. However enthusiastic you may be about getting on with the job in hand, do take the time to ensure that your safety is not put at risk. A moment's lack of attention can result in an accident, as can failure to observe certain elementary precautions.

There will always be new ways of having accidents, and the following points do not pretend to be a comprehensive list of all dangers; they are intended rather to make you aware of the risks and to encourage a safety-conscious approach to all work you carry out on your vehicle.

Essential DOs and DON'Ts

DON'T rely on a single jack when working underneath the vehicle. Always use reliable additional means of support, such as axle stands, securely placed under a part of the vehicle that you know will not give way.

DON'T attempt to loosen or tighten high-torque nuts (e.g. wheel hub nuts) while the vehicle is on a jack; it may be pulled off.

DON'T start the engine without first ascertaining that the transmission is in neutral (or 'Park' where applicable) and the parking brake applied.

DON'T suddenly remove the filler cap from a hot cooling system – cover it with a cloth and release the pressure gradually first, or you may get scalded by escaping coolant.

DON'T attempt to drain oil until you are sure it has cooled sufficiently to avoid scalding you.

DON'T grasp any part of the engine, exhaust or catalytic converter without first ascertaining that it is sufficiently cool to avoid burning you.

DON'T allow brake fluid or antifreeze to contact vehicle paintwork.

DON'T syphon toxic liquids such as fuel, brake fluid or antifreeze by mouth, or allow them to remain on your skin.

DON'T inhale dust – it may be injurious to health (see *Asbestos* below).

DON'T allow any spilt oil or grease to remain on the floor – wipe it up straight away, before someone slips on it.

DON'T use ill-fitting spanners or other tools which may slip and cause injury.

DON'T attempt to lift a heavy component which may be beyond your capability – get assistance.

DON'T rush to finish a job, or take unverified short cuts.

DON'T allow children or animals in or around an unattended vehicle.

DO wear eye protection when using power tools such as drill, sander, bench grinder etc, and when working under the vehicle.

DO use a barrier cream on your hands prior to undertaking dirty jobs – it will protect your skin from infection as well as making the dirt easier to remove afterwards; but make sure your hands aren't left slippery.

DO keep loose clothing (cuffs, tie etc) and long hair well out of the way of moving mechanical parts.

DO remove rings, wristwatch etc, before working on the vehicle – especially the electrical system.

DO ensure that any lifting tackle used has a safe working load rating adequate for the job.

DO keep your work area tidy – it is only too easy to fall over articles left lying around.

DO get someone to check periodically that all is well, when working alone on the vehicle.

DO carry out work in a logical sequence and check that everything is correctly assembled and tightened afterwards.

DO remember that your vehicle's safety affects that of yourself and others. If in doubt on any point, get specialist advice.

IF, in spite of following these precautions, you are unfortunate enough to injure yourself, seek medical attention as soon as possible.

Asbestos

Certain friction, insulating, sealing, and other products – such as brake linings, brake bands, clutch linings, torque converters, gaskets, etc – contain asbestos. *Extreme care must be taken to avoid inhalation of dust from such products since it is hazardous to health.* If in doubt, assume that they *do* contain asbestos.

Fire

Remember at all times that petrol (gasoline) is highly flammable. Never smoke, or have any kind of naked flame around, when working on the vehicle. But the risk does not end there – a spark caused by an electrical short-circuit, by two metal surfaces contacting each other, by careless use of tools, or even by static electricity built up in your body under certain conditions, can ignite petrol vapour, which in a confined space is highly explosive.

Always disconnect the battery earth (ground) terminal before working on any part of the fuel or electrical system, and never risk spilling fuel on to a hot engine or exhaust.

It is recommended that a fire extinguisher of a type suitable for fuel and electrical fires is kept handy in the garage or workplace at all times. Never try to extinguish a fuel or electrical fire with water.

Fumes

Certain fumes are highly toxic and can quickly cause unconsciousness and even death if inhaled to any extent. Petrol (gasoline) vapour comes into this category, as do the vapours from certain solvents such as trichloroethylene. Any draining or pouring of such volatile fluids should be done in a well ventilated area.

When using cleaning fluids and solvents, read the instructions carefully. Never use materials from unmarked containers – they may give off poisonous vapours.

Never run the engine of a motor vehicle in an enclosed space such as a garage. Exhaust fumes contain carbon monoxide which is extremely poisonous; if you need to run the engine, always do so in the open air or at least have the rear of the vehicle outside the workplace.

If you are fortunate enough to have the use of an inspection pit, never drain or pour petrol, and never run the engine, while the vehicle is standing over it; the fumes, being heavier than air, will concentrate in the pit with possibly lethal results.

The battery

Never cause a spark, or allow a naked light, near the vehicle's battery. It will normally be giving off a certain amount of hydrogen gas, which is highly explosive.

Always disconnect the battery earth (ground) terminal before working on the fuel or electrical systems.

If possible, loosen the filler plugs or cover when charging the battery from an external source. Do not charge at an excessive rate or the battery may burst.

Take care when topping up and when carrying the battery. The acid electrolyte, even when diluted, is very corrosive and should not be allowed to contact the eyes or skin.

If you ever need to prepare electrolyte yourself, always add the acid slowly to the water, and never the other way round. Protect against splashes by wearing rubber gloves and goggles.

When jump starting a car using a booster battery, for negative earth (ground) vehicles, connect the jump leads in the following sequence: First connect one jump lead between the positive (+) terminals of the two batteries. Then connect the other jump lead first to the negative (–) terminal of the booster battery, and then to a good earthing (ground) point on the vehicle to be started, at least 18 in (45 cm) from the battery if possible. Ensure that hands and jump leads are clear of any moving parts, and that the two vehicles do not touch. Disconnect the leads in the reverse order.

Mains electricity

When using an electric power tool, inspection light etc, which works from the mains, always ensure that the appliance is correctly connected to its plug and that, where necessary, it is properly earthed (grounded). Do not use such appliances in damp conditions and, again, beware of creating a spark or applying excessive heat in the vicinity of fuel or fuel vapour.

Ignition HT voltage

A severe electric shock can result from touching certain parts of the ignition system, such as the HT leads, when the engine is running or being cranked, particularly if components are damp or the insulation is defective. Where an electronic ignition system is fitted, the HT voltage is much higher and could prove fatal.

Buying
spare parts and vehicle identification numbers

Buying spare parts

Spare parts are available from many sources, for example: Datsun garages, other garages and accessory shops, and motor factors. Our advice regarding spare parts is as follows:

Officially appointed Datsun garages - This is the best source of parts which are peculiar to your car and otherwise not generally available (eg; complete cylinder heads, internal gearbox components, badges, interior trim etc). It is also the only place at which you should buy parts if your car is still under warranty; non-Datsun components may invalidate the warranty. To be sure of obtaining the correct parts it will always be necessary to give the storeman your car's engine and chassis number, and if possible, to take the old part along for positive identification. Remember that many parts are available on a factory exchange scheme - any parts returned should always be clean! It obviously makes good sense to go straight to the specialists on your car for this type of part for they are best equipped to supply you.

Other garages and accessory shops - These are often very good places to buy material and components needed for the maintenance of your car (eg; oil filters, spark plugs, bulbs, fan belts, oils and grease, touch-up paint, filler paste etc). They also sell general accessories, usually have convenient opening hours, charge lower prices and can often be found not far from home.

Motor factors - Good factors will stock all of the more important components which wear out relatively quickly (eg; clutch components, pistons, valves, exhaust systems, brake cylinders/pipes/hoses/seals/shoes and pads etc). Motor factors will often provide new or reconditioned components on a part exchange basis - this can save a considerable amount of money.

Vehicle identification numbers

Modifications are a continuing and unpublished process in vehicle manufacture quite apart from major model changes. Spare parts manuals and lists are compiled upon a numerical basis, the individual vehicle numbers being essential to correct identification of the component required.

The vehicle identification is on a plate situated on the right-hand side of the bulkhead, with the car number stamped nearby.

The car number is always preceded by the vehicle model identification which is as follows:

E10	*Right-hand Drive Saloon*
LE10	*Left-hand Drive Saloon*
WE10	*Right-hand Drive Estate Car*
WLE10	*Left-hand Drive Estate Car*

The above identifications are further sub-divided into individual vehicle identifications as follows:

2-door Standard Saloon	E10SRUT (R.H. Drive)
2-door Standard Saloon	LE10SRUT (L.H. Drive)
4-door Standard Saloon	E10SUT (R.H. Drive)
4-door Standard Saloon	LE10SUT (L.H. Drive)
4-door De Luxe Saloon	E10UT (R.H. Drive)
4-door De Luxe Saloon	LE10T (L.H. Drive)
Estate Car, Standard Model	WE10SRUT (R.H. Drive)
Estate Car, Standard Model	WLE10SRT (R.H. Drive)
Coupe, 2-doors	

The engine serial number is stamped on the rear right-hand side of the cylinder block. The engine serial number is preceded by the engine model reference 'A10'. ('A12' for the 120A Coupe).

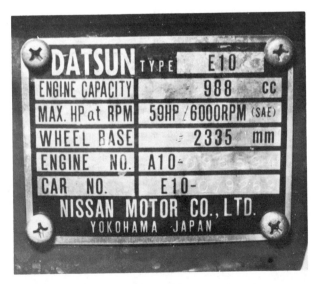

Chassis number

Engine number

Routine maintenance

Maintenance is essential for ensuring safety and desirable for the purpose of getting the best in terms of performance and economy from the car. Over the years the need for periodic lubrication - oiling, greasing and so on - has been drastically reduced if not totally eliminated. This has unfortunately tended to lead some owners to think that because no such action is required the items either no longer exist or will last for ever. This is a serious delusion. It follows therefore that the largest initial element of maintenance is visual examination. This may lead to repairs or renewals.

In the summary given here the 'essential for safety' items are shown in **bold type**. These **must** be attended to at the regular frequencies shown in order to avoid the possibility of accidents and loss of life. Neglect results in unreliability, increased running costs, more rapid wear and more rapid depreciation of the vehicle in general.

Every 250 miles (400 km) travelled or weekly - whichever comes first

---

Steering
Check the tyre pressures.
Examine tyres for wear or damage.
Is steering smooth and accurate?

Brakes
Check reservoir fluid level.
Is there any fall off in braking efficiency?
Try an emergency stop. Is adjustment necessary?

Lights, wipers and horns
Do all bulbs work at the front and rear?
Are the headlamp beams aligned properly?
Do the wipers and horns work?
Check windscreen washer fluid level.

Engine
Check the sump oil level and top-up if required.
Check the radiator coolant level and top-up if required.
Check the battery electrolyte level and top-up the level of the plates with distilled water as needed.

3,000 miles (4,800 km)

Every 3,000 miles (4,800 km) or 4 monthly, whichever comes first, or earlier if indications suggest that safety items in particular are not performing correctly.

Steering
Examine all steering linkage rods, joints and bushes for signs of wear or damage.
Check front wheel hub bearings and adjust if necessary.

Check for free-play between the steering wheel and roadwheels. Check steering gear if play is found.

Brakes
Examine disc pads and drum shoes to determine the amount of friction material left. Renew if necessary.
Examine all hydraulic pipes, cylinders and unions for signs of chafing, corrosion, dents or any other form of deterioration or leaks.
Adjust drum type brakes.

Suspension
Examine all nuts, bolts and shackles securing the suspension units, front and rear. Tighten if necessary.
Examine the rubber bushes for signs of wear and play.

Engine
Change oil.
Check distributor points gap.
Check and clean spark plugs.

Transmission
Check oil level and top-up if necessary.
Check driveshafts for broken gaiters on the constant velocity joints.

Clutch
Grease cable lubrication point (mechanical type operation).
Check fluid reservoir level and top-up if necessary (hydraulic type).

Body
Lubricate all locks and hinges.
Check that water drain holes at bottom of doors are clear.

6,000 miles (9600 km)

Engine
Check fan belt tension and adjust if necessary.
Check cylinder head bolt torque setting.
Check valve clearances and adjust if necessary.
Renew oil filter.
Lubricate distributor.
Clean air cleaner element.
Clean fuel pump.

Steering
Rotate roadwheels and rebalance if necessary.

Brakes
Check pedal free-movement and for oil leakage at cylinders.

Clutch
Check pedal free-movement, and adjust if necessary.

Engine sump drain plug

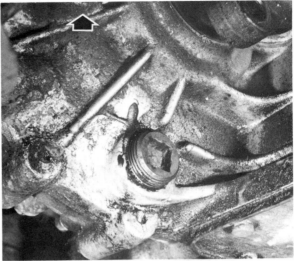

Transmission drain plug (filler plug arrowed)

Changing the oil filter

Spare wheel and jack

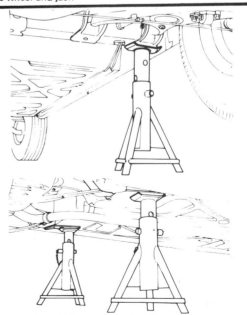

Top left Front jacking points

Top right Rear jacking points (Saloon)

Bottom right Rear jacking points (Estate)

12,000 miles (19,000 km)

Engine
Check crankcase fume emission valve.
Check fuel storage evaporative emission control system.
Check exhaust emission control system
Fit new spark plugs.
Fit new distributor points.
Clean carburettor float chamber and jets.
Renew fuel line filter unit.
Check HT ignition leads for deterioation.

Steering
Check wheel alignment.

Suspension
Check shock absorber operation.

Transmission
Check security of driveshaft bolts.

24,000 miles (38,000 km)

Engine
Flush cooling system and refill with antifreeze mixture.
Renew air cleaner element.

Brakes
Lubricate handbrake linkage

30,000 miles (48,000 km)

Transmission
Drain transmission and refill with fresh oil.
Check driveshaft universal joints for wear and replace if necessary.

Headlights
Check beams and adjust if required.

Brakes
Check brake master and wheel cylinders.
Ensure the differential pressure valve is working correctly

48,000 miles (77,000 km)

Brakes
Drain hydraulic system, renew all cylinder seals and refill with fresh fluid. Bleed system.

Clutch
Drain hydraulic system, renew master and slave cylinder seals, refill with fresh fluid. Bleed system. If it is a mechanical system it is sound practise to replace the cable.

Additionally the following items should be attended to as time can be spared:-

Cleaning
Examination of components requires that they be cleaned. The same applies to the body of the car, inside and out, in order

that deterioration due to rust or unknown damage may be detected. Certain parts of the body frame, if rusted badly, can result in the vehicle being declared unsafe and it will not pass the annual test for roadworthiness.

Exhaust system
An exhaust system must be leakproof, and the noise level below a certain minimum. Excessive leaks may cause carbon monoxide fumes to enter the passenger compartment. Excessive noise constitutes a public nuisance. Both these faults may cause the vehicle to be kept off the road. Repair or replace defective sections when symptoms are apparent.

Other aspects of Routine Maintenance

1 Jacking-up
Always chock a wheel on the opposite side, in front and behind. Always support the car on stands as well as on the jack. Use only the jacking strong points shown in the associated illustrations.

2 Wheel nuts
These should be cleaned and lightly smeared with grease as necessary during work, to keep them moving easily. If the nuts are stubborn to undo due to dirt and overtightening, it may be necessary to hold them by lowering the jack till the wheel rests on the ground. Normally if the wheel brace is used across the hub centre a foot or knee held against the tyre will prevent the wheel from turning, and so save the wheels and nuts from wear if the nuts are slackened with weight on the wheel. After replacing a wheel make a point later of rechecking the nuts again for tightness.

3 Safety
Whenever working, even partially, under the car, put an extra strong box or piece of timber underneath onto which the car will fall rather than on you.

4 Cleanliness
Whenever you do any work allow time for cleaning. When something is in pieces or components removed to improve access to other areas, give an opportunity for a thorough clean. This cleanliness will allow you to cope with a crisis on the road without getting yourself dirty. During bigger jobs when you expect a bit of dirt it is less extreme and can be tolerated at least whilst removing a component. When an item is being taken to pieces there is less risk of ruinous grit finding its way inside. The act of cleaning focuses your attention onto parts and you are more likely to spot trouble. Dirt on the ignition part is a common cause of poor starting. Large areas such as the engine compartment, inner wings or bulkhead should be brushed thoroughly with a solvent like Gunk, allowed to soak and then very carefully hosed down. Water in the wrong places, particularly the carburettor or electrical components will do more harm than dirt. Use petrol or paraffin and a small paintbrush to clean the more inaccessible places.

5 Waste disposal
Old oil and cleaning paraffin must be destroyed. Although it makes a good base for a bonfire the practice is dangerous. It is also illegal to dispose of oil and paraffin down domestic drains. By buying your new engine oil in one gallon cans you can refill with old oil and take back to the local garage who have facilities for disposal.

6 Long journeys
Before taking the car on long journeys, particularly such trips as continental holidays, make sure that the car is given a thorough check in the form of the next service due, plus a full visual inspection well in advance so that any faults found can be rectified in time.

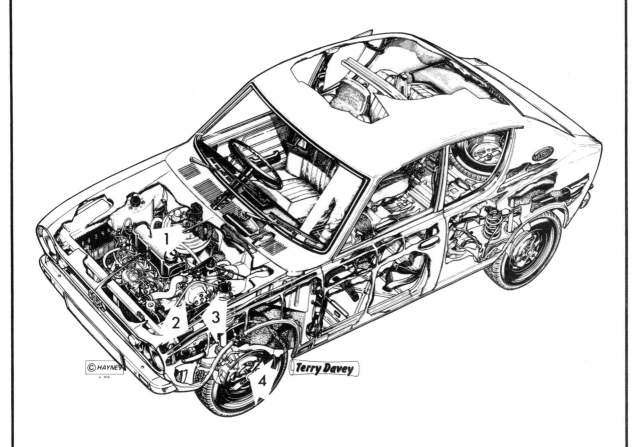

Recommended lubricants

Component	Castrol Product
1 Engine	Castrol GTX
2 Gearbox/final drive	Castrol Hypoy Light (80 EP)
3 Rack and pinion unit	Castrol Hypoy (90 EP)
4 Wheel bearings	Castrol LM Grease
Chassis general	Castrol LM Grease

Note: The above are general recommendations. Lubrication requirements vary from territory-to-territory and also with vehicle range — Consult the operators handbook supplied with your car.

Chapter 1 Engine

Contents

Specifications

(all dimensions in inches unless otherwise stated).

		A12 (120A Cherry)	A10 (100A Cherry)
Cylinder block			
Material	... ...	cast iron	cast iron
Type ...	... ...	four cylinders, in-line, overhead valve	four cylinders, in-line, over-head valve
Capacity	... ...	1171 cc	988 cc
Bore ...	... ...	2,874	2,874
Stroke	... ...	2.756	2.323
Firing order ...	... ...	1 3 4 2	1 3 4 2
Compression ratio	... ...	9 : 1	9 : 1
Oil pressure (hot) at 2000 rev/min.	... ...	43 - 50 lb sq in	50 - 57 lb sq in
Ignition timing	... ...	Refer to Chapter 4	
Cylinder head			
Material	... ...	aluminium alloy	aluminium alloy
Pistons			
Type	... ...	aluminium, concave head	aluminium, flat head
Bore clearance	... ...	0.023 to 0.043	0.023 to 0.043
Diameter:			
Standard ...	... ...	2.8727 to 2.8747	2.8727 to 2.8747
Oversize 50	... ...	2.8924 to 2.8944	2.8924 to 2.8944
Oversize 100	... ...	2.9121 to 2.9140	2.9121 to 2.9140
Oversize 150	... ...	2.9318 to 2.9337	2.9318 to 2.9337
Piston rings			
Number	... ...	two compression (top) one oil control	two compression (top) one oil control
Ring groove width:			
Compression	... ...	0.0787	0.0787
Oil control	... ...	0.1575	0.1575

	A12 (120A Cherry)	A10 (100A Cherry)
Ring side clearance in groove:		
Compression	0.0016 to 0.0027	0.0016 to 0.0027
Oil control	0.0016 to 0.0031	0.0016 to 0.0031
Ring end gap:		
Compression	0.0079 to 0.0138	0.0079 to 0.0138
Oil control	0.0118 to 0.0354	0.0118 to 0.0354

Gudgeon pins

Diameter	0.6869 to 0.6871	0.6869 to 0.6871
Length	2.5681 to 2.5779	2.5681 to 2.5779
Clearance in piston	0.0002 to 0.0003 (at 20°C/ 168°F ambient)	0.0002 to 0.0003 (at 20°C/ 168°F ambient)
Interference fit in small end of connecting rod	0.0007 to 0.0013	0.0007 to 0.0013

Crankshaft

Number and type of main bearings...	five, shell, detachable	three, shell, detachable
Journal diameter	1.9666 to 1.9671	1.9666 to 1.9671
Maximum journal ovality	less than 0.0012	less than 0.0012
Crankpin diameter	1.7706 to 1.7701	1.7706 to 1.7701
Maximum crankpin ovality	less than 0.0012	less than 0.0012
Main bearing thickness	0.0722 to 0.0719	0.0722 to 0.0719
Main bearing clearance	0.0008 to 0.0024	0.0008 to 0.0024
Main bearing clearance (wear limit)	0.0059	0.0059
Endfloat	0.0029 to 0.0059 (max. 0.0118)	0.0029 to 0.0059 (max. 0.0118)

Connecting rods

Bearing thickness	0.0591 to 0.0594	0.0591 to 0.0594
Big-end endfloat	0.0079 to 0.0012	0.0079 to 0.0012
Big-end endfloat (wear limit)	less than 0.016	less than 0.016
Big-end bearing clearance	0.0008 to 0.0020	0.0008 to 0.0020
Weight difference between rods	not more than 0.18 oz	not more than 0.18 oz
Distance between centres	4.7812 to 4.7788	4.6112 to 4.6075

Camshaft

Number of bearings	five, bored in line	five, bored in line
Endfloat	0.0004 to 0.0020	0.0004 to 0.0020
Lobe lift	0.222	0.211
Journal diameter:		
1st	1.7237 to 1.7242	1.7237 to 1.7242
2nd	1.6647 to 1.7046	1.6647 to 1.7046
3rd	1.6844 to 1.6849	1.6844 to 1.6849
4th	1.6647 to 1.6652	1.6647 to 1.6652
5th	1.6224 to 1.6229	1.6224 to 1.6229
Bearing inner diameter:		
1st	1.7261 to 1.7257	1.7261 to 1.7257
2nd	1.7056 to 1.7060	1.7056 to 1.7060
3rd	1.6868 to 1.6865	1.6868 to 1.6865
4th	1.6667 to 1.6663	1.6667 to 1.6663
5th	1.6247 to 1.6243	1.6247 to 1.6243

Valves

Clearance (hot) inlet and exhaust	0.0138 (0.35 mm)	0.0138 (0.35 mm)
Clearance (cold) inlet and exhaust	0.0098 (0.25 mm)	0.0098 (0.25 mm)
Valve head diameter:		
Inlet	1.457 to 1.465	1.457 to 1.465
Exhaust	1.181 to 1.189	1.181 to 1.189
Valve stem diameter:		
Inlet	0.3138 to 0.3144	0.3138 to 0.3144
Exhaust	0.3128 to 0.3134	0.3128 to 0.3134
Valve length - inlet and exhaust	4.034 to 4.041	4.034 to 4.041
Valve lift	0.3346	0.2953
Valve spring free-length	1.831	1.799
Valve guide length	1.929	1.929
Valve guide height from cylinder head surface	0.709	0.709
Valve guide inner diameter - inlet and exhaust	0.3156 to 0.3150	0.3156 to 0.3150
Valve guide outer diameter - inlet and exhaust	0.4816 to 0.4820	0.4816 to 0.4820
Valve stem to guide clearnace:		
Inlet	0.0006 to 0.0018	0.0006 to 0.0018
Exhaust	0.0016 to 0.0028	0.0016 to 0.0028
Valve seat width:		
Inlet	0.0512	0.0512
Exhaust	0.0709	0.0709

Valve seat angle - inlet and exhaust	45°	45°
Valve seat interference fit - inlet and exhaust	0.0025 to 0.0038	0.0025 to 0.0038
Valve guide interferene fit - inlet and exhaust	0.0009 to 0.0017	0.0009 to 0.0017

Timing chain

Type	double roller	double roller

Oil pump and lubrication

Type (pump)	rotor, camshaft gear driven	rotor, camshaft gear driven
Type (system)	pressure, feed	pressure, feed
Filter	canister, disposable, full-flow type	canister, disposable, full-flow type
Pressure relief valve	ball and spring, non adjustable	ball and spring, non adjustable
Sump and filter capacity	6¼ pints, 3.05 litres	6¼ pints, 3.05 litres

Torque wrench settings

	A12		A10	
	lb f ft	kg f m	lb f ft	kg f m
Cylinder head bolts	51 - 54	7.0 - 7.5	43 - 47	6.0 - 6.5
Connecting rod nuts...	23 - 28	3.2 - 3.8	22 - 26	3 - 3.6
Flywheel bolts	47 - 54	6.5 - 7.5	41 - 43	5.6 - 6.0
Main bearing cap bolts	36 - 43	5 - 6	36 - 43	5 - 6
Camshaft gear bolts	29 - 35	4 - 4.8	29 - 35	4 - 4.8
Sump bolts	2.9 - 4.3	0.4 - 0.6	2.9 - 4.3	0.4 - 0.6
Oil pump bolts	6.5 - 10	0.9 - 1.4	6.5 - 10	0.9 - 1.4
Oil strainer bolts	6.5 - 10	0.9 - 1.4	6.5 - 10	0.9 - 1.4
Crank pulley bolts	108 - 145	15 - 20	108 - 145	15 - 20
Front cover bolts	3.6 - 5.1	0.5 - 0.7	3.6 - 5.1	0.5 - 0.7

1 General description

The engine fitted to the Cherry 100A is the A10. It is a three-bearing 988 cc engine transversely installed and inclined at 5° from the vertical on a subframe.

The Cherry 120A engine is virtually identical, except that it has a five-bearing crankshaft and a capacity of 1171 cc. This engine is designated the A12.

Apart from the difference in the number of crankshaft bearings, and the capacity, the following description encompasses both engines. All of the photographs in the ensuring Sections are of the A10 engine, but are nearly all applicable to the A12 engine.

Both engines are four-cylinder, in-line overhead valve, water-cooled design. The crankshaft is of forged steel construction and incorporates oil drillings for lubrication of the main bearings.

The pistons are made of aluminium with flat crowns on the A10 engine, and with concave crowns on the A12 engine. The connecting rods are of forged steel with gudgeon pins which are an interference fit in the connecting rod small ends but fully floating in the pistons.

The cylinder head is of aluminium with pressed in valve seats. A cast iron camshaft is fitted, which is supported by replaceable bearings, the number depending on engine type, and driven by a double roller chain from the crankshaft. The overhead valve mechanism comprises conventional camshaft operated tappets, push rods and rocker shaft and arms. The valves are fitted with single coil springs and split cotters are employed to retain the valve spring caps.

The inlet manifold is aluminium and the exhaust manifold is cast iron and incorporates a quick warm-up valve.

The power unit is mounted at three points, one at the sump, one at the clutch housing and one on the transmission housing. The mountings are of bonded rubber/metal acting under compression of steel brackets.

2 Major operations possible with the engine in position in the car

The following major operations can be carried out to the engine with it in place in the bodyframe:
1 *Removal and replacement of the cylinder head assembly*
2 *Removal and replacement of the oil pump.*
3 *Removal and replacement of the engine front mountings.*
4 *Removal and replacement of the engine/transmission rear mounting.*

3 Major operations requiring engine removal

The following major operations can be carried out with the engine out of the bodyframe and on the bench or floor:
1 *Removal and replacement of the main bearings.*
2 *Removal and replacement of the crankshaft.*
3 *Removal and replacement of the flywheel.*
4 *Removal and replacement of the crankshaft rear bearing oil seal.*
5 *Removal and replacement of the camshaft.*
6 *Removal and replacement of big-end bearings, pistons and con-rods*

4 Method of engine removal

The engine and transmission are removed together as an integral unit. The engine cannot be removed as a separate entity because of the method of utilizing the clutch housing as part of the transmission casing and the limited access to split them in the vehicle.

5 Engine - removal with transmission

1 The complete unit can be removed easily in about four hours. It is essential to have a good hoist, and two strong axle stands if an inspection pit is not available. Removal will be much easier if there is someone to assist, especially during the later stages.

2 With few exceptions, it is simplest to lift out the engine with all ancillaries (alternator, distributor, carburettor, exhaust manifold) still attached.

3 Before beginning work it is worthwhile to get all dirt cleaned off the engine at a garage equipped with steam or high pressure air and water cleaning equipment. This makes the job quicker, easier and of course much cleaner.

4 Using a pencil or scriber mark the outline of the bonnet hinge on either side to act as a datum for refitting. An assistant should now take the weight of the bonnet.

5 Undo and remove the two bolts and washers that secure the

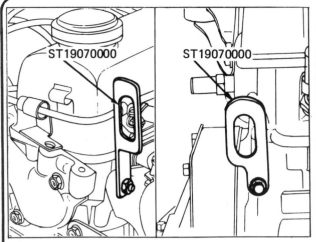

Fig. 1.1. Positions for engine lifting hooks. The arrowed numbers merely indicate Datsun part numbers for these hooks. Other hooks are equally acceptable

5.7 Disconnecting the battery

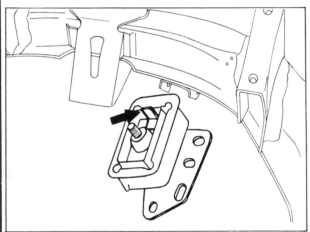

Fig. 1.2. Rear mounting locking pawl

5.9 Lifting out the radiator

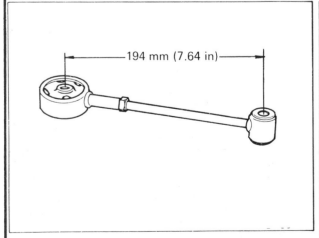

←— 194 mm (7.64 in) —→

Fig. 1.3. Engine buffer rod - optimum length

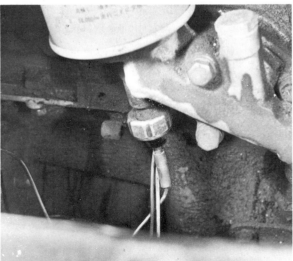

5.11 Leads to the oil pressure switch

bonnet to the hinge and carefully lift the bonnet up and then over the front of the car. Store in a safe place where it will not be scratched. Push down the hinges to stop accidents.

6   Protect the top surface of the front wings with thick covers to prevent scratching during the removal operations. Remove the front grille.

7   Disconnect the earth lead from the negative terminal of the battery.

8   Drain the cooling system by means of the radiator tap and retain the coolant (if mixed with antifreeze) in a suitable receptacle for further use unless it is rusty or contaminated.

9   Disconnect the two radiator hoses, and, if it is an electrically-operated fan mounted on the radiator, disconnect the two leads to the fan. Next, remove the four bolts that secure the radiator and lift the radiator out. If the fan is mounted on the water pump, and is belt-driven, it will be necessary to remove the fan and the ducting shrouds in accordance with Chapter 2.

10 Disconnect the coil to distributor HT lead.

11 Disconnect the leads to the oil pressure switch and the water temperature transmitter.

12 Disconnect the LT lead from the distributor.

13 Disconnect the cable from the starter motor.

14 Disconnect the fuel supply hose at the fuel pump and plug the hose to prevent loss of fuel.

15 Disconnect the cables from the alternator.

16 Disconnect the heater flow and return water hoses.

17 Remove the air cleaner and then disconnect the accelerator and choke controls from the carburettor.

18 Disconnect the clutch operating cable at its forked clevis (right-hand drive vehicles) or an left-hand drive vehicles, remove the slave cylinder (one bolt) after disconnecting the operating rod from the clutch release arm. The slave cylinder may then be swung up out of the way without disturbing the hydraulic circuit which would necessitate subsequent bleeding of the system.

19 Disconnect the exhaust pipe down tube from the manifold by unscrewing the two flange securing nuts.

20 Disconnect the speedometer drive.

21 Next, since one has to work under the vehicle, it is better to jack-up and support it on axle stands or some other equally solid support. If available, a pit is ideal.

22 Disconnect the bracket from the exhaust pipe to the differential (not just the clamp).

23 Disconnect the cables from the reverse lamp switch.

24 Unhook the return spring on the gearchange linkage, then disconnect the radius link assembly from the differential case by removing the two bolts. Now disconnect the spring clip at the end of the control rod; this will enable you to ease away the radius link from the control rod, but be ready to collect the spring and nylon inserts from inside the joint. The main rod will now drop away.

25 Unclip the remaining single linkage from the selector mechanism on the differential.

26 Remove the three bolts that secure each driveshaft to the inner flexible joint. Lower the driveshafts to rest on the sub-frame.

27 Remove the single mounting nut on the assembly rear mounting.

28 Return to the engine bay and disconnect the two stabiliser bars.

29 Remove the nuts on the engine front mountings. Before connecting a hoist and sling to the engine, have a good look around the engine bay and ensure there are no more items to disconnect.

30 The engine can be removed either by a sling placed round each end of the assembly, or by attaching lifting hooks in the appropriate place (refer to Fig. 1.1. for details).

31 With lifting tackle connected to the lifting hooks or with slings round the engine as previously described, take the weight of the engine/transmission unit.

32 The engine mountings are lifted out together with the engine.

33 The engine/transmission unit can now be lifted out.

5.18 Removing the clutch operating cable

5.20 Disconnecting the speedometer drive

5.22 Disconnecting the bracket from the exhaust pipe to the differential ...

5.23 ... and the cables from the reverse light switch

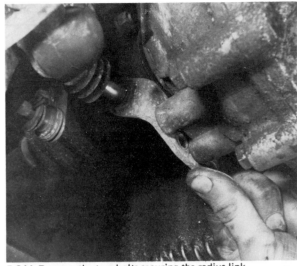

5.24A Remove the two bolts securing the radius link assembly ...

5.24B ... then lift the link away and collect the spring and nylon inserts

5.27 Single mounting nut on rear mounting

5.28 Disconnect the stabiliser bars

5.29 Remove the front mounting nuts

5.31 Lifting out the combined engine/transmission

5.33A General view of the engine and transmission
when clear of the vehicle

5.33B General view of the engine and transmission
when clear of the vehicle

5.33C General view of the engine and transmission
when clear of the vehicle

6 Engine and transmission - separation

1 With the combined engine and transmission removed from
the vehicle, the next task is to split the two major assemblies;
this is necessary whether one is working on the engine or transmission.
2 Details of this sequence are contained in Chapter 6, because
some of the operations relate to dismantling the primary input
gear.
3 When the two major assemblies have been separated the
engine dismantling sequence can continue as detailed in Section
8.

7 Interchangeability - A10 and A12 components

Although the engines for the two models are similar, it would
be unwise, should the contingency arise, to assume that
components are interchangeable. The best recourse is to take
advice from your Datsun agent.

8 Dismantling the engine - general

1 It is best to mount the engine on a dismantling stand but if

one is not available, then stand the engine on a strong bench so
as to be at a comfortable working height. Failing this, the engine
can be stipped down on the floor.
2 During the dismantling process the greatest care should be
taken to keep the exposed parts free from dirt. As an aid to
achieving this, it is a sound scheme to thoroughly clean down the
outside of the engine, removing all traces of oil and congealed
dirt.
3 Use paraffin or a good grease solvent such as 'Gunk'. The
latter compound will make the job much easier, as, after the
solvent has been applied and allowed to stand for a time, a
vigorous jet of water will wash off the solvent and all the grease
and filth. If the dirt is thick and deeply embedded, work the
solvent into it with a wire brush.
4 Finally wipe down the exterior of the engine with a rag and
only then, when it is quite clean should the dismantling process
begin. As the engine is stripped clean each part in a bath of
paraffin or petrol.
5 Never immerse parts with oilways in paraffin, ie; the crankshaft, but to clean, wipe down carefully with a petrol dampened
rag. Oilways can be cleaned out with wire. If an air line is present
all parts can be blown dry and the oilways blown through as an
added precaution.
6 Re-use of old engine gaskets is false economy and can give
rise to oil and water leaks, if nothing worse. To avoid the possibility or trouble after the engine has been reassembled always

Fig. 1.4. Cylinder head bolt tightening sequence
Note: No. 1 bolt, marked with a 'T', is of a different diameter from the others and can only be used in the No. 1 position

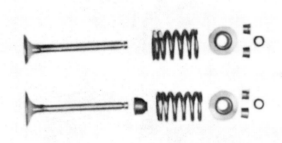

Fig. 1.5. Valve assembly components

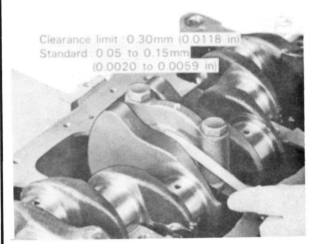

Clearance limit : 0.30mm (0.0118 in)
Standard : 0.05 to 0.15mm
(0.0020 to 0.0059 in)

Fig. 1.6. Measuring crankshaft endplay

Fig. 1.7. Measuring piston ring end-clearance in the bore

use new gaskets throughout.

7   Do not throw the old gaskets away as it sometimes happens that an immediate replacement cannot be found and the old gasket is then very useful as a template. Hang up the old gaskets as they are removed on a suitable hook or nail.

8   To strip the engine it is best to work from the top down. The sump provides a firm base on which the engine can be supported in an upright position. When this stage where the sump must be removed is reached, the engine can be turned on its side and all other work carried out with it in this position.

9   Wherever possible, replace nuts, bolts and washers fingertight from wherever they were removed. This helps avoid later loss and muddle. If they cannot be replaced then lay them out in such a fashion that it is clear from where they came.

9   Removing ancillary engine components

1   With the engine removed from the vehicle and separated from the gearbox, the ancillary components should now be removed before dismantling of the engine unit commences.

2   Loosen the alternator mounting bolts and the adjustment strap bolt. Push the alternator in towards the engine and remove the driving belt. Remove the alternator mounting bolts and adjustment strap bolt and lift the unit away.

3   Unscrew the crankshaft pulley securing bolt. This is achieved by using a ring spanner. One or two hefty clouts with a club hammer on the shaft of the spanner should loosen the nut. It is useless to attempt to unscrew the pulley bolt using hand-pressure as the engine will simply rotate as force is applied.

4   Remove the crankshaft pulley, using two tyre levers if necessary.

5   Unscrew and remove the cartridge type oil filter. It may be necessary to employ a small chain or strap wrench where the filter is stuck tight.

6   Unscrew and remove the bolts which secure the oil pump body to the exterior of the crankcase. Withdraw the oil pump complete with drive gear.

7   Unscrew and remove the spark plugs.

8   Disconnect and remove the vacuum tube which runs between the distributor vacuum capsule and the carburettor.

9   Unscrew and remove the setscrew which retains the distributor plate to the engine crankcase. Withdraw the distributor from its crankcase location.

10 Disconnect the fuel pump to carburettor fuel pipe at the

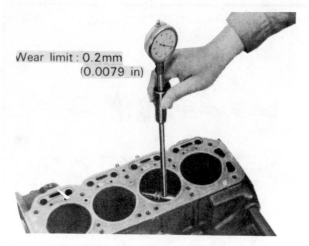

Wear limit : 0.2mm
(0.0079 in)

Fig. 1.8. Measuring the cylinder bore

Clearance limit :
0.2mm (0.0079 in)

Fig. 1.9. Checking ring clearance in the grooves

Clearance limit : 0.1mm (0.0039 in)
Standard : 0.02 to 0.08mm
(0.0008 to 0.0031 in)

Fig. 1.10. Measuring camshaft thrust plate clearance

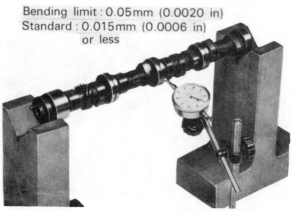

Bending limit : 0.05mm (0.0020 in)
Standard : 0.015mm (0.0006 in)
or less

Fig. 1.11. Alignment check on the camshaft

carburettor end. Unscrew and remove the four carburettor to manifold flange nuts and washers. Lift the carburettor away.

11 Unscrew and remove the rocker cover screws and lift off the rocker cover.

12 Unscrew and remove the two thermostat cover retaining bolts and lift the cover away. If it is stuck do not insert a blade and attempt to prise it off as this will damage the mating faces. Tap it sideways with a plastic faced hammer until it is free.

13 Withdraw the thermostat. If it is stuck in its seating, do not try and pull it out with a pair of pliers but cut round its periphery with a sharp pointed knife to free it.

14 Unscrew and remove the manifold securing nuts and withdraw the manifold and gasket.

15 Unscrew and remove the four fan securing bolts and remove the fan and pulley assembly. On some models the fan is not fitted and it is only necessary to remove the pulley.

16 Unscrew and remove the five nuts which secure the water pump to the upper front face of the timing cover.

17 Unscrew and remove the two securing nuts from the fuel pump and lift it from its crankcase location. Carefully note the exact number and sequence of gaskets and spacers between the pump and crankcase.

9.4 Remove the crankshaft pulley

9.11 Removing the rocker cover

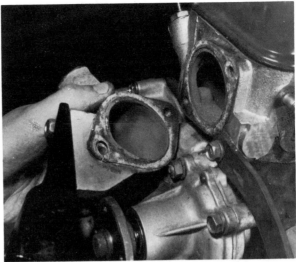
9.13 Thermostat and cover removed

9.15 Removing the pulley (no fan on this model)

9.16A Unscrew the nuts ...

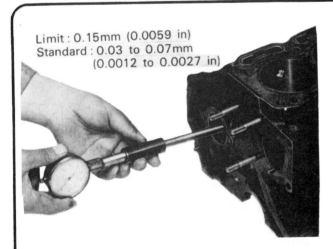

Limit : 0.15mm (0.0059 in)
Standard : 0.03 to 0.07mm
(0.0012 to 0.0027 in)

Fig. 1.12. Measuring the camshaft bearings

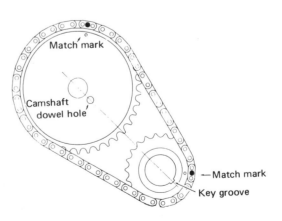

Match mark

Camshaft
dowel hole

Match mark

Key groove

Fig. 1.13. Correct alignment of the timing chain and sprockets

Fig. 1.14. Correct timing chain tensioner adjustment

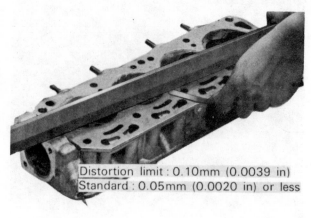

Fig. 1.15. Checking the cylinder head for distortion

10 Cylinder head - removal

1 Unscrew and remove the five rocker shaft pillar securing bolts. Lift the rocker shaft assembly from the cylinder head.
2 Unscrew each of the cylinder head bolts a turn or two each at a time in the sequence shown in Fig. 1.4 finally removing them.
3 Withdraw each of the pushrods and keep them in sequence so that they can be returned to their original positions. A piece of wood with two rows of holes drilled in it and numbered will provide a very useful rack for both pushrods and valves.
4 Lift off the cylinder head. Should it be stuck, do not attempt to prise it from the engine block but tap it all round using a hardwood block or plastic faced mallet. Remove the cylinder head gasket.

11 Valves - removal

1 The valves can be removed from the cylinder head by the following method. Compress each spring in turn with a valve spring compressor until the two halves of the collets can be removed. Release the compressor and remove the spring and spring retainer.
2 If, when the valve spring compressor is screwed down, the valve spring retaining cap refuses to free to expose the split collet, do not continue to screw down on the compressor as there is a likelihood of damaging it.
3 Gently tap the top of the tool directly over the cap with a light hammer. This will free the cap. To avoid the compressor jumping off the valve spring retaining cap when it is tapped, hold the compressor firmly in position with one hand.
4 Slide the rubber oil control seal off the top of each valve stem and then drop out each valve through the combustion chamber.
5 It is essential that the valves are kept in their correct sequence unless they are so badly worn that they are to be renewed.

12 Dismantling the rocker assembly

1 Components of the rocker assembly are removed simply by sliding the rocker pillars, rocker arms and springs from the shaft, Fig. 1.5.
2 If the original components are to be refitted, identify their fitting sequence with a piece of masking tape.

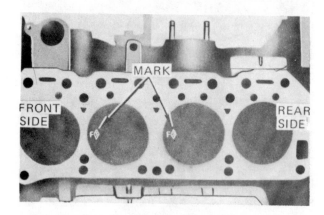

Fig. 1.16. Correct assembly of pistons

13 Sump - removal

1 Unscrew and remove the sump drain plug, catching the oil in a container of adequate capacity. Refit the plug.
2 Unscrew and remove the sump retaining bolts and lift the sump away.
3 The gauze strainer and oil intake pipe will not be exposed and should be detached by removal of the two intake pipe flange securing bolts.

14 Timing cover, gear and chain - removal

1 Unscrew and remove the timing cover securing bolts.
2 Remove the timing cover (the crankshaft pulley already having been removed, Section 9 paragraph 3). The timing cover will incorporate a chain slipper.
3 Withdraw the oil thrower disc from the crankshaft.
4 Unbolt and remove the timing chain tensioner from the front face of the engine block.
5 Unscrew and remove the camshaft gearwheel securing bolt.
6 Remove the camshaft and crankshaft gearwheels simultaneously complete with double roller chain. Use tyre levers behind each gear and lever them equally and a little at a time. If

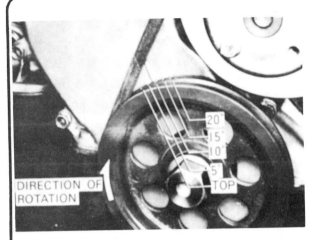

Fig. 1.17. Timing marks on pulley and timing cover. Check the Specifications for the correct timing for the particular model

Fig. 1.18. Correct position of rotor arm after the distributor has been replaced

9.16B ... and remove the water pump

10.1 Lift away the rocker shaft

10.3 Remove the pushrods ...

10.4 ... and lift off the cylinder head

13.2A Release the sump bolts ...

13.2B ... and lift away the sump

13.3 Now remove the oil strainer and pipe

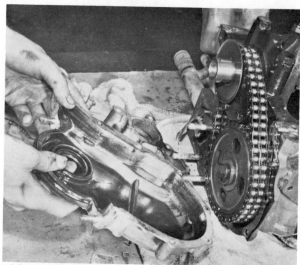
14.2 Remove the timing cover ...

14.3 ... then the oil thrower disc

14.4 Unbolt the timing chain tensioner ...

they are stuck on their shafts, the use of a puller may be required.

7   When the gearwheels and chain are removed, extract the two Woodruff keys from the crankshaft and retain safely. Some spacer washers may also be found on some models.

15 Pistons, connecting rods and big-end bearings - removal

1   With the cylinder head and sump removed undo the big-end retaining bolts.

2   The connecting rods and pistons are lifted out from the top of the cylinder block, after the carbon or 'wear' ring at the top of the bore has been scraped away.

3   Remove the big-end caps one at a time, taking care to keep them in the right order and the correct way round. Also ensure that the shell bearings are kept with their correct connecting rods and caps unless they are to be renewed. Normally, the numbers 1 to 4 are stamped on adjacent sides of the big-end caps, and connecting rods, indicating which cap fits on which rod and which way round the cap fits. If no numbers or lines can be found then, with a sharp screwdriver or file, scratch mating marks across the joint from the rod to the cap. One line for connection rod No. 1, two for connection rod No. 2 and so on. This will ensure there is no confusion later as it is most important that the caps go back in the correct position on the connecting rods from which they were removed.

4   If the big-end caps are difficult to remove they may be gently tapped with a soft hammer.

5   To remove the shell bearings, press the bearings opposite the groove in both the connecting rod, and the connecting rod caps and the bearings will slide out easily.

6   Withdraw the pistons and connecting rods, upwards and ensure they are kept in the correct order for replacement in the same bore. Refit the connecting rod, caps and bearings to the rods if the bearings do not require renewal, to minimise the risk of getting the caps and rods muddled.

16 Flywheel - removal

1   Remove the clutch, as described in Chapter 5.

2   Lock tabs are fitted under the six bolts which hold the flywheel to the flywheel flange on the rear of the crankshaft.

3   Unscrew the bolts and remove them.

4   Lift the flywheel away from the crankshaft flange.

Note: Some difficulty may be experienced in removing the bolts by the rotation of the crankshaft every time pressure is put on the spanner. To lock the crankshaft in position while the bolts are removed, wedge a block of wood between the crankshaft and the side of the block inside the crankcase.

5   The endplate behind the flywheel can now be removed.

17 Main bearings and crankshaft - removal

1   Unscrew and remove the securing bolts from the main bearing caps. On the 3-bearing crankshaft engine fitted to the 100A model, the main bearing cap at the timing case end has a raised circular flange in the centre. The other two bearing caps can easily be confused so it is well to identify them before dismantling. On the 5-bearing crankshaft engine fitted to 120A models the caps are numbered 1 to 5 starting from the timing cover end of the engine and arrows are marked on the caps and these point towards the timing cover to ensure correct orientation of the caps when refitting.

2   Withdraw the bearing caps complete with the lower halves of the shell bearings.

3   Remove the rear oil seal.

4   Lift the crankshaft from the crankcase and then remove each of the upper halves of the shell bearings.

5   Remove the baffle plate and the mesh screen from the crankcase, (120A models only).

14.5 ... and the camshaft gear retaining bolt

14.6 Remove the chain and gears simultaneously

14.7 Showing one of the two Woodruff keys and two spacer washers

15.1 Removing the big-end bearing cap ...

15.2 ... then the connecting rod and piston

15.3 Identification of conrods and bearing caps

16.3 Unscrew the retaining bolts ...

16.4 ... then remove the flywheel and the endplate

17.2A Remove the centre main bearing cap ...

17.2B ... and the flywheel end bearing cap

17.4 Lifting out the crankshaft

17.6A Remove the camshaft endplate ...

17.6B ... and then the camshaft

6   With the engine block still inverted, unscrew and remove the two bolts which secure the camshaft end plate. Remove the plate and carefully withdraw the camshaft. Rotate the camshaft during the removal operation and take particular care not to damage the camshaft bearings as the lobes of the cams pass through them.

7   The tappet blocks may now be lifted from their original sequence so that they may be refitted in exactly the same order.

8   The engine is now completely dismantled and the individual components should be examined and serviced as described in later Sections of this Chapter.

18 Piston rings - removal

1   Each ring should be sprung open only just sufficiently to permit it to ride over the lands of the piston body.

2   Once a ring is out of its groove, it is helpful to cut three ¼ in wide strips of tin and slip them under the ring at equidistant points.

3   Using a twisting motion this method of removal will prevent the ring dropping into a empty groove as it is being removed from the piston.

19 Gudgeon pins - removal

1   The gudgeon pins are an interference fit in the connecting rod small ends. It is recommended that removal of the gudgeon pin be left to a service station having a sufficiently powerful press to remove them.

2   Where a press is available to carry out the work yourself, the body of the piston must be supported on a suitably shaped distance piece into which the gudgeon pin may be ejected.

20 Lubrication system - description

The engine lubrication system is of the pressure feed type. An oil pump mounted on the right-hand side of the cylinder block is driven by a meshing gear on the camshaft which also drives the distributor drive shaft. Oil is drawn from the sump through a filter screen and tube, pumped by the rotor type pump, through the full flow oil filter to the main crankcase oil gallery.

The main oil gallery supplies oil to the crankshaft main bearings and big-end bearings through drillings and a regulated quantity of oil ejected from small holes in the connecting rods lubricate the gudgeon pins and cylinder walls.

The timing chain is fed with oil from the main gallery and the chain tensioner is held against the timing chain partly by oil pressure and partly by a coil spring.

The camshaft bearings are lubricated with oil from the main gallery and the rocker shaft and valve gear obtain their lubrication through a drilling from the camshaft centre bearing.

21 Oil pump - inspection and servicing

1 Having removed the oil pump as previously described, unscrew and remove the two cover bolts, extract the inner and outer rotors and drive shaft.
2 Clean all components in paraffin and then check the following clearances using feeler gauges.

Side clearance between inner and outer rotors, not to exceed 0.0047 in (0.11 mm).

Clearance between outer rotor and the pump body, between 0.0059 and 0.0083 in (0.15 and 0.20 mm).

The endfloat with the cover fitted should be between 0.0016 and 0.0047 in (0.037 and 0.11 mm).

Where measurements are outside the specified tolerances then the oil pump should be renewed as an assembly.
3 Apply a thin coating of gasket cement to the mating surfaces of the body and cover before reassembling and always use a new gasket when refitting the pump to the crankcase.

22 Oil pressure relief valve - inspection and servicing

1 The oil pressure relief valve assembly is screwed into the rear face of the oil pump body. Unscrew the sealing plug and extract the shim, spring and valve.
2 The adjustment of the valve is provided for and the only check that can be carried out is to measure the length of the spring. This should be 1.71 in (44 mm). The best way to check this is to compare it with a new one.
3 Refit the relief valve components in their correct sequence, check the plug sealing washer and tighten the plug to between 29 and 36 lb/ft (4 and 4.97 kg/m) torque.
4 In the event of low oil pressure being indicated by the oil warning lamp lighting up, it must not be assumed that the fault lies with the pressure relief valve on the oil pump. Check for (i) blocked filter cartridge (ii) sump oil level correct (iii) oil pressure switch faulty and (iv) general excessive wear in main and big-end bearings. All these factors may be the cause of low oil pressure being indicated.

23 Crankcase ventilation control system - description and servicing

1 The system is designed to extract gas which has passed the pistons and entered the crankcase. These fumes are drawn through a closed circuit with valve to the inlet manifold.
2 During part-throttle openings the vacuum created in the inlet manifold draws fumes through a valve screwed into the side of the inlet manifold and air to replace them is drawn into the clean side of the air cleaner through a hose which connects the air cleaner to the rocker cover and thence to the crankcase. Some models are fitted with two hoses.
3 During full throttle operation, the inlet manifold vacuum is insufficient to draw the crankcase fumes through the valve and the flow is therefore in the reverse direction through the rocker cover to air cleaner hose.
4 The spring loaded valve which is essential to the accurate control of the system should be checked periodically in the following manner. With the engine idling, remove the hose from the valve. If the valve is operating correctly a hissing noise will be evident to prove that air is being admitted by the valve. A high vacuum should also be felt if a finger is placed over the valve inlet. Where these factors are not observed then the valve must

be renewed.
5 Occasionally check the hoses for splits and security of connections. Pull a piece of rag through them to clean them.
6 A flame trap is interposed between the air cleaner and the rocker cover to prevent a blow-back from the carburettor reaching the engine interior. Check that this is securely fixed in the hose and regularly wash it free from oil contamination in paraffin, **not petrol**.

24 Engine mountings - renewal

1 With time the bonded rubber insulators, will perish causing undue vibration and noise from the engine. Severe juddering when reversing or when moving off from rest is also likely and is a further sign of worn mounting rubbers.
2 The mounting rubber insulators can be changed with the engine in the car.
3 Apply the handbrake firmly, jack-up the front of the car, and place stands under the front of the car.
4 Lower the jack, and place the jack under the sump to take the weight of the engine.
5 Undo the large bolt which holds each of the engine mountings to the subframe.
6 Raise the engine sufficiently high to enable the mounting insulator brackets to be disconnected from the sump, clutch housing and transmission. If the engine is raised too high the buffer rods and exhaust pipe could be damaged. If you are uncertain it is better to disconnect them.
7 Fitting new flexible insulators is a reversal of removal but note the following points:

1 *When installing rear insulator to subframe, check to be sure that locking pawl is properly positioned. Do not damage locking pawl while fitting.*
2 *The front insulator should be installed so that arrow on side is pointing toward up.*
3 *Avoid placing "set" in insulator. Noise is transferred inside if this caution is neglected.*
4 *Adjust length of buffer rods and then install in their correct positions.*

25 Examination and renovation - general

With the engine stripped down and all parts thoroughly cleaned, it is now time to examine everything for wear. The following items should be checked and where necessary renewed or renovated as described in the following Sections.

26 Crankshaft and main bearings - inspection and renovation

1 Examine the crankpin and main journal surfaces for signs of scoring or scratches. Check the ovality of the crankpins at different positions with a micrometer. If more than 0.001 in out of round the crankpin will have to be reground. It will also have to be reground if there are any scores or scratches present. Also check the journals in the same fashion.
2 If it is necessary to regrind the crankshaft and fit new bearings your local Datsun garage or engineering works will be able to decide how much metal to grind off and the size of new bearing shells.
3 Full details of crankshaft regrinding tolerances and bearing undersizes are given in Specifications.
4 The main bearing clearances may be established by using a strip of Plastigage between the crankshaft journals and the main bearing/shell caps. Tighten the bearing cap bolts to a torque of between 36 and 44 lb/ft (4.97 and 6 kg/m). Remove the cap and compare the flattened Plastigage strip with the index provided. The clearance should be compared with the tolerances in Specifications.
5 Temporarily refit the crankshaft to the crankcase having

refitted the upper halves of the shell main bearings in their locations. Fit the centre main bearing cap only, complete with shell bearing and tighten the securing bolts to between 36 and 44 lb/ft (4.97 and 6 kg/m) torque. Using a feeler gauge, check the endfloat by pushing and pulling the crankshaft (Fig. 1.6). Where the endfloat is outside the specified tolerance, the centre bearing cap will have to be renewed.

27 Connecting rods and bearings - examination and renovation

1 Big-end bearing failure is indicated by a knocking from within the crankcase and a slight drop in oil pressure.
2 Examine the big-end bearing surfaces for pitting and scoring. Renew the shells in accordance with the size specified in Specifications. Where the crankshaft has been reground, the correct undersize big-end shell bearings will be supplied by the repairer.
3 Should there be any suspicion that a connection rod is bent or twisted or the small end bush no longer provides an interference fit for the gudgeon pin then the complete connecting rod assembly should be exchanged for a reconditioned one but ensure that the comparative weight of the two rods is within 0.18 oz.
4 Measurement of the big-end bearing clearances may be carried out in a similar manner to that described for the main bearings in the previous Section but tighten the securing nuts on the cap bolts to between 23 and 28 lb/ft (3.179 and 3.87 kg/m).

28 Cylinder bores and crankcase - examination and renovation

1 The cylinder bores must be examined for taper, ovality, scoring and scratches. Start by carefully examining the top of the cylinder bores. If they are at all worn a very slight ridge will be found on the thrust side. This marks the top of the piston ring travel. The owner will have a good indication of the bore wear prior to dismantling the engine, or removing the cylinder head. Excessive oil consumption accompanied by blue smoke from the exhaust is a sure sign of worn cylinder bores and piston rings.
2 Measure the bore diameter just under the ridge with a micrometer and compare it with the diameter at the bottom of the bore, which is not subject to wear. If the difference between the two measurements is more than 0.008 in (0.20 mm) then it will be necessary to fit special pistons and rings or to have the cylinders rebored and fit oversize pistons. If no micrometer is available remove the rings from a piston and place the piston in each bore in turn about ¾ in (19.05 mm) below the top of the bore. If an 0.0012 in (0.03 mm) feeler gauge slide between the piston and cylinder wall requires more than a pull of between 1.1 and 3.3 lbs (0.46 and 1.38 kg) to withdraw it, using a spring balance, then remedial action must be taken. Oversize pistons are available as listed in Specifications.
3 These are accurately machined to just below the indicated measurements so as to provide correct running clearances in bores bored out to the exact oversize dimensions.
4 If the bores are slightly worn but not so badly worn as to justify reboring them, then special oil control rings and pistons can be fitted which will restore compression and stop the engine burning oil. Several different types are available and the manufacturer's instructions concerning their fitting must be followed closely.
5 If new pistons are being fitted and the bores have not been reground, it is essential to slightly roughen the hard glaze on the sides of the bores with fine glass paper so the new piston rings will have a chance to bed in properly.

29 Pistons and piston rings - examination and renovation

1 If the original pistons are to be refitted, carefully remove the piston rings, as described in Section 18.
2 Clean the grooves and rings free from carbon, taking care not

to scratch the aluminium surfaces of the pistons.
3 If new rings are to be fitted, then order the top compression ring to be stepped to prevent it impinging on the 'wear ring' which will almost certainly have been formed at the top of the cylinder bore.
4 Before fitting the rings to the pistons, push each ring in turn down to the part of its respective cylinder bore (use an inverted piston to do this and to keep the ring square in the bore) and measure the ring end gap. For compression rings the end-gap (measured with a feeler blade) should be between 0.0079 and 0.0138 in (0.20 and 0.35 mm) and for oil control rings 0.0118 to 0.0354 in (0.30 to 0.8 mm).
5 The rings should now be tested in their respective grooves for side clearance. With new rings and pistons the clearance should be between 0.0015 and 0.0027 in (0.037 and 0.07 mm) for the top two compression rings and between 0.0015 and 0.0031 in (0.037 and 0.80 mm) for the bottom oil control ring. Where original rings are being refitted, the maximum side clearance of all rings is 0.0079 in. (0.195 mm).
6 Where necessary a piston ring which is slightly tight in its groove may be rubbed down holding it perfectly squarely on an oilstone or a sheet of fine emery cloth laid on a piece of plate glass. Excessive thickness can only be rectified by having the grooves machined out.
7 The gudgeon pin should be a push fit into the piston at room temperature. If it appears slack, then both the piston and gudgeon pin should be renewed.

30 Camshaft and camshaft bearings - examination and renovation

1 Carefully examine the camshaft bearings for wear. If the bearings are obviously worn or pitted then they must be renewed. This is an operation for your local Datsun dealer or local engineering works as it demands the use of specialized equipment. The bearings are removed with a special drift after which new bearings are pressed in, and in-line bored, care being taken to ensure the oil holes in the bearings line up with those in the block.
2 The camshaft itself should show no signs of wear, but, if very slight scoring on the cams is noticed, the score marks can be removed by very gently rubbing down with a very fine emery cloth. The greatest care should be taken to keep the cam profiles smooth.
3 Examine the skew gear for wear, chipped teeth or other damage.
4 Carefully examine the camshaft thrust plate. Excessive endfloat (more than 0.0039 in/0.10 mm) will be visually self evident and will require the fitting of a new plate.

31 Valves and valve seats - examination and renovation

1 Examine the heads of the valves for pitting and burning, especially the heads of the exhaust valves. The valve seatings should be examined at the same time. If the pitting on valve and seat is very slight the marks can be removed by grinding the seats and valves together with coarse, and then fine, valve grinding paste.
2 Where bad pitting has occurred to the valve seats it will be necessary to recut them and fit new valves. If the valve seats are so worn that they cannot be recut, then it will be necessary to fit new valve seat inserts. These latter two jobs should be entrusted to the local Datsun agent or engineering works. In practice it is very seldom that the seats are so badly worn that they require renewal. Normally, it is the valve that is too badly worn for replacement, and the owner can easily purchase a new set of valves and match them to the seats by valve grinding.
3 Valve grinding is carried out as follows:
 Smear a trace of coarse carborundum paste on the seat face and apply a suction grinder tool to the valve head. With a semi-rotary motion, grind the valve head to its seat, lifting the valve

occasionally to redistribute the grinding paste. When a dull matt even surface finish is produced on both the valve seat and the valve, wipe off the paste and repeat the process with fine carborundum paste, lifting and turning the valve to redistribute the paste as before. A light spring placed under the valve head will greatly ease this operation. When a smooth unbroken ring of light grey matt finish is produced, on both valve and valve seat faces, the grinding operation is completed.

4   Scrape away all carbon from the valve head and the valve stem. Carefully clean away every trace of grinding compound, taking great care to leave none in the ports or in the valve guides. Clean the valves and valve seats with a paraffin soaked rag then with a clean rag, and finally, if an air line is available, blow the valves, valve guides and valve ports clean.

32 Valve guides - examination and renovation

1   Test each valve in its guide for wear. After a considerable mileage, the valve guide bore may wear oval. This can best be tested by inserting a new valve in the guide and moving it from side to side. If the top of the valve stem deflects by about 0.0080 in (0.20 mm) then it must be assumed that the tolerance between the stem and guide is greater than the permitted maximum (0.0039 in/0.10 mm)

2   New valve guides (oversize available - see Specifications) may be pressed or drifted into the cylinder head after the worn ones have been removed in a similar manner. The cylinder head must be heated to 200°C (392°F) before carrying out these operations and although this can be done in a domestic oven, it must be remembered that the new guide will have to be reamed after installation and it may therefore be preferable to leave this work to your Datsun dealer.

33 Timing gears and chain - examination and renovation

1   Examine the teeth on both the crankshaft gear wheel and the camshaft gear wheel for wear. Each tooth forms an inverted 'V' with the gearwheel periphery, and if worn the side of each tooth under tension will be slightly concave in shape when compared with the other side of the tooth (ie; one side of the inverted 'V' will be concave when compared with the other). If any sign of wear is present the gearwheels must be renewed.

2   Examine the links of the chain for side slackness and renew the chain if any slackness is noticeable when compared with a new chain. It is a sensible precaution to renew the chain at about 30,000 miles (48,000 km) and at a lesser mileage if the engine is stripped down for a major overhaul. The actual rollers on a very badly worn chain may be slightly grooved.

34 Rockers and rocker shaft - examination and renovation

1   Thoroughly clean the rocker shaft and then check the shaft for straightness by rolling it on plate glass. It is most unlikely that it will deviate from normal, but if it does, purchase a new shaft. The surface of the shaft should be free from any worn ridges, caused by the rocker arms. If any wear is present, renew the shaft.

Check the rocker arms for wear of the rocker bushes, for wear at the rocker arm face which bears on the valve stem, and for wear of the adjusting ball ended screws. Wear in the rocker arm bush can be checked by gripping the rocker arm tip and holding the rocker arm in place on the shaft, noting if there is any lateral rocker arm shake. If shake is present, and the arm is very loose on the shaft, a new bush or rocker arm must be fitted.

Check the top of the rocker arm where it bears on the valve head for cracking or serious wear on the case hardening. If none is present reuse the rocker arm. Check the lower half of the ball on the end of the rocker arm adjusting screw. Check the push-rods for straightness by rolling them on the bench. Renew any that are bent.

35 Tappets (cam followers) - examination and renovation

Examine the bearing surface of the mushroom tappets which lie on the camshaft. Any indentation in this surface or any cracks indicate serious wear and the tappets should be renewed. Thoroughly clean them out, removing all traces of sludge. It is most unlikely that the sides of the tappets will prove worn, but, if they are a very loose fit in their bores and can readily be rocked, they should be exchanged for new units. It is very unusual to find any wear in the tappets, and any wear is likely to occur only at very high mileages.

36 Flywheel starter ring gear - examination and renovation

1   If the teeth on the flywheel starter ring are badly worn, or if some are missing then it will be necessary to remove the ring and fit a new one, or preferably exchange the flywheel for a reconditioned unit.

2   Either split the ring with a cold chisel after making a cut with a hacksaw blade between two teeth, or use a soft headed hammer (not steel) to knock the ring off, striking it evenly and alternately at equally spaced points. Take great care not to damage the flywheel during this process.

3   Heat the new ring in either an electric oven to about 200°C (392°F) or immerse in a pan of boiling oil.

4   Hold the ring at this temperature for five minutes and then quickly fit it to the flywheel so the chamfered portion of the teeth faces the gearbox side of the flywheel.

5   The ring should be tapped gently down onto its register and left to cool naturally when the contraction of the metal on cooling will ensure that it is a secure and permanent fit. Great care must be taken not to overheat the ring, indicated by it turning light metallic blue, as if this happens the temper of the ring will be lost.

37 Cylinder head - decarbonising and examination

1   With the cylinder head removed, us a blunt scraper to remove all traces of carbon and deposits from the combustion spaces and ports. Remember that the cylinder head is aluminium alloy and can be damaged easily during the decarbonising operations. Scrape the cylinder head free from scale or old pieces of gasket or jointing compound. Clean the cylinder head by washing it in paraffin and take particular care to pull a piece of rag through the ports and cylinder head bolt holes. Any grit remaining in these recesses may well drop onto the gasket or cylinder block mating surface as the cylinder head is lowered into position and could lead to a gasket leak after reassembly is complete.

2   With the cylinder head clean test for distortion if a history of coolant leakage has been apparent. Carry out this test using a straight-edge and feeler gauge or a piece of plate glass. If the surface shows any warping in excess of 0.0039 in (0.10 mm) then the cylinder head will have to be resurfaced which is a job for a specialist engineering company.

3   Clean the pistons and top of the cylinder bores. If the pistons are still in the block then it is essential that great care is taken to ensure that no carbon gets into the cylinder bores as this could scratch the cylinder walls or cause damage to the piston and rings. To ensure this does not happen, first turn the crankshaft so that two of the pistons are at the top of their bores. Stuff rag into the other two bores or seal them off with paper and masking tape. The waterways should also be covered with small pieces of masking tape to prevent particles of carbon entering the cooling system and damaging the water pump.

There are two schools of thought as to how much carbon should be removed from the piston crown. One school recommends that all carbon should be removed from the piston head. The other recommends that a ring of carbon should be left round the edge of the piston and on the cylinder bore wall as an aid to low oil consumption. Although this is probably true for early engines with worn bores, on later engines the thought of the second school can be applied: which is that for effective decarbonisation all traces of carbon should be removed.

If all traces of carbon are to be removed, press a little grease into the gap between the cylinder walls and the two pistons which are to be worked on. With a blunt scraper carefully scrape away the carbon from the piston crown, taking great care not to scratch the aluminium. Also scrape away the carbon from the surrounding lip of the cylinder wall. When all carbon has been removed, scrape away the grease which will now be contaminated with carbon particles, taking care not to press any into the bores. To assist prevention of carbon build-up the piston crown can be polished with a metal polish such as brasso. Remove the rags or masking tape from the other two cylinders and turn the crankshaft so that the two pistons which were at the bottom are now at the top. Place rag or masking tape in the cylinders which have been decarbonised and proceed as just described.

If a ring of carbon is going to be left round the piston then this can be helped by inserting an old piston ring into the top of the bore to rest on the piston and ensure that the carbon is not accidentally removed. Check that there are no particles of carbon in the cylinder bores. Decarbonising is now complete.

38 Engine reassembly - general

1 To ensure maximum life with minimum trouble from a rebuilt engine, not only must everything be correctly assembled, but everything must be spotlessly clean, all the oilways must be clear, locking washers and spring washers must always be fitted where indicated and all bearing and other working surfaces must be thoroughly lubricated during assembly.
2 Before assembly begins renew any bolts or studs the threads of which are in any way damaged, and whenever possible use new spring washers.
3 Apart from your normal tools, a supply of clean rag, an oil can filled with engine oil (an empty plastic detergent bottle thoroughly cleaned and washed out, will invariably do just as well); a new supply of assorted spring washers; a set of new gaskets; and a torque spanner, should be collected together.

39 Assembling the engine

1 Check the cylinder block for cracks, probe the oil passages and holes with a piece of wire and clean the external surfaces.
2 Renew all gaskets and seals and use plenty of clean engine oil to lubricate the components as they are installed. Observe absolute cleanliness.
3 Lubricate and refit the tappet blocks to their original locations with the engine block in the inverted position.
4 Oil the camshaft bearings and gently slide the camshaft into position taking care not to scratch or damage the bearing surfaces as the cam lobes pass through.
5 Fit the camshaft locking plate so that the world 'lower' is to the bottom when the engine is the right way up. Tighten the securing bolts to 3.6 lb/ft (0.5 kg/m).
6 Install the main bearing shells into their crankcase locations and into the bearing caps. Oil the bearing surfaces and carefully lower the crankshaft into position in the crankcase. Apply some Lithium based grease to the inner face of the rear oil seal. It can now be positioned approximately on the crankshaft boss.
7 Fit the main bearing caps complete with shells. Refer to Section 17, paragraph 1 for the difference between 100A and 120A main bearing caps. Tighten the main bearing cap bolts to a torque of between 36 and 43 lb/ft (4.97 and 5.94 kg/m).
8 Check the crankshaft rotates smoothly and test the endfloat (Section 26).
9 Position the new rear oil seal and then fit the endplate. Next, assemble the flywheel to the crankshaft using new locking tabs and tightening the bolts to between 47 and 54 lb/ft (6.5 and 7.46 kg/m).
10 The piston rings will have been fitted to the pistons (Section

29) and the connecting rods fitted with new bearings, pistons and gudgeon pins, as required (Sections 27 and 29). Arrange the piston ring gaps, each at an equidistant point of a circle so that they do not line up and cause gas blow-by. Liberally lubricate the rings and piston surfaces and insert the connecting rod into the cylinder bore so that the mark 'F' faces towards the timing cover. If you have a model that is not marked with an 'F', ensure the oil hole in the connecting rod big-end is toward the right side of the cylinder (ie; where it will mate with the oil hole in the crankshaft). Ensure that if the original pistons are being fitted then they are returned to their original cylinders.
11 Using a piston ring compressor, place the shaft of a hammer on the piston crown and strike the hammer head with the hand. This force should be quite sufficient to drive the piston, rod assembly down its bore. Where this action does not have the desired effect then the piston rings have not be sufficiently compressed or the piston ring end gaps are incorrect.
12 Connect each big-end to its appropriate crankshaft journal and fit the big-end cap complete with shell. The caps and rods are numbered 1 to 4 commencing at the timing gear end of the engine and when correctly fitted will have the cap and rod numbers adjacent. Tighten the big-end bolt nuts to between 23 and 27.5 lb/ft (3.179 and 3.5 kg/m). Use plenty of oil when fitting the connecting rods to the crankshaft and turn the crankshaft so that each big-end bearing is engaged when the respective crankshaft journal is at its lowest point.
13 Check the endfloat of each connecting rod big-end after installation, this should be between 0.0079 and 0.0118 in (0.20 and 0.30 mm) when the crankshaft is aligned (120A engines only).
14 Refit the crankcase baffle and gauze filter screen.
15 Temporarily refit the camshaft and crankshaft sprockets.
16 Place the crankshaft and camshaft sprockets within the timing chain and fit both sprockets complete with timing chain to the crankshaft and camshaft simultaneously. When correctly installed, a line drawn through the sprocket centres should also pass through the crankshaft dowel hole and the crankshaft sprocket keyway. A double check is the alignment of the sprocket dot punch marks and the matching marks on the chain side plates (Fig. 1.13). Installation of the timing gear will call for rotation of the camshaft and the crankshaft and repositioning of the camshaft sprocket within the loop of the chain on a trial and error basis until the alignment is correct.
17 When the timing is correct, tighten the camshaft sprocket securing bolt to between 29 and 35 lb/ft (4 and 4.83 kg/m) torque.
18 Fit the timing chain tensioner and tighten the securing bolts.
19 Check that the gap between the body of the tensioner and the rear face of the slipper does not exceed 0.591 in (18.01 mm) Fig. 1.14. If the gap is greater than specified, either the chain has stretched badly or the tensioner slipper has worn away and in either event the component must be renewed.
20 Fit the oil thrower disc to the crankshaft ensuring that the projecting rim is towards the timing cover.
21 Drift out the timing cover oil seal using a piece of tubing for this purpose. Fit a new seal, ensuring that the lips face inwards. Renew the chain slipper if it is worn.
22 Apply a thin film of gasket cement to the mating surfaces of the timing cover and the cylinder block. Stick a new gasket in aligned with it. Secure the cover with the retaining bolts and tighten them to a torque of 5 lb/ft (0.69 kg/m).
23 Refit the oil pump intake pipe and gauze filter.
24 Apply a thin film of gasket cement to the lower face of the crankcase and stick a new sump gasket into position so that the hole in the gasket are in alignment with the bolt holes of the crankcase. Apply more gasket cement to the mating surfaces of the sump, being particularly liberal with it at the front and rear and in the corners adjacent to the main bearing caps and timing cover. Offer up the sump and insert the securing bolts. Tighten them progressively in diametrically opposite sequence.
25 The cylinder head should now be reassembled ready for bolting to the engine. Place the cylinder head on its side and having oiled the valve guides, insert the valves in their original

17.7 Lift out the tappet blocks

39.5 Note the position of the word 'lower'

39.6A Fit the oil seal on the crankshaft

39.6B Install the main bearing shells ...

39.6C ... and lower the crankshaft into position

39.7A Fit the pulley end main bearing cap ...

39.7B ... and the centre cap ...

39.7C ... and then the flywheel end main bearing cap

39.9A Tap-up the oil seal flush with the bearing cap

39.9B Tighten the flywheel bolts and knock over the lockwashers

39.11A Compress the piston rings ...

39.11B ... and then tap home

39.12 Connecting the big-end bearing caps

39.15 Fit the crankshaft sprocket over the Woodruff key

39.20 Oil thrower assembled to crankshaft sprocket

39.21 Fit the new seal, lip innermost ...

39.22 ... then refit the timing case cover

39.23 Refit the oil pipe and strainer

locations or the seats into which they were previously ground (Section 31).

26 To each valve in turn, fit a new oil seal, a new valve spring (if the engine has covered more than 20,000 miles/32,000 km) the valve spring cup and insert. Compress each spring in turn sufficiently to permit the split cotters to be inserted in the cut-out in the valve stem. Release the compressor gently and check that the cotters have not be displaced.

27 When all valves have been fitted, place the cylinder head face down on the bench and using a hammer and a block of wood strike the end of each valve stem squarely to settle the valve components.

28 Thoroughly clean the faces of the cylinder head and the cylinder block using a non-fluffy rag and fuel.

29 The cylinder head gasket is of laminated type, having a steel sheet surface on one side and this surface should make contact with the face of the cylinder block. Due to the possibility of oil leakage from the cylinder head gasket on the pushrod side, the gasket has been partially treated with sealant in this area only. It is recommended however that both the mating faces of head and block are smeared with a thin coat of non-setting gasket cement as this will help to protect the surface of the alloy head against corrosion as well as providing a reliable seal.

30 Place the gasket in position on the block (steel side down, jointing material visible). Lightly smear the threads of the cylinder head bolts with heavy grade grease and push two of the bolts through the head so that as the head is gently lowered into position they will serve as locating dowels to locate the gasket and head.

31 Note that one bolt head is marked T; this must be screwed into number one position (Fig. 1.4).

32 Fit the remaining bolts and tighten them progressively a turn or two at a time each, in the sequence shown, to a torque of between 43 and 47 lb/ft (6.0 and 6.5 kg/m).

33 Refit the pushrods in their original locations.

34 Refit the rocker shaft assembly tightening the pillar bolts to a torque of between 15 and 18 lb/ft (2.07 and 2.48 kg/m). Tighten the centre bolts first and work outwards.

35 Fit a new exhaust manifold gasket and fit the manifold, securing nuts and washers. Tighten to a torque of between 6.5 and 10 lb/ft (0.9 and 1.38 kg/m).

36 Oil the crankshaft pulley shank and having checked that the Woodruff key is in position, push it carefully into position through the timing cover oil seal. Tighten the pulley securing bolt to between 109 and 116 lb/ft (15.06 and 16.03 kg/m). The teeth of the flywheel ring gear may be jammed with a large screwdriver to prevent the pulley and crankshaft rotating during the tightening operation.

37 The valve clearances should now be adjusted. Rotate the engine during the adjustment procedure by using a spanner or socket on the crankshaft pulley bolt.

38 The valve clearances obviously will have to be set with the engine cold to start with but when the unit is refitted to the vehicle and run up to normal operating temperature then they will have to be checked and readjusted when the engine is hot.

39 The valve adjustments may be made with the engine cold but are more accurate when the engine is hot. The importance of correct rocker arm/valve stem clearances cannot be overstressed as they vitally affect the performance of the engine. If the clearances are set too open, the efficiency of the engine is reduced as the valves open late and close earlier than was intended.

40 It is important that the valve clearance is set when the tappet of the valve being adjusted is on the heel of the cam (the lowest point) so that the valve is fully seated. One of two methods may be employed, first place a finger over No 1 spark plug hole, turn the engine and as soon as compression is felt, either observe the piston crown until it reaches its highest point (TDC) and descends about 1/8th inch (3.175 mm) or using a length of wire as a measure stop rotating the engine when the wire has passed its highest point and descended about 1/8th inch (3.175 mm). Both the valves for No 1 cylinder may be set (inlet and exhaust valve clearance given in the Specifications).

41 The firing order is 1-3-4-2 and the alternative method of valve clearance adjustment which avoids the necessity of turning the engine excessively is to apply the adjustment sequence shown in the following table.

Valve fully open	Check & Adjust
Valve No. 8	Valve No. 1
Valve No. 6	Valve No. 3
Valve No. 4	Valve No. 5
Valve No. 7	Valve No. 2
Valve No. 1	Valve No. 8
Valve No. 3	Valve No. 6
Valve No. 5	Valve No. 4
Valve No. 2	Valve No. 7

Counting from the timing cover end of the engine, inlet valves are nos. 2-3-6-7, exhaust valves are nos. 1-4-5-8.

42 Adjustment of the clearance is made by conventional screw and locknut. Insert the feeler blade between the rocker arm face and the valve stem end face. Loosen the locknut, turn the screw until the blade cannot be withdrawn and then loosen the screw until the blade can be withdrawn just, (stiffly), by a hard pull. Holding the slotted adjustment screw quite still, tighten the lock-nut with a ring spanner. When all the valve clearances have been adjusted, recheck them again before fitting the rocker box cover complete with a new sealing gasket.

43 Using a new gasket, fit the oil pump to the crankcase, checking that the drive gear meshes correctly.

44 Screw a new oil filter cartridge into position. Lightly grease the rubber sealing ring before fitting it and tighten it by hand pressure only.

45 Using new gaskets, refit the thermostat, thermostat cover, water pump and fan. On some models there is no fan, but the pulley will still have to be replaced.

46 Fit the alternator to its mountings and reconnect the slotted adjustment strap.

47 Locate the fan belt over the crankshaft, water pump and alternator pulleys and then prise the alternator away from the engine until the belt has a total deflection of ½ in at the centre of its longest run. Tighten the adjustment strap bolt and mounting bolts of the alternator.

48 Fit the carburettor to the manifold (if not previously combined with the exhaust manifold) and the fuel pump to the crankcase, ensuring that new gaskets similar to those originally fitted are used.

49 Reconnect the fuel pipe between the pump and the carburettor.

50 The distributor should now be refitted. To do this, turn the engine until No 1 cylinder is at TDC. This position can be observed from the alignment of the crankshaft pulley and timing cover marks (Fig. 1.17). A secondary check can be made by seeing that both the inlet and exhaust valves of No 1 cylinder are fully closed.

51 When installed, the distributor rotor should take up the position shown in Fig. 1.18. To achieve this, hold the distributor over the engine and position the rotor as shown. Now turn the rotor approximately 60° in a clockwise direction, this is to compensate for movement of the rotor as the distributor is pushed into mesh with the camshaft gear. The action of meshing will return the rotor to the position illustrated which shows the rotor point to No. 1 spark plug HT lead segment in the distributor cap. Tighten the distributor clamp plate bolt. It will be necessary to check the ignition timing in accordance with Chapter 4, when the engine is installed.

52 Fit the spark plugs, correctly cleaned and gapped (Chapter 4).

53 Connect the plug leads and crankcase ventilation hose.

54 Refit the clutch assembly to the flywheel (Chapter 5), and mate the transmission with the engine, as described in Chapter 6.

39.24 Mating the sump with the crankcase

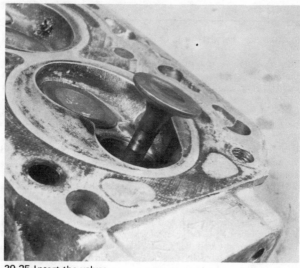

39.25 Insert the valves ...

39.26A ... valve spring seat ...

39.26B ... spring ...

39.26C ... spring retainer and then secure with collets

39.30 Refit the cylinder head

39.31 The special 'T' bolt

39.33 Refit the pushrods ...

39.34 ... then the rocker shaft assembly

39.35 Refit the combined inlet and exhaust manifold

39.36A Fit the crankshaft pulley ...

39.36B ... and bolt it in position

39.42A Adjusting the valve clearances

39.42B Refitting the rocker cover

39.43 Inserting the oil pump drive

39.45A Assemble the thermostat ...

39.45B ... and then its cover

39.45C Fitting the drive belt pulley

39.47 Adjusting the fan belt tension

39.50 Insert the distributor

39.53 Refit the plug leads

39.54 Assemble the clutch to the flywheel

55 Once the transmission is coupled to the engine block, refit the engine mounting brackets.

56 Fit suitable slings to the engine/gearbox unit and prepare the hoist for lifting the power unit back into the vehicle.

40 Engine/transmission replacement - general

1 Although the engine can be replaced by one man using a suitable winch, it is easier if two are present: one to lower the assembly into the engine compartment and the other to guide the assembly into position and to ensure it does not foul anything.

2 At this stage one or two tips may come in useful. Ensure all the loose leads, cables, etc. are tucked out of the way. If not it is easy to trap one and so cause much additional work after the engine is replaced.

3 Two pair of hands are better than one when refitting the bonnet. Do not tighten the bonnet securing bolts fully until it is ascertained that the bonnet is on straight.

41 Engine/transmission - refitting to the vehicle

1 Raise the engine/transmission unit and either roll the vehicle forward under it or if the hoist is mobile roll it forward so that

the unit is suspended above the engine compartment.

2 Lower the assembly into the engine compartment. Ensure that nothing is foulded during the operation.

3 The engine is installed by following, in the reverse order, the procedures given for removal. The following points must be noted:

(a) *Do not let the weight of the engine be fully taken on the mounting insulators until the bolts have been tightened.*

(b) *The rear insulator has a locking pawl attached to the rubber mount. Take care that this part is not damaged whilst lowering the engine into position.*

(c) *Tighten the exhaust pipe by starting at the manifold connection. Install the buffer rods only after the engine mounting insulators have been tightened. The buffer rods must not be installed under stress. The standard length of the rod (centres of the mounting holes) is 194 mm (7.64 in). Commence installation with the rods at this length but adjust, if necessary, to remove any stress in the engine mountings.*

4 Reconnect the driveshafts (Chapter 7).

5 Reconnect the gearchange linkage.

6 Reconnect the speedometer drive,

7 Remove the plug and reconnect the fuel line to the fuel pump.

8 Reconnect the reversing lamp leads.

9 Reconnect the alternator leads.

10 Reconnect the clutch cable or hydraulic slave cylinder according to vehicle type.

11 Reconnect the choke and accelerator controls and refit the air cleaner.

12 Reconnect the LT lead to the distributor, the HT lead between the distributor and the coil.

13 Connect the oil pressure and water temperature leads.

14 Refit the radiator and heater hoses. Reconnect the leads to the fan, if an electrically-operated fan is fitted.

15 Connect the negative battery lead.

16 Refit the bonnet.

17 Refill the cooling system (Chapter 2).

18 Refill the engine sump with the correct grade and quantity of oil.

19 Check the level of oil in the transmission.

42 Engine adjustment after major overhaul

1 With the engine refitted to the vehicle, give a final visual check to see that everything has been reconnected and that no loose rags or tools have been left within the engine compartment.

2 Turn the engine slow running screw in about ½ turn (to increase slow running once the engine is started). (Chapter 3).

3 Pull the choke fully out and start the engine. This may take a little longer than usual as the fuel pump and carburettor bowl will be empty and need initial primary.

4 As soon as the engine starts, push the choke in until the engine runs at a fast tickover and examine the engine for leaks. Check particularly the water hoses and oil filter and fuel hose unions.

5 Run the vehicle on the road until normal operating temperature is reached. Check the valve clearances while the engine is hot, as described in Section 39, of this Chapter. Re-adjust engine tickover.

6 After 500 miles (800 km) running, the engine oil should be changed particularly where the majority of the internal components have been renewed or reconditioned.

7 After 500 miles (800 km) check the torque setting of the cylinder head bolts with the cylinder head cold. Follow the tightening sequence given in Fig. 1.4.

43 Fault diagnosis - engine

Symptom	Reason/s	Remedy
Engine will not turn over when starter switch is operated	Flat battery Bad battery connections Bad connections at solenoid switch and/or starter motor Starter motor jammed	Check that battery is fully charged and that all connections are clean and tight. Where a pre-engaged starter is fitted rock the car back and forth with a gear engaged. If this does not free pinion remove starter.
	Defective solenoid	Bridge the main terminals of the solenoid switch with a piece of heavy duty cable in order to operate the starter.
	Starter motor defective	Remove and overhaul starter motor.
Engine turns over normally but fails to start	No spark at plugs	Check ignition system according to procedures given in Chapter 4.
	No fuel reaching engine	Check fuel system according to procedures given in Chapter 3.
	Too much fuel reaching the engine (flooding)	Check the fuel system as above.
Engine starts but runs unevenly and misfires	Ignition and/or fuel system faults	Check the ignition and fuel systems as though the engine had failed to start.
	Incorrect valve clearances	Check and reset clearances.
	Burnt out valves	Remove cylinder head and examine and overhaul as necessary.
	Worn out piston rings	Remove cylinder head and examine pistons and cylinder bores. Overhaul as necessary.
Lack of power	Ignition and/or fuel system faults	Check the ignition and fuel systems for correct ignition timing and carburattor settings.
	Incorrect valve clearances	Check and reset the clearances.
	Burnt out valves	Remove cylinder head and examine and overhaul as necessary.
	Worn out piston rings	Remove cylinder head and examine pistons and cylinder bores. Overhaul as necessary.
Excessive oil consumption	Oil leaks from crankshaft rear oil seal, timing cover gasket and oil seal, rocker cover gasket, oil filter gasket, sump gasket, sump plug washer.	Identify source of leak and renew seal as appropriate.
	Worn piston rings or cylinder bores resulting in oil being burnt by engine	Fit new rings or rebore cylinders and fit new pistons, depending on degree of wear.
	Worn valve guides and/or defective valve stem seals	Remove cylinder heads and recondition valve stem bores and valves and seals as necessary.

Excessive mechanical noise from engine	Wrong valve to rocker clearances	Adjust valve clearances
	Worn crankshaft bearings	Inspect and overhaul where necessary.
	Worn cylinders (piston slap)	
	Slack or worn timing chain and sprockets	Adjust chain and/or inspect all timing mechanism.

Note: When investigating starting and uneven running faults do not be tempted into snap diagnosis. Start from the beginning of the check procedure and follow it through. It will take less time in the long run. Poor performance from an engine in terms of power and economy is not normally diagnosed quickly. In any event the ignition and fuel systems must be checked first before assuming any further investigation needs to be made.

Chapter 2 Cooling system

Contents

Specifications

System type	thermo syphon with pump assistance
Radiator type	corrugated fin
Filler cap opening pressure	13 lb/in^2

Thermostat

Type	wax pellet
Start to open	82°C $\pm$ 1.5°C
Maximum valve lift	Above 8 mm at 95°C

Coolant capacity

With heater	5.4 litres (9.5 pints)
Without heater	4.8 litres (8.2 pints)

Torque wrench settings

	lb f ft	kg f m
Water pump body securing nuts	7 - 10	0.967 - 1.382

1 General description

The cooling system comprises the radiator, top and bottom water hoses, water pump, cylinder head and block water jackets, radiator cap with pressure relief valve and flow and return heater hoses. Some models are fitted with an expansion tank. On some models, since the engine is transversely mounted, a shroud is fitted over the cooling fan to duct air from the radiator. The shroud is in two sections; upper and lower. On other models an electrically operated and controlled fan is fitted directly on the radiator, which obviates the need for shrouds. The thermostat is located in a recess at the front of the cylinder head. The principle of the system is that cold water in the bottom of the radiator circulates upwards through the lower radiator hose to the water pump, where the pump impeller pushes the water round the cylinder block and head through the various cast-in passages to cool the cylinder bores, combustion surfaces and valve seats. When sufficient heat has been absorbed by the cooling water, and the engine has reached an efficient working temperature, the water moves from the cylinder head past the now open thermostat into the top radiator hose and into the radiator header tank.

The water then travels down the radiator tubes when it is rapidly cooled by the in-rush of air, when the vehicle is in forward motion.

The water, now cooled, reaches the bottom of the radiator and the cycle is repeated.

When the engine is cold the thermostat remains closed until the coolant reaches a pre-determined temperature (see Specifications). This assists rapid warming-up.

Water temperature is measured by an electro-sensitive capsule located immediately below the thermostat housing. Connection between the transmitter capsule and the facia gauge is made by a single cable and Lucar type connector. The cooling system also provides the heat for the heater. The heater matrix is fed directly with water from the hottest part of the cylinder - the cylinder head - returning through a connection on the bottom radiator hose.

On some models the cooling fan is mounted on the water

pump and is driven by a pulley belt from the crankshaft. Other models are equipped with an electrical fan on the radiator.

2 Cooling system - draining

1 Should the system have to be left empty for any reason both the cylinder block and radiator must be drained, otherwise with a partly drained system corrosion of the water pump impeller seal face may occur with subsequent early failure of the pump seal and bearing.

2 Place the car on a level surface and have ready a container having a capacity of two gallons which will slide beneath the radiator and sump.

3 Move the heater control on the facia to 'H' and unscrew and remove the radiator cap. If hot, unscrew the cap very slowly, first covering it with a cloth to remove the danger of scalding when the pressure in the system is released.

4 Unscrew the radiator drain tap at the base of the radiator and then when coolant ceases to flow into the receptable, repeat the operation by unscrewing the cylinder block plug located on the engine. Retain the coolant for further use, if it contains anti-freeze.

3 Cooling system - flushing

1 The radiator and waterways in the engine after some time may become restricted or even blocked with scale or sediment which reduce the efficiency of the cooling system. When this condition occurs or the coolant appears rusty or dark in colour the system should be flushed. In severe cases reverse flushing may be required as described later.

2 Place the heater controls to the 'H' position and unscrew fully the radiator and cylinder block drain taps.

3 Remove the radiator filler cap and place a hose in the filler neck. Allow water to run through the system until it emerges from both drain tabs quite clear in colour. Do not flush a hot engine with cold water.

4 In severe cases of contamination of the coolant or in the system, reverse flush by first removing the radiator cap and disconnecting the lower radiator hose at the radiator outlet pipe.

5 Remove the top hose at the radiator connection end and remove the radiator, as described in Section 6.

6 Invert the radiator and place a hose in the bottom outlet pipe. Continue flushing until clear water comes from the radiator top tank.

7 To flush the engine water jackets, remove the thermostat as described later in this Chapter and place a hose in the thermostat location until clear water runs from the water pump inlet. Cleaning by the use of chemical compounds is not recommended.

4 Cooling system - filling

1 Place the heater control to the 'H' position.

2 Screw in the radiator drain tap finger tight only and close the cylinder block drain tap.

3 Pour coolant slowly into the radiator so that air can be expelled through the thermostat pin hole without being trapped in a waterway.

4 Fill to the correct level which is 1 inch (25.4 mm) below the radiator filler neck and replace the filler cap.

5 Run the engine, check for leaks and recheck the coolant level.

6 On vehicles fitted with an expansion tank, check that the radiator overflow tube is correctly connected and that the tank is filled with coolant to the level indicated.

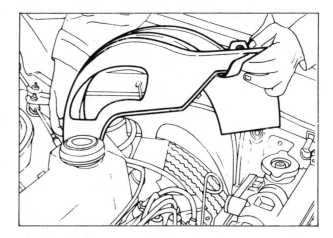

Fig. 2.1. Removing the fan upper shroud

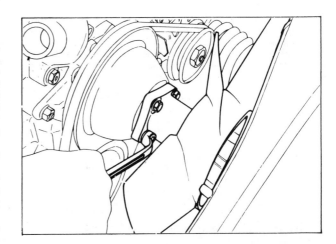

Fig. 2.2. Disconnecting the fan and spacer

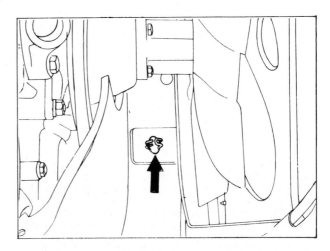

Fig. 2.3. Radiator hose clamp in the lower shroud

5 Antifreeze mixture

1   The cooling system should be filled with Castrol Antifreeze solution in early Autumn. The heater matrix and radiator bottom tank are particularly prone to freeze if antifreeze is not used. Modern antifreeze solutions of good quality will also prevent corrosion and rusting and they may be left in the system to advantage all year round, draining and refilling with fresh solution each year.

2   Before adding antifreeze to the system, check all hose connections and check the tightness of the cylinder head bolts as such solutions are searching. The cooling system should be drained and refilled with clean water as previously explained, before adding antifreeze.

3   The quantity of antifreeze which should be used for various levels of protection is given in the table below, expressed as a percentage of the system capacity.

Antifreeze volume	Protection to	Safe pump circulation
25%	−26°C (−15°F)	−12°C (10°F)
30%	−33°C (−28°F)	−16°C (3°F)
35%	−39°C (−38°F)	−20°C (− 4°F)

4   Where the cooling system contains an antifreeze solution any topping-up should be done with a solution made up in similar proportions to the original in order to avoid dilution.

5   On vehicles fitted with an expansion tank, ensure that it is filled to the correct level with the same strength of antifreeze mixture.

6 Radiator - removal, inspection and refitting

1   Drain the cooling system, as described in Section 2.

2   Disconnect the top hose from the radiator header tank pipe and the overflow tube from the reservoir (if fitted).

3   Remove the raditor/fan upper shroud by releasing the belts at the bottom shroud (four) and the single bolt at the bonnet ledge.

4   Remove the fan and spacer, then ease off the fan pulley and belt. You may have to loosen the alternator bolts and reduce the belt tension to achieve this.

5   Press out the radiator hose clamp from the lower shroud by applying finger pressure.

6   Loosen the screws securing the lower shroud so that it can be taken out when the radiator is removed.

7   Disconnect the radiator lower hose.

8   Remove the front grille and the radiator securing bolts. Remove the radiator together with the lower shroud.

9   Remove the radiator lower shroud.

10 With the radiator away from the car any leaks can be soldered or repaired with a plastic filler. Clean out the inside of the radiator by flushing as described earlier in this Chapter. When the radiator is out of the car it is advantageous to turn it upside down and reverse flush. Clean the exterior of the radiator by carefully using a compressed air jet or a strong jet of water to clear away any road dirt, flies etc.

11 Inspect the radiator hoses for cracks, internal or external perishing and damage by overtightening of the securing clips. Also inspect the overflow pipe. Renew the hoses if suspect. Examine the radiator hose clips and renew them if they are rusted or distorted.

12 The drain plug and washer should be renewed if leaking or with worn threads, but first ensure that the leak is not caused by a damaged washer.

13 Replacement of the radiator is a reversal of the removal procedure. Refill and check for leaks, as described in Section 4.

7 Radiator and fan - removal and refitting

1   On some models the cooling fan is electrically operated and is mounted on the back of the radiator. If the radiator has to be

Fig. 2.4. Removing the radiator bolts

Fig. 2.5. Removing the thermostat

1 Thermostat   2 Water outlet

Fig. 2.6. Removing the water pump

removed, it is easier to remove the fan integrally with the radiator.

2 Disconnect the top and bottom hoses after first draining the cooling system.

3 Locate the electrical connections to the fan; these are joined to the main cable loom by in-line Lucar connectors underneath the windscreen washer bag. Disconnect the cables.

4 Disconnect the reservoir pipe (if fitted).

5 Remove the four bolts that retain the radiator and lift out the combined radiator and fan unit.

6 Cleaning and inspection of the radiator is the same as for earlier models, but if the radiator is to be washed down or flushed it is advisable to remove the fan first.

7 Replacement is a reverse of removal techniques.

8 Thermostat - removal, testing and refitting

1 A faulty thermostat can cause overheating or slow engine warm up. It will also affect the performance of the heater.

2 Drain off enough coolant through the radiator drain tap so that the coolant level is below the thermostat housing joint face. A good indication that the correct level has been reached is when the cooling tubes are exposed when viewed through the radiator filler cap.

3 Unscrew and remove the two retaining bolts and withdraw the thermostat cover sufficiently to permit the thermostat to be removed from its seat in the cylinder head.

4 To test whether the unit is serviceable, suspend the thermostat by a piece of string in a pan of water being heated. Using a thermometer, with reference to the opening and closing temperature in Specifications, its operation may be checked. The thermostat should be renewed if it is stuck open or closed or it fails to operate at the specified temperature. The operation of a thermostat is not instantaneous and sufficient time must be allowed for movement during testing. Never replace a faulty unit - leave it out if no replacement is available immediately.

5 Replacement of the thermostat is a reversal of the removal procedure. Ensure the mating faces of the housing are clean. Use a new gasket with jointing compound. The word 'TOP' which appears on the thermostat face must be visible from above.

9 Water pump - description

The water pump is of conventional impeller type, driven by a pulley belt that also drives the fan on early models. The impeller chamber is built into, and forms part of, the timing cover. The water pump detachable body is of die-cast aluminium in which runs the shaft. The shaft is fitted with bearings which are a shrink fit in the body and in the event of leakage or failure of the water pump, then it must be renewed as an assembly on an exchange basis.

10 Water pump - removal and refitting

1 Drain the cooling system, retaining the coolant if required for further use.

2 Slacken the alternator mountings and adjustment strap bolt, push the alternator in towards the engine and slip the belt from the driving pulleys.

3 Unscrew and remove the four bolts which secure the fan and pulley to the water pump flange, remove the fan and pulley. The fan is not fitted on later models.

4 Unscrew and remove the securing nuts and bolts from the water pump housing flange and withdraw the water pump. Should the pump be stuck to the face of the timing cover, do not attempt to prise the mating flange apart as this will damage the soft aluminium and cause leaks after refitting. Grip the shaft extension housing firmly and lever from side to side to break the seal.

5 Refitting is a reversal of removal but ensure that the mating

7.2 Disconnecting the top hose at the thermostat

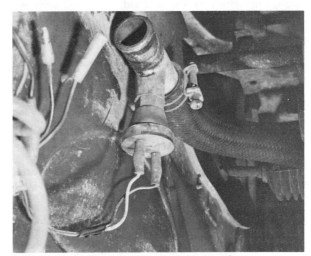

7.3 Lower hose disconnected at the thermostat fan switch 'T' piece, and also disconnected electrical leads to the fan

7.5 Lifting out the combined fan and radiator

faces are clean and free from old pieces of gasket. Use a new gasket coated both sides with jointing compound and tighten the securing nuts to a torque of between 7 and 10 lb/ft (0.967 and 1.382 kg/m).
6 Adjust the tension of the fan belt, as described in Section 11 of this Chapter.
7 Refill the cooling system (Section 4).

11 Fan belt - adjustment, removal and refitting

1 The correct tension of the fan belt must be maintained, for it is very important. If it is overtightened then the bearings in the water pump and the alternator may wear prematurely. If it is slack, it will slip and cause overloading and a discharged battery through low alternator output.
2 The fan belt is correctly tensioned when a total movement of ½ in can be obtained at the centre of the longest run of the belt.
3 Always adjust the fan belt with the engine cold. Slacken the alternator mounting bolts and the slotted adjustment strap bolt. Prise the alternator away from the engine until the correct tension is obtained. It will be easier to achieve the correct tension if the alternator bolts are only slackened sufficiently to permit it to move stiffly. Always apply leverage to the drive end housing when tilting the alternator and never to the diode end housing, or the alternator will be damaged at the casing. Always recheck the fan belt tension after the alternator mounting and adjustment strap bolts have been tightened.

12 Electrical cooling fan - testing and removal

1 If the water temperature gauge is showing a high reading then one obviously suspect the thermostat or cooling fan, if nothing more obvious like coolant leaks are the case.
2 In the case of an electrical cooling fan it is not easy to determine when, or if, it is working, especially since it is thermostatically controlled and is not always running.
3 Obviously, if the engine has been working hard (eg; after climbing a longish hill), then one simply looks at the fan and sees whether its working or not. If it is then you have some other reason for the high temperature, and should check the fault diagnosis chart in this Chapter.

4 Having decided the fan is not working; proceed as follows. First, turn on the ignition and then short-circuit the thermostat switch: this is in the insert pipe in the bottom hose on the left-hand side, and stands up like a tee-piece. If the fan now runs the thermostat is faulty and should be replaced. If not, check that the white feed cable to the thermostat is live, using a test lamp or voltmeter.
5 If all is satisfactory so far check the black/white cable at the fan relay: this should be live when the thermostat is short-circuited. If it is, next check the yellow cable at the fan relay: this should always be live. If not check the fused end of the cable at the fuse box.
6 If all tests have been satisfactory so far, next check the blue wire at the fan relay: this should only be live when the thermostat is short-circuited. If ok it indicates that the fan motor is probably defective: this must be removed and replaced.
7 Disconnect the Lucar connectors to the fan and then remove the four bolts that secure it to the radiator. The fan can now be lifted out. Replacement is the reverse of removal.

13 Water temperature gauge - fault finding

1 Correct operation of the water temperature gauge is very important as the engine can otherwise overheat without it being observed.
2 The gauge is an electrically operated instrument comprising a transmitter unit screwed into the front of the cylinder head and transmitting through a Lucar type connector and cable to the dial mounted on the facia instrument panel. The instrument only operates when the ignition is switched on.
3 Where the water temperature gauge reads high-low intermittently, or not at all, then first check the security of the connecting cable between the transmitter unit and the gauge.
4 Disconnect the Lucar connector from the transmitter unit, switch on the ignition when the gauge should read COLD. Now earth the cable to the engine block when the gauge needle should indicate HOT. This test proves the gauge to be functional and the fault must therefore lie in the calbe or transmitter unit. Renew as appropriate.
5 If the fuel gauge shows signs of malfunction at the same time as the water temperature gauge then a fault in the voltage stabilizer may be the cause.

14 Fault diagnosis - cooling system

Symptom	Reason/s	Remedy
Overheating	Electrical fan faulty (if fitted)	Trace fault
	Low coolant level	Top up
	Slack fan belt	Adjust tension
	Thermostat not operating	Renew
	Radiator pressure cap faulty or of wrong type	Renew
	Defective water pump	Renew
	Cylinder head gasket blowing	Fit new gasket
	Radiator core clogged	Clean
	Radiator blocked	Reverse flush
	Binding brakes	Rectify
	Bottom hose or tank frozen	Drain and refill with antifreeze
	Shrouds missing or broken	Recitfy
Engine running too cool	Defective thermostat	Renew
	Faulty water temperature gauge	Renew
Loss of coolant	Leaking radiator or hoses	Renew or tighten
	Cylinder head gasket leaking	Renew gasket
	Leaking cylinder block core plugs	Renew
	Faulty radiator filler cap or wrong type fitted	Replace with correct type

Chapter 3 Carburation;
fuel and exhaust systems

Contents

Specifications

Fuel pump ... ...   mechanical, driven by camshaft eccentric

    Static fuel pressure ... ... 2.56 lb/in^2 (A12); 3.41 lb/in^2 (A10)

    Output ... ...   600 cc per minute

Fuel tank

    Location ... ...   rear mounted

    Capacity:

       saloon ... ...   7.9 Imp. gals/36 litres/9.5 US gals

       estate and coupe ... ...   7.7 Imp. gals/35 litres/9.3 US gals

Air cleaner

    Type ... ...   normal, paper element

Carburettors

    Type:

       A12 engine ... ...   Hitachi DCG 306 - 6D

       A10 engine ... ...   Hitachi DCG 286 - 6D

	DCG 306 - 6D		DCG 286 - 6D	
	Primary	Secondary	Primary	Secondary
Outer diameter	1.024 in (26 mm)	1.181 in (30 mm)	1.024 in (26 mm)	1.102 in (28 mm)
Venturi diameter	0.787 in (20 mm)	1.024 in (26 mm)	0.748 in (19 mm)	0.945 in (24 mm)
Main jet	96	150	92	140
Main air bleed	80	80	80	80
Slow jet	43	50	43	50
Slow air bleed	220	100	220	100
Power jet	60		45	

1 General description

The fuel system comprises a fuel tank at the rear of the vehicle, a mechanical fuel pump located on the front of the engine and a Hitachi carburettor. A renewable paper element air cleaner is fitted as standard.

The fuel pump draws petrol from the fuel tank and delivers it to the carburettor installation. The level of petrol in the carburettor is controlled by a float operated needle valve. Petrol flows past the needle unit the float rises sufficiently to close the valve. The pump will then free wheel under slight back pressure until the petrol level drops. The needle valve will then open and petrol continue to flow until the level rises again.

One of three types of emission control systems may be fitted to the Datsun Cherry range of vehicles. The crankcase emission control system is the standard system used in all vehicles. The exhaust emission control system or evaporative emission control system are used in models exported to Canada and USA.

Vehicle being operated in areas controlled by the US Federal

Regulations on air pollution must have their engines and ancilliary equipment modified and accurately tuned so that carbon monoxide, hydrocarbons and nitrogen produced by the engine are within finely controlled limits.

To achieve this there are several systems used. Depending on the pollution standard required, the systems may be fitted either singly or a combination of them all. The solution to the problem is achieved by modifying various parts of the engine and fuel supply system as will be seen in subsequent Sections.

2 Air cleaner - servicing

1 The standard air cleaner comprises a body in which is housed a paper element type filter, a lid and the necessary connecting hoses and brackets.
2 Every 24,000 miles the element should be renewed. Other than renewal, no servicing is required.
3 Unscrew and remove the wing nut which secures the air cleaner lid in position, remove the lid and extract the paper element.
4 Wipe the interior of the aid cleaner body free from oil and dirt and install the new element.
5 On some models a WINTER/SUMMER selector lever is used on the air inlet. The lever should be set accordingly and in winter will admit air heated from proximity to the exhaust manifold.

3 Fuel filter - servicing

1 the fuel filter is located in the tank to pump hose and is of the sealed paper element type.
2 Every 12,000 miles, renew the filter. It is preferable to carry out this operation when the fuel tank level is low otherwise when the fuel hoses are disconnected from the filter, the tank line will have to be plugged to prevent loss of fuel.
3 Check that the new filter is installed in the correct attitude, (Fig. 3.1).

4 Fuel tank and fuel lines - description and servicing

1 The fuel tank is rear mounted and varies in capacity according to vehicle model. Filler tube, vent pipes and fuel lines are connected to the tank by flexible tubing. The fuel level gauge (next Section) is mounted in the top of the tank and a drain plug is conveniently located. The tank on the estate car is of a different shape and is mounted in a slightly different manner.

2.3A Removing the lid

2.3B Showing the element

2.3C With the element removed

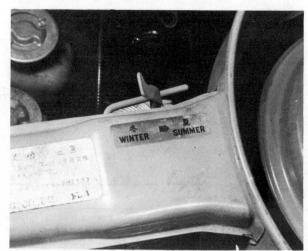
2.5 The winter/summer selector lever

2 To remove the fuel tank, drain the tank and then disconnect the fuel line connector.
3 Loosen the clamps at the fuel filler hose and ventilation tube. Disconnect the sender unit cable harness.
4 Unscrew and remove the securing bolts and anchor plates from the fuel tank flanges. When working on the saloon or estate, work should commence at the bolts at the front of the tank. The estate car tank should be lowered just far enough to rest against the rear axle before removing the remaining bolts.
5 Withdraw the tank from its location.
6 If the tank contains a lot of sediment or sludge, shake it vigorously using two or three changes of paraffin and then allow it to drain thoroughly.
7 Should a leak develop in the fuel tank do not be tempted to solder over the hole. Fuel tank repair is a specialist job and unless lengthy safety precautions are observed can be a very dangerous procedure. It is probably as cheap these days to buy a new tank rather than have the faulty one repaired.
8 Occasionally drain the tank when there is very little fuel left in it so that any accumulated water or sediment will be flushed out and discarded. This action will safeguard the tank against corrosion and help to prevent clogging of the fuel line filter.
9 Refitting the fuel tank is a reversal of removal, check that the vent tubes which are connected to the filler neck are not trapped and are securely clipped in position. Do not forget to install spring and plain washers on tank mounting bolts since the mounting holes in the tank flange are elongated to provide for adjustment.

5 Fuel pump - description

The fuel pump is actuated by the movement of its rocker arm on a camshaft eccentric. This movement is transferred to a flexible diaphragm with draws the fuel from the tank and pumps

Fig. 3.1. Fuel system in-line filter

it under pressure to the carburettor float chamber. Inlet and out valves are incorporated to control the flow of fuel irrespective of engine speed.

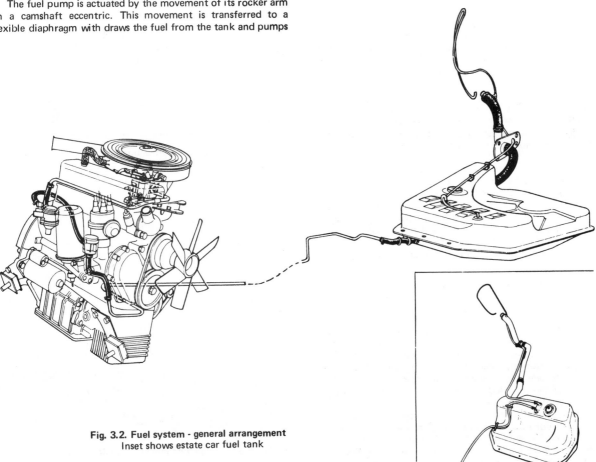

Fig. 3.2. Fuel system - general arrangement
Inset shows estate car fuel tank

6 Fuel pump - testing

Presuming that the fuel lines and unions are in good condition and that there are no leaks anywhere, check the performance of the fuel pump in the following manner: Disconnect the fuel pipe at the carburettor inlet union, and the high tension lead to the coil, and with a suitable container or a large rag in position to catch the ejected fuel, turn the engine over on the starter motor solenoid. A good spurt of petrol should emerge from the end of the pipe every second revolution.

7 Fuel pump - removal and refitting

1 Disconnect the fuel pipes by unscrewing their two unions on the fuel pump which is located on the front of the engine. Where the fuel tank contains more than a small amount of fuel it will probably be necessary to plug the inlet fuel line from the tank.
2 Remove the two nuts which secure the fuel pump to the crankcase. Lift away the pump noting carefully the number of gaskets used between the pump and crankcase mating faces.

8 Fuel pump - dismantling, inspection and reassembly

1 Scratch a mark across the edges of the upper and lower body flange to ensure easy refitting.
2 Unscrew and remove the body securing screws (17) and their lock washers (18) (Fig. 3.7).
3 Remove the cover screw (7) washer (8) cover (5) and the gasket (6).
4 Unscrew and remove the inlet and outlet fuel pipe connecting stubs.
5 Unscrew and remove the two screws from the valve retainer (3). Withdraw the two valves (1) and the valve washers (2).
6 Press the diaphragm (13) downwards and then grip the top of the pull rod and move the bottom end of the rod so that a sideways movement will disengage it from the rocker arm link. The diaphragm, diaphragm spring, lower body and washer may then be withdrawn.
7 The rocker arm pin (10) is an interference fit and if it is essential to remove it, then it should be pressed or drifted out.
8 Check all components for wear and renew as necessary. Hold the diaphragm up to the light and inspect for splits or pin holes. Check the upper and lower body halves for cracks.
9 Reassembly is a reversal of dismantling. Apply grease to the rocker arm mechanism and install a new cover gasket.
10 When the pump has been reassembled, test its efficiency by either placing a finger over the inlet pipe and actuating the rocker arm when a good suction noise should be heard by connecting it to the tank fuel line and after actuating the rocker arm a few times, each successive stroke should be accompanied by a well defined spurt of fuel from the outlet pipe.
11 Refit the pump as described in the preceding Section.

9 Fuel tank level transmitter - removal and refitting

1 Disconnect the battery.
2 Provided the fuel tank is not too full the transmitter may be removed without draining the tank, although access is not easy.
3 Jack-up the rear of the car and support it on blocks.
4 Disconnect the electrical lead from the unit.
5 Using a screwdriver, unscrew the locking plate which secures the unit to the tank orifice by a bayonet action.
6 Withdraw the unit and sealing washer taking care not to damage or bend the float mechanism.
7 Refitting is a reversal of removal but always use a new sealing washer. It is not possible to interchange sending units between saloon and estate car models. A simple test to determine unit serviceability is to earth the lead disconnected from the unit. This should result in a fullscale deflection on the gauge. If not, suspect the cable or the fuel gauge.

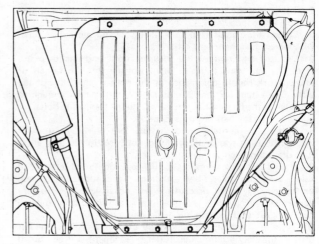

Fig. 3.3. Fuel tank retaining bolts - Saloon

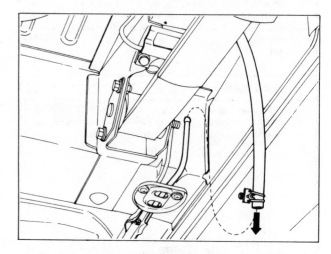

Fig. 3.4. Fuel pipe disconnection to drain tank - Estate

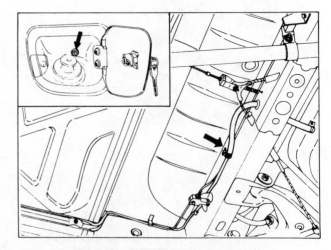

Fig. 3.5 Fuel pipe disconnection to drain tank - saloon

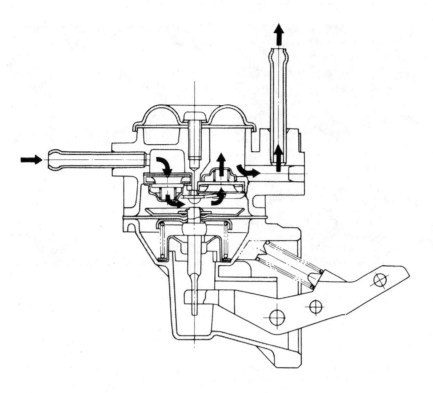

Fig. 3.6. Sectional view of fuel pump showing direction of fuel flow

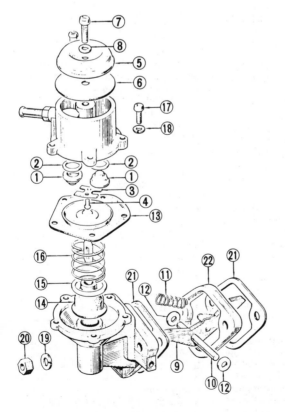

Fig. 3.7. Exploded view of fuel pump

1 Valve assembly
2 Packing
3 Retainer
4 Screw
5 Cap
6 Gasket
7 Screw
8 Washer
9 Rocker arm
10 Rocker pin
11 Rocker arm spring
12 Spacer
13 Diaphragm assembly
14 Oil seal
15 Retainer
16 Diaphragm spring
17 Screw
18 Washer
19 Washer
20 Nut
21 Packing
22 Spacer

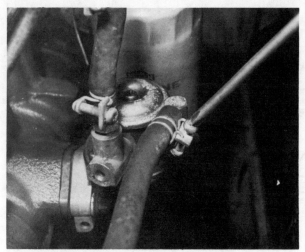

7.1 Disconnecting the fuel lines

7.2 Lifting away the pump. Note the number of gaskets and the position of the spacer carefully

10 Accelerator linkage - adjustment

1 After a considerable mileage, the accelerator cable may stretch and the following adjustment may be carried out to remove the slackness.
2 Check the security of the inner cable to the accelerator pedal and the threaded portion of the outer cable which is held by a nut to the engine bulkhead. Loosen clamp (1) and pull the outer cable in the direction 'P' (Fig. 3.8), until any further movement would cause the throttle arm on the carburettor to move. Now ease the outer cable in the opposite direction 'Q' no more than 0.050 in (1.27 mm). Tighten the clamp.
3 The accelerator pedals on left and right-hand drive models are fitted with an adjustable stop and although the pedal pad itself differs in design between the two models, each must have a clearance with the pedal fully depressed and the throttle lever on the carburettor fully open. The ideal clearance to aim at is 0 - 0.039 in (0 to 1 mm) (Fig. 3.9).
4 Never attempt to bend the accelerator pedal arm to correct the clearance but only adjust the stop bolt by first loosening the locknut. Before carrying out any adjustment to the stop bolt always check the cable setting as described earlier in this Section.

11 Carburettor - general description

The carburettor fitted to all models is of a downdraught twin choke type. A manually operated choke version DCG 306, is fitted to A12 engines while a DCG 286 is fitted to A10 engines. The carburettors are basically identical, except that the DCG 306 version is fitted with a secondary slow air bleed, as slow jet, and a power valve mechanism. Full specifications of the carburettors used in all vehicles of the range are given in the Specifications Section of this Chapter.

The carburettor is conventional in operation and incorporates a primary and main jet system and a mechanically operated accelerator pump.

Manually operated choke: This comprises a butterfly valve which closes one of the venturi choke tubes and is so synchronized with the throttle valve plate that the latter opens sufficiently to provide a rich mixture and an increased slow running speed for easy starting.

For idling and slow running, the fuel passes through the slow running jet, the primary slow air bleed and the secondary slow air bleed. The fuel is finally ejected from the bypass and idle holes (Figs. 3.11 and 3.12).

The accelerator pump is synchronized with the throttle valve. During periods of heavy acceleration, the pump which is of simple piston and valve construction, provides an additional metered quantity of fuel to enrich the normal mixture. The

quantity of fuel metered can be varied according to operating climatic conditions by adjusting the stroke of the pump linkage.

The secondary system provides a mixture for normal motoring conditions by means of a main jet and air bleed. The float chamber is fed with fuel pumped by the mechanically operated pump on the crankcase. The level in the chamber is critical and must at all times be maintained as specified. The power valve system utilizes the vacuum in the intake manifold to open or close the valve. During light load running the valve is closed, but is opened during full load running or acceleration, thus furnishing more fuel.

12 Slow running - adjustment

1 Run the engine to normal operating temperature and then set the throttle adjusting screw (Fig. 3.17) to provide an engine speed of 600 rpm.

If the vehicle is fitted with a tachometer then the setting of engine speed will be no problem. Where an instrument is not available then a useful guide may be obtained from the state of the ignition warning lamp. This should be just going out at the correct idling speed.
2 Setting of the mixture screw may be carried out using 'Color-tune' or a vacuum gauge attached to the inlet manifold. In either case follow the equipment manufacturer's instructions.
3 In certain territories, the use of a CO_1 meter is essential and if this is used then the throttle adjusting screw and the mixture screw must be turned to provide a reading on the meter of 1.5% ± 0.5% at the specified engine idling speed.
4 As a temporary measure, the adjustment screws may be rotated progressively, first one and then the other until the engine idles at the correct speed without any 'hunting' or stalling. Turning the mixture screw clockwise weakens the mixture and anti-clockwise richens it. Never screw the mixture screw in too far so that it forced into its seat or damage to the needle point of the screw will result. On later type carburettors this cannot happen as a travel stop is fitted.

13 Float level - adjustment

1 Where the appropriate adjustments have been carried out and there is evidence of fuel starvation or conversely, flooding or excessively rich mixture, the float level should be checked.
2 Remove the carburettor, as described in Section 16.
3 Disconnect choke connecting rod, accelerator pump lever and return spring.
4 Unscrew and remove the five securing screws which secure the upper choke chamber to the main body.
5 Turn the float chamber upside down and check the

dimension 'H' with the float hanging down under its own weight. This should be 0.472 in (12.0 mm) (Fig. 3.18).

6 Now gently push the float upwards to the full extent of its travel and check the clearance between the endface of the inlet needle valve and the float tongue. This should be 0.0512 to 0.0669 in (1.3 to 1.7 mm). Adjustment to correct either of these dimensions is carried out by bending the float tongue or the stopper tag.

14 Fast idle adjustment - manually operated choke

1 Ensure that the choke control is fully out and that the air cleaner having been removed, the choke butterfly valve can be seen to be in the fully closed position.
2 Check the position of the primary throttle valve plate. This should be open sufficiently to give a clearance of 0.048 in (1.219 mm) between the edge of the plate and the venturi wall, (GI in Fig. 3.19).
3 Where adjustment is required, bend the choke connecting rod.

15 Primary and secondary throttle butterfly valves - adjustment of interlock mechanism

1 Actuate the primary throttle valve until the secondary throttle valve is just about to open. Measure the distance between the edge of the primary valve plate and the wall of the bore, this should be 0.23 in (6 mm) (G2 in Fig. 3.20).
2 If the clearance requires adjustment, bend the rod which connects the two throttle plates.

16 Carburettor - removal and refitting

1 Remove the air cleaner assembly.
2 Disconnect the fuel and vacuum hoses from the carburettor, also the choke and accelerator controls.
3 Remove the four nuts and washers which secure the carburettor to the inlet manifold.
4 Lift the carburettor from the manifold and discard the flange gasket.
5 Refitting is a reverse of removal, always use a new flange gasket.

17 Carburettors - dismantling and reassembly (general)

1 With time the components parts of the Hitachi carburettor will wear and petrol consumption will increase. The diameter of drillings and jet may alter, and air and fuel leaks may develop round spindles and other moving parts. Because of the high degree of precision involved it is recommended that an exchange rebuilt carburettor is purchased. This is one of the few instances where it is better to buy a new component rather than to rebuild the old one.
2 The accelerator pump itself may need attention and gaskets may need renewal. Providing care is taken there is no reason why the carburettor may not be completely reconditioned at home, but ensure a full repair kit can be obtained before you strip the carburettor down. **Never** poke out jets with wire or similar to clean them but blow them out with compressed air or air from a car tyre pump.

18 Carburettor - dismantling and reassembly

1 The main jets and needle valves are accessible from the exterior of the carburettor.
2 These should be unscrewed, removed and cleaned by blowing them through with air from a tyre pump; **never** probe a jet or needle valve seat with wire.

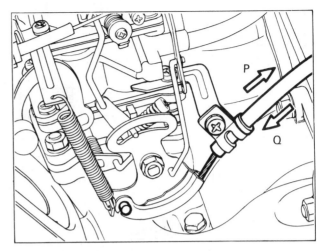

Fig. 3.8. Adjusting accelerator cable linkage

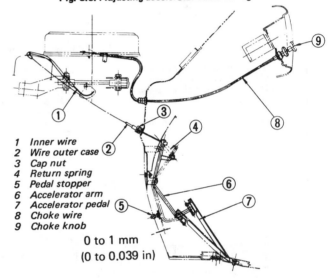

1 Inner wire
2 Wire outer case
3 Cap nut
4 Return spring
5 Pedal stopper
6 Accelerator arm
7 Accelerator pedal
8 Choke wire
9 Choke knob

0 to 1 mm
(0 to 0.039 in)

Fig. 3.9. Accelerator and choke linkage details - RHD vehicles

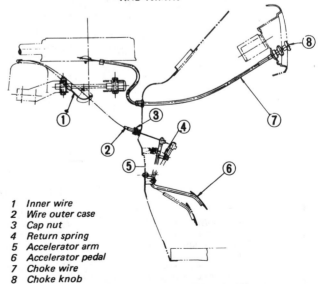

1 Inner wire
2 Wire outer case
3 Cap nut
4 Return spring
5 Accelerator arm
6 Accelerator pedal
7 Choke wire
8 Choke knob

Fig. 3.10. Accelerator and choke linkage details - LHD vehicles

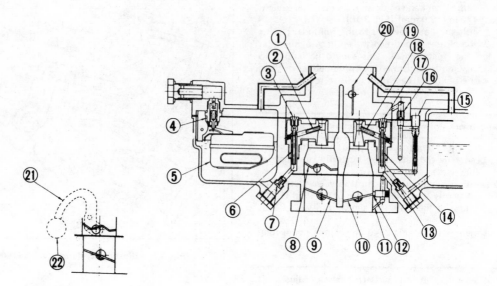

Fig. 3.11. Sectional view of DCG 286 carburettor

1	Secondary air vent pipe
2	Secondary main nozzle
3	Secondary main air bleed
4	Needle valve
5	Float
6	Secondary emulsion tube
7	Secondary main jet
8	Auxiliary valve
9	Secondary throttle valve
10	Primary throttle valve
11	Idle hole
12	By-pass hole
13	Primary main jet
14	Primary emulsion tube
15	Primary slow jet
16	Primary slow air bleed
17	Primary main air bleed
18	Primary main nozzle
19	Primary air vent pipe
20	Choke valve
21	Counter lever
22	Counterweight

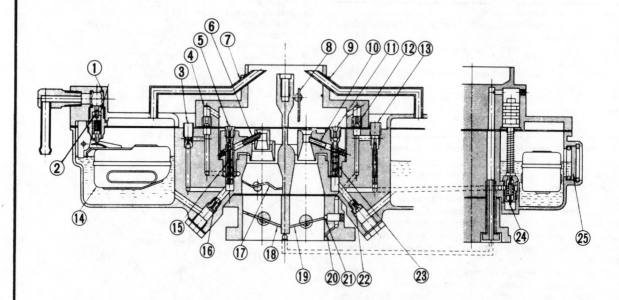

Fig. 3.12. Sectional view of DCG 306 carburettor

1	Filter
2	Needle valve
3	Secondary slow jet
4	Secondary slow air bleed
5	Secondary main air bleed
6	Secondary main nozzle
7	Secondary air vent pipe
8	Choke valve
9	Primary air vent pipe
10	Primary main nozzle
11	Primary main air bleed
12	Primary slow air bleed
13	Primary slow jet
14	Float
15	Secondary emulsion tube
16	Secondary main jet
17	Auxiliary valve
18	Secondary throttle valve
19	Primary throttle valve
20	Idle hole
21	Bypass hole
22	Primary main jet
23	Primary emulsion tube
24	Power valve
25	Level gauge

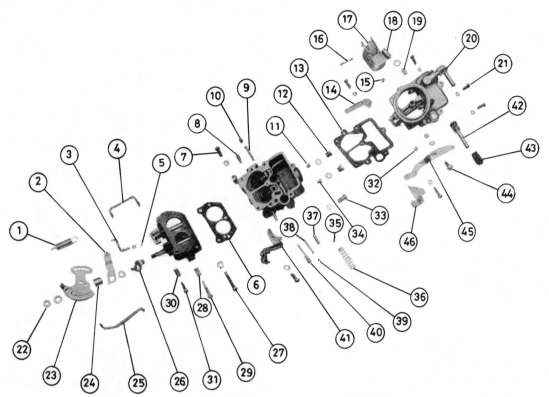

Fig. 3.13. Carburettor components - DCG 306

1	Throttle return spring	17	Float	32	Primary slow air bleed
2	Starting lever	18	Needle valve	33	Power valve
3	Connecting rod	19	Filter	34	Primary main jet
4	Choke connecting rod	20	Choke chamber assembly	35	Ball
5	Cotter pin - 1 mm dia.	21	Screw - 5 mm dia.	36	Piston return spring
6	Throttle chamber	22	Nut - 8 mm dia.	37	Injector weight
7	Screw - 6 mm dia.	23	Throttle lever	38	Primary emulsion tube
8	Secondary slow jet	24	Sleeve	39	Primary main air bleed
9	Secondary emulsion tube	25	Pump rod	40	Primary slow jet
10	Secondary main air bleed	26	Adjust plate	41	Throttle wire arm
11	Secondary main jet	27	Screw - 6 mm dia.	42	Piston
12	Drain plug	28	Idle adjust screw spring	43	Pump cover
13	Float chamber gasket	29	Idle adjust screw	44	Pump lever shaft
14	Spring hanger	30	Throttle adjust screw spring	45	Pump lever
15	Secondary slow air bleed	31	Throttle adjust screw	46	Choke wire arm
16	Float shaft				

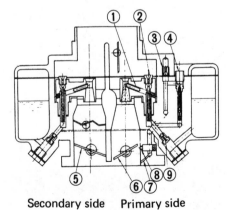

Secondary side   Primary side

Fig. 3.14. Carburettor under light load

1	Primary main nozzle	6	Primary throttle valve
2	Primary main air bleed	7	Idle hole
3	Primary slow air bleed	8	Bypass hole
4	Primary slow jet	9	Primary main jet
5	Secondary throttle valve		

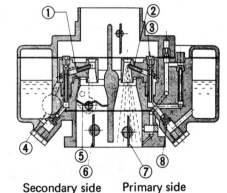

Secondary side   Primary side

Fig. 3.15. Carburettor fully open - low speed

1	Counter lever	5	Auxiliary valve
2	Primary main nozzle	6	Secondary throttle valve
3	Primary main air bleed	7	Primary throttle valve
4	Counterweight	8	Primary main jet

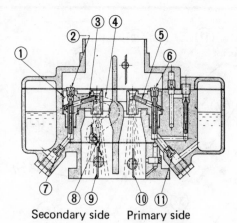

Fig. 3.16. Carburettor fully open - high speed

Secondary side   Primary side

1	Counter weight	7	Secondary main jet
2	Secondary main air bleed	8	Auxiliary valve
3	Secondary main nozzle	9	Secondary throttle valve
4	Counter lever	10	Primary throttle valve
5	Primary main nozzle	11	Primary main jet
6	Primary main air bleed		

16.2A Disconnecting the throttle cable ...

MIXTURE SCREW

THROTTLE SCREW

Fig. 3.17. Carburettor adjustment screws

16.2B ... and its retaining clip

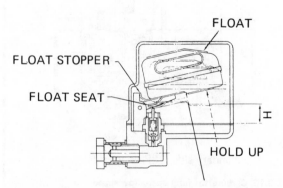

FLOAT

FLOAT STOPPER

FLOAT SEAT

HOLD UP

H

Clearance: 1.3 to 1.7 mm (0.0512 to 0.0669 in)

Fig. 3.18. Float adjustment

16.2C Disconnecting the choke cable

3 Detach the choke chamber by removing the connecting rod, accelerator pump lever, return spring and the five securing screws.

4 The primary and secondary emulsion tubes are accessible after removing the main air bleeds.

5 Remove the accelerator pump cover, retaining the spring, piston and ball valve carefully.

6 Separate the float chamber from the throttle housing by un-screwing and removing three securing screws. Slide out the float pivot pin and remove the float.

7 Unless imperative, do not dismantle the throttle butterfly valves from their spindles.

8 Take great care when disconnecting the interlock rods that they are not bent or twisted or the settings and adjustments will be upset.

9 With the carburettor dismantled, clean all components in clean fuel and blow through the internal body passages with air from a tyre pump.

10 Inspect all components for wear and the body and chamber castings for cracks.

11 Clean the small gauze filter and if corroded or clogged, renew it.

12 If wear is evident in the throttle spindle, the carburettor should be renewed on an exchange basis.

13 Check all ket and air bleed sizes with those specified in Speci-fications in case a previous owner has changed them for ones of incorrect size.

14 Check the ejection of fuel when the accelerator pump is actuated.

15 Reassembly is a reversal of dismantling using all the items supplied in the repair kit.

16 When the carburettor is being reassembled, check the float movement (Section 13) and when it is refitted to the engine, carry out all the checks and adjustments described in this Chapter.

19 Evaporative emission control (fuel storage) - description and checking

1 This system is designed to prevent vapour from the tank escaping to atmosphere and is fitted to vehicles operating in areas where stringent anti-pollution regulations are enforced.

2 The system comprises a tight sealing filler cap, a vapour-liquid separator, a vent line and a flow guide valve.

3 The principle of operation is such that with the engine switched off, the vent line, the separator and fuel tank are filled with fuel vapour. When the pressure of this vapour reaches a pre-determined level it actuates a flow guide valve and passes to the crankcase. When the engine is started, the vapour which has accumulated in the crankcase, manifold and air cleaner is drawn into the inlet manifold for combustion within the engine cylinders. When the vapour pressure in the system becomes negative, then the flow guide valve will permit entry of fresh air to the fuel tank from the air cleaner.

4 Periodic preventative maintenance of the system should be carried out. Inspect all hoses and the fuel filler cap for damage or deterioration. Leakage at the fuel cap can only be determined by fitting a three-way connector, cock and manometer (U shaped glass tube will do) into the vent line as shown (Fig. 3.21).

5 Blow through the cock until the level in the 'U' tube is approximately at the higher level illustrated. Close the cock and after a period of 2½ minutes check that the level in the 'U' tube has not dropped more than indicated in the illustration. If the levels in the 'U' tube quickly become equalised, then the filler cap is not sealing correctly.

6 Assuming the previous test has proved satisfactory, again blow into the 'U' tube and shut the cock. Remove the filler cap quickly when the height of the liquid in the 'U' tube should immediately drop to zero, failure to do this will indicate a clogged or obstructed vent line.

7 The fuel filler cap incorporates a vacuum release valve and

this may be checked by gently sucking with the mouth. A slight resistance accompanied by a click shows the valve is in good condition. Further suction will cause the resistance to cease as soon as the valve clicks.

8 To check the operation of the flow guide valve, apply air pressure from a tyre pump in the following sequence:

 a) *Air applied to fuel tank nozzle should emerge freely from crankcase nozzle.*

 b) *Air applied to crankcase nozzle should not enter or emerge from any other nozzles.*

 c) *Air applied to air cleaner nozzle should emerge from one of both of the other two nozzles.*

Any deviations from the foregoing tests will necessitate renewal of the components as assemblies.

20 Exhaust system - description and servicing

1 All models in the range are fitted wiht a two section exhaust system. The front downpipe is connected to a socket at the forward end of the silencer and the silencer body and tailpipe are a combined unit. The estate version is slightly different in that the pipe run is changed and an additional pipe joint is introduced in front of the silencer.

2 The system is suspended at the front pipe by brackets bolted to the chassis and at the tailpipe by a flexible strap.

3 Examination of the exhaust pipe and silencers at regular intervals is worthwhile as small defects may be repairable when, if left they will almost certainly require renewal of one of the sections of the system. Also, any leaks, apart from the noise factor, may cause poisonous exhaust gases to get inside the car which can be unpleasant, to say the least, even in mild concen-trations. Prolonged inhalation could cause sickness and giddiness.

4 As the sleeve connections and clamps are usually very difficult to separate it is quicker and easier in the long run to remove the complete system from the car when renewing a section. It can be expensive if another section is damaged when trying to separate a bad section from it.

5 To remove the system first remove the bolts holding the tail pipe bracket to the body. Support the rear silencer on something to prevent cracking or kinking the pipes elsewhere.

6 Disconnect the front pipe at the chassis and differential support brackets.

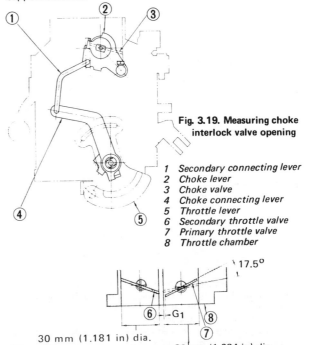

Fig. 3.19. Measuring choke interlock valve opening

1 *Secondary connecting lever*
2 *Choke lever*
3 *Choke valve*
4 *Choke connecting lever*
5 *Throttle lever*
6 *Secondary throttle valve*
7 *Primary throttle valve*
8 *Throttle chamber*

17.5°

30 mm (1.181 in) dia.

26 mm (1.024 in) dia.

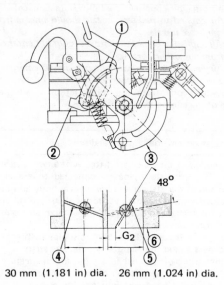

Fig. 3.20. Adjusting interlock opening

1   Connecting rod   4   Secondary throttle valve
2   Secondary connecting lever 5   Primary throttle valve
3   Throttle lever   6   Throttle chamber

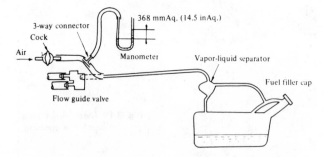

Fig. 3.21. Diagram for checking serviceability of components used in the fuel storage system fume emission control system

7   Disconnect the manifold to downpipe connecting flange and then withdraw the complete exhaust system from below and out to the rear of the vehicle. If necessary, jack-up the rear of the vehicle to provide more clearance.

8   When separating the damaged section to be renewed cut away the damaged part from the adjoining good section rather than risk damaging the latter.

9   If small repairs are being carried out it is best, if possible, not to try and pull the sections apart.

10 Refitting should be carried out after connecting the two sections together. De-burr and grease the connecting socket and make sure that the clamp is in good condition and slipped over the front pipe but do not tighten it at this stage.

11 Connect the system to the manifold and connect the rear support strap. Now adjust the attitude of the silencer so that the following clearances are obtainable:

>   Saloon
>   Silencer to tank flange clearance: 30 mm (1.18 in) or more
>   Silencer to suspension arm clearance (with arm closest): 20 mm (0.787 in) or more
>   Estate car
>   Front pipe to tank flange clearance: 40 mm (1.575 in) or more
>   Front pipe to forward left corner of tank: 60 mm (2.362 in) or more
>   Front pipe to hand brake lever clearance: 10 mm (0.394 in) or more

12 Tighten the pipe clamp, the manifold flange nuts and the rear suspension strap bolts. Check that the exhaust system will not knock against any part of the vehicle when deflected slightly in a sideways or upward direction.

21 Exhaust emission control system - adjustment and maintenance

1   The maintenance of a 'clean exhaust' without loss of power or economy is dependent not only upon the correct adjustment of the specific components described in this Section but also upon the correct tune of other components of the engine.

2   Regularly check the adjustment of the following:
    a) Valve clearance
    b) Ignition timing
    c) Contact breaker points
    d) Spark plugs
    e) Crankcase fume emission control (Chapter 1)
    f) All the carburettor adjustments described for carburettors in this Chapter.

3   A throttle opening device is fitted which is designed to open the throttle slightly during engine deceleration and to reduce the concentration of unburned hydrocarbons in the exhaust system by admitting a mixture sufficient to maintain complete combustion within the cylinders. The device comprises a servo diaphragm attached to the carburettor and a control valve bolted to the inlet manifold. the system is actuated by vacuum within the inlet manifold.

4   To adjust the system, disconnect the electric lead from the air cleaner vacuum valve.

5   Start the engine and adjust the slow running speed to 700 rpm checking with a tachometer.

6   Refer to Fig. 3.24 and detach tube (6) from the inlet manifold. Disconnect the servo to valve tube and fit this directly to the manifold, thus by-passing the valve. The tachometer should now register between 1700 and 1800 rpm. If the reading is outside that specified, loosen the locknut (2) and adjust the screw (1) until the reading is correct (Fig. 3.25).

7   Reconnect the vacuum tubes in their original positions and then increase the engine speed to 3000 rpm moving the throttle lever by hand. Release the throttle lever abruptly and time the period taken for the engine speed to drop to 1000 rpm this should be between 3.5 and 4.5 seconds. If the time taken for the engine speed to drop is outside the specified limits, loosen the locknut on the valve and adjust the screw, clockwise to increase the period, anticlockwise to reduce it (Fig. 3.25).

8   In the event of failure to respond to adjustment with either component, renew as assemblies as they are not capable of repair.

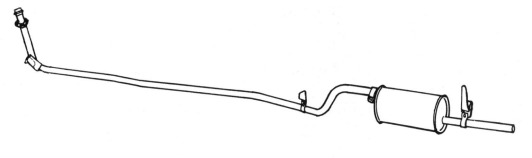

Saloon

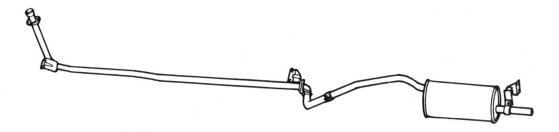

Estate

Fig. 3.22. Exhaust systems

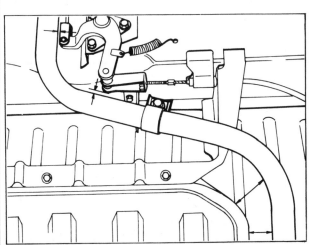

Fig. 3.23. Clearance between exhaust pipe and handbrake lever -
Estate car

18.8 General view of the interlock rods

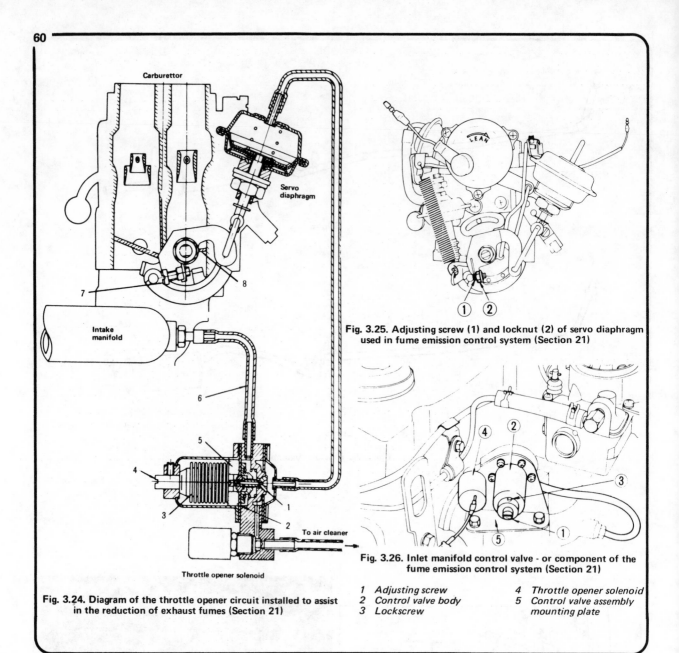

Fig. 3.25. Adjusting screw (1) and locknut (2) of servo diaphragm used in fume emission control system (Section 21)

Fig. 3.26. Inlet manifold control valve - or component of the fume emission control system (Section 21)

1 Adjusting screw
2 Control valve body
3 Lockscrew
4 Throttle opener solenoid
5 Control valve assembly
   mounting plate

Fig. 3.24. Diagram of the throttle opener circuit installed to assist in the reduction of exhaust fumes (Section 21)

22 Fault diagnosis - fuel system and carburation

Symptom	Reason/s	Remedy
Fuel consumption excessive	Air cleaner choked and dirty giving rich mixture	Remove, clean, renew element and replace air cleaner
	Fuel leaking from carburettor, fuel pump or fuel lines	Check for and eleminate all fuel leaks. Tighten fuel line union nuts.
	Float chamber flooding	Check and adjust float level.
	Generally worn carburettor	Remove, overhaul and replace.
	Distributor condenser faulty	Remove and fit new unit.
	Balance weights or vacuum advance mechanism in distributor faulty	Remove and overhaul distributor.
	Carburettor incorrectly adjusted mixture too rich	Tune and adjust carburettor.
	Idling speed too high	Adjust idling speed
	Contact breaker gap incorrect	Check and reset gap
	Valve clearances incorrect	Check rocker arm to valve stem clearances and adjust as necessary.
	Incorrectly set spark plugs	Remove, clean and re-gap.
	Tyres under-inflated	Check tyre pressures and inflate if necessary
	Wrong spark plugs fitted	Remove and replace with correct units.
	Brakes dragging	Check and adjust brakes.
Insufficient fuel delivery or weak mixture due to air leaks	*Petrol tank air vent restricted	Remove petrol cap and clean out air vent
	Partially clogged filters in pump and carburettors	Remove and clean filters. Remove and clean out float chamber and needle valve assembly.
	Incorrectly seating valves in fuel pump	Remove, and overhaul or fit new fuel pump.
	Fuel pump diaphragm leaking or damaged	Remove, and overhaul or fit new fuel pump.
	Gasket in fuel pump damaged	Remove, and overhaul or fit new fuel pump.
	Fuel pump valves sticking due to petrol gumming	Remove and overhaul or thoroughly clean fuel pump.
	Too little fuel in fuel tank (prevalent when climbing steep hills)	Refill fuel tank.
	Union joints on pipe connections loose	Tighten joints and check for air leaks.
	Split in fuel pipe on suction side of fuel pump	Examine, locate and repair.
	Inlet manifold to head or inlet manifold to carburettor gasket leaking	Test by pouring oil along joints - bubbles indicate leak. Renew gasket as appropriate.

*Not applicable where exhaust emission modifications have been made.

Chapter 4 Ignition system

Contents

Specifications

System type	12V negative earth (−); battery, coil and distributor
Firing order	1 3 4 2 (no. 1 cylinder at the fan belt end)
Static ignition timing	7° BTDC at 600 rpm
Spark plugs	
Type:	
Up to 1972	Hitachi L46 or NGK BP—6E (14 mm)
1973 and later models	NGK B5ES or BR5ES
Gap:	
Up to 1972	0.031 to 0.035 in (0.78 to 0.88 mm)
1973 and later models	0.028 to 0.032 in (0.71 to 0.81 mm)
Coil	
Make	Hanskin or Hitachi oil-filled
Type	HP5 - 13E or C6R - 200
Resistor (matched with coil)	RC15 or 556OR - 1510
Condenser	
Capacity	0.20 to 0.24 uf
Distributor	
Make	Hitachi
Type	D411 - 61 or D412 - 63
Direction of rotation of rotor	anticlockwise
Contact breaker points gap	0.018 to 0.022 in. (0.45 to 0.55 mm)
Servicing data (all models)	
Lower shaft diameter	0.4902 in. wear limit 0.0008 in.
Shaft to housing clearance	0.0004 to 0.0015 in.
Shaft (upper section) diameter	0.3150 in. wear limit 0.0006 in.
Shaft to cam clearance	0.0002 to 0.0011 in.
Counterweight hole diameter	0.1969 in. wear limit 0.0007 in.
Counterweight hole to pivot clearance	0.0002 to 0.0018 in.

Torque wrench settings	**lb f ft**	**kg f m**
Spark plugs	11 to 15 lb/ft	1.5 to 2.1 kg/m

1 General description

In order that the engine can run correctly it is necessary for an electrical spark to ignite the fuel/air mixture in the combustion chamber at exactly the right moment in relation to engine speed and load. The ignition system is based on feeding low tension (LT) voltage from the battery to the coil where it is converted to high tension (HT) voltage. The high tension voltage is powerful enough to jump the spark plug gap in the cylinders many times a second under high compression pressures,

providing that the system is in good condition and that all adjustments are correct.

The ignition system is divided into two circuits. The low tension circuit and the high tension circuit.

The low tension (sometimes known as the primary) circuit consists of the battery lead to the control box, lead to the ignition switch, lead from the ignition switch to the low tension or primary coil windings (terminal SW), and the lead from the low tension coil windings (coil terminal CB) to the contact breaker points and condenser in the distributor.

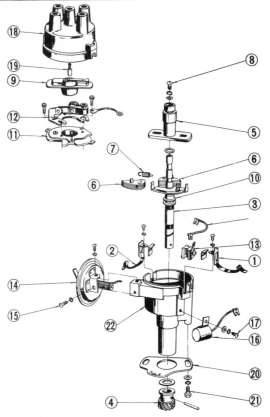

Fig. 4.1. Exploded view of distributor

1 Assembly clamp cap	9 Assembly rotor head	16 Assembly condenser
2 Assembly clamp cap	10 Washer thrust	17 Screw
3 Assembly shaft	11 Assembly breaker plate	18 Assembly cap distributor
4 Pinion	12 Set contact	19 Assembly point carbon
5 Assembly cam	13 Assembly terminal	20 Plate fixing
6 Assembly weight governor	14 Assembly control vacuum	21 Bolt
7 Spring governor	15 Screw	22 Housing
8 Screw		

The high tension circuit consists of the high tension or secondary coil windings, the heavy ignition lead from the centre of the coil to the centre of the distributor cap, the rotor arm, and the spark plug leads and spark plugs.

The system functions in the following manner. Low tension voltage is changed in the coil into high tension voltage by the opening and closing of the contact breaker points in the low tension circuit. High tension voltage is then fed via the carbon brush in the centre of the distributor cap to the rotor arm of the distributor cap, and each time it comes in line with one of the four metal segments in the cap, which are connected to the spark plug leads, the opening and closing of the contact breaker points causes the high tension voltage to build up, jump the gap from the rotor arm to the appropriate metal segment and so via the spark plug lead to the spark plug, where it finally jumps the spark plug gap before going to earth.

The ignition is advanced and retarded automatically, to ensure the spark occurs at just the right instant for the particular load at the prevailing engine speed.

The ignition advance is controlled both mechanically and by a vacuum operated system. The mechanical governor mechanism comprises two lead weights, which move out from the distributor shaft as the engine speed rises due to centrifugal force. As they move outwards they rotate the cam relative to the distributor shaft, and so advance the spark. The weights are held in position by two light springs and it is the tension of the

springs which is largely responsible for correct spark advancement.

The vacuum control consits of a diaphragm, one side of which is connected via a small bore tube to the carburettor, and the other side to the contact breaker plate. Depression in the inlet manifold and carburettor, which varies with engine speed and throttle opening, causes the diaphragm to move, so moving the contact breaker plate, and advancing or retarding the spark. A fine degree of control is achieved by a spring in the vacuum assembly.

2 Contact breaker - adjustment

1 To adjust the contact breaker points to the correct gap, first pull off the two clips securing the distributor cap to the distributor body, and lift away the cap. Clean the cap inside and out with a dry cloth. It is unlikely that the four segments will be badly burned or scored, but if they are the cap will have to be renewed.

2 Inspect the carbon brush contact located in the top of the cap - see that it is unbroken and stands proud of the plastic surface.

3 Check the contact spring on the top of the rotor arm. It must be clean and have adequate tension to ensure good contact.

4 Gently prise the contact breaker points open to examine the

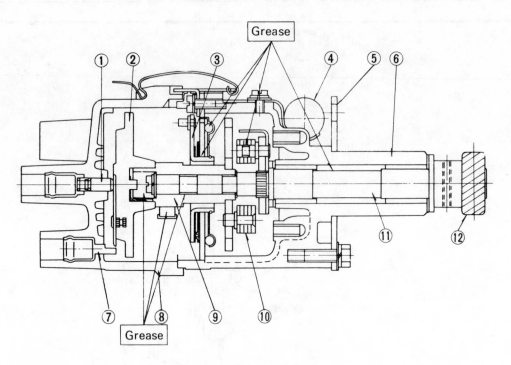

Fig. 4.2. Sectional view of distributor

1	Centre carbon	5	Fixing plate	9	Cam
2	Rotor head	6	Housing	10	Governor weight
3	Breaker plate	7	Side plug	11	Shaft
4	Condenser	8	Cap	12	Pinion

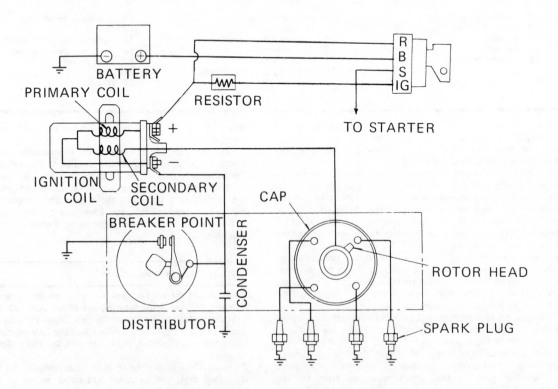

Fig. 4.3. Ignition system - theoretical diagram

condition of their faces. If they are rough, pitted, or dirty, it will be necessary to remove them for resurfacing, or for replacement points to be fitted.

5 Presuming the points are satisfactory, or that they have been cleaned and replaced, measure the gap between the points by turning the engine over until the heel of the breaker arm is on the highest point of the cam.

6 An 0.020 in (0.50 mm) feeler gauge should now just fit between the points. The specifications allow a tolerance of 0.018 in (0.45 mm) to 0.022 in (0.55 mm) but the optimum gap of 0.020 in (0.50 mm) should be set if possible. This will allow the normal changes in the gap due to wear, to still fall in the permitted tolerance.

7 If the gap varies from this amount slacken the contact plate securing screw.

8 Adjust the contact gap by inserting a screwdriver in the notched hole, in the breaker plate. Turn clockwise to increase and anticlockwise to decrease the gap. When the gap is correct tighten the securing screw and check the gap again.

9 Making sure the rotor is in position replace the distributor cap and clip the spring blade retainers into position.

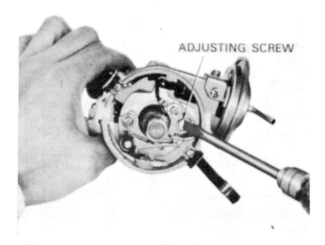

Fig. 4.4. Contact breaker adjusting screw

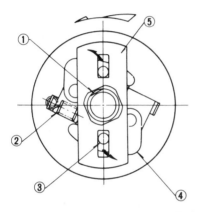

Fig. 4.5. Installation of governor spring and cam

1   Rotor positioning tip
2   Governor spring (A)
3   Weight pin
4   Governor weight
5   Cam
6   Governor spring (B)

2.6 Measuring the contact breaker gap

2.7 Adjusting the gap

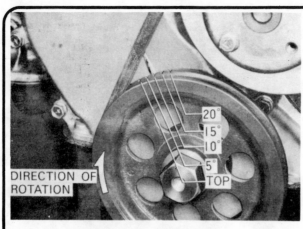

Fig. 4.6. Timing marks

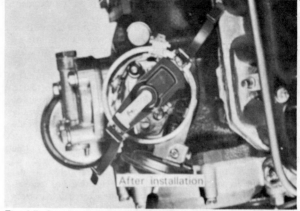

Fig. 4.7. Correct position of distributor after installation, with
No. 1 cylinder at T.D.C.

3 Contact breaker points - removal and refitting

1 Slip back the spring clips which secure the distributor cap in
position. Remove the distributor cap and lay it to one side, only
removing one or two of the HT leads from the plugs. If necessary
to provide greater movement of the cap.
2 Pull the rotor from the distributor shaft.
3 Unscrew the contact breaker securing screws a turn or two
and disconnect the LT lead from the contact breaker arm.
4 If necessary, unscrew the securing screws a turn or two more
and slide the contact breaker arms sideways to remove them.
5 Inspect the faces of the contact points. If they are only
lightly burned or pitted then they may be ground square on an
oilstone or by rubbing a carborundum strip between them.
Where the points are found to be severely burned or pitted, then
they must be renewed and at the same time the cause of the
erosion of the points established. This is most likely to be due to
poor earth connections from the battery negative lead to body
earth or the engine to earth strap. Remove the connecting bolts
at these points, scrape the surfaces free from rust and corrosion
and tighten the bolts using a star type lock washer. Other screws
to check for security are: the baseplate to distributor body
securing screws, the condenser securing screw and the distributor
body to lockplate bolt. Looseness in any of these could
contribute to a poor earth connection. Check the condenser
(Section 4).
6 Refitting the contact breaker assembly is a reversal of
removal and when fitted, adjust the points gap as described in
the preceding Section.

4 Condenser (capacitor) - removal, testing and refitting

1 The condenser ensures that with the contact breaker points
open, the sparking between them is not excessive as this would
cause severe pitting.
2 Testing for an unserviceable condenser may be effected by
switching on the ignition and separating the contact points by
hand. If this action is accompanied by a blue flash then
condenser failure is indicated. Difficult starting, missing of the
engine after several miles running badly pitted points are other
indications of a faulty condenser.
3 The surest test is by substitution of a new unit.
4 Removal of the condenser is by means of withdrawing the
screw which retains it to the distributor. Replacement is a
reversal of this procedure.

5 Distributor - removal and refitting

1 To remove the distributor complete with cap from the

engine, begin by pulling the plug lead terminals off the four
spark plugs. But first mark the leads so that you know where to
replace them. Free the HT lead from the centre of the coil to the
centre of the distributor by undoing the lead retaining cap from
the coil.
2 Pull off the rubber pipe holding the vacuum tube to the
distributor vacuum advance and retard take off pipe.
3 Disconnect the low tension wire from the coil.
4 Undo and remove the bolt which holds the distributor clamp
plate to the distributor and lift out the distributor. Mark the
relative positions of the distributor and the block to aid replacement if the engine is not going to be turned.
5 To refit the distributor, if the engine has been rotated, turn
the engine by hand using a spanner on the crankshaft pulley
securing bolt until number one piston is at TDC. This position is
indicated when the TDC mark on the crankshaft pulley is in
alignment with the pointer on the timing cover (compression
stroke, both number one cylinder valves closed).
6 When correctly installed, the distributor rotor should take up
the position shown in Fig. 4.7. Due to the meshing action of
the distributor and camshaft drive gears however, the distributor
drive shaft must be turned back (clockwise) by about 60° from
the position it will finally take up. Insert the distributor into its
crankcase location and when fully inserted, check the rotor
alignment the top of which should be opposite number 2 contact
in the distributor cap.
7 Reconnect the HT and LT leads and then time the ignition as
described in the following Section.

6 Ignition - timing

1 This operation should be required only if the distributor has
been removed and refitted or adjustment is necessary due to a
change of fuel or engine condition.
2 Connect a timing light (stroboscope) between number one
spark plug and number one HT lead terminal.
3 Mark the timing cover pointer and the specified BTDC mark
(see Specification Sections) on the crankshaft pulley. Loosen the
distributor to clamp plate bolt.
4 Start the engine which should be normal operating temperature and let it run at the specified idling speed (600 rpm).
5 By directing the timing light onto the chalked marks, the
mark on the crankshaft pulley will appear to be stationary.
Having previously loosened the distributor body clamp plate
bolt, the distributor may be rotated slightly until the timing
marks are in alignment. Where the limited adjustment provided
by the oval clamp plate bolt hole is found to be insufficient to
attain the correct alignment, then the distributor must be
removed and re-meshed with the camshaft as described in the
preceding Section.

Measuring plug gap. A feeler gauge of the correct size (see ignition system specifications) should have a slight 'drag' when slid between the electrodes. Adjust gap if necessary

Adjusting plug gap. The plug gap is adjusted by bending the earth electrode inwards, or outwards, as necessary until the correct clearance is obtained. Note the use of the correct tool

Normal. Grey-brown deposits, lightly coated core nose. Gap increasing by around 0.001 in (0.025 mm) per 1000 miles (1600 km). Plugs ideally suited to engine, and engine in good condition

Carbon fouling. Dry, black, sooty deposits. Will cause weak spark and eventually misfire. Fault: over-rich fuel mixture. Check: carburettor mixture settings, float level and jet sizes; choke operation and cleanliness of air filter. Plugs can be re-used after cleaning

Oil fouling. Wet, oily deposits. Will cause weak spark and eventually misfire. Fault: worn bores/piston rings or valve guides; sometimes occurs (temporarily) during running-in period. Plugs can be re-used after thorough cleaning

Overheating. Electrodes have glazed appearance, core nose very white – few deposits. Fault: plug overheating. Check: plug value, ignition timing, fuel octane rating (too low) and fuel mixture (too weak). Discard plugs and cure fault immediately

Electrode damage. Electrodes burned away; core nose has burned, glazed appearance. Fault: pre-ignition. Check: as for 'Overheating' but may be more severe. Discard plugs and remedy fault before piston or valve damage occurs

Split core nose (may appear initially as a crack). Damage is self-evident, but cracks will only show after cleaning. Fault: pre-ignition or wrong gap-setting technique. Check: ignition timing, cooling system, fuel octane rating (too low) and fuel mixture (too weak). Discard plugs, rectify fault immediately

5.4A The distributor securing bolt

5.4B Lifting out the distributor

6.5A Distributor clamp plate and retaining bolt, showing the advance-and-retard adjustment

6.5B Securing advance/retard mechanism

6   When the timing is correct, tighten the distributor body to clamp plate bolt.

7   An alternative method is to turn the engine in the normal direction of rotation until on the compression stroke (felt by placing finger over No 1 plug hole) the timing cover pointer and the timing mark on the pulley are aligned (see Specifications for correct timing).

8   Rotate the engine in an anticlockwise direction just past the mark then clockwise so that the mark and the timing cover pointer are aligned. The foregoing procedure ensures that all backlash is removed from the timing assembly.

9   Remove the distributor cap and check that the rotor arm points towards No 1 cylinder firing position. Reference to the No 1 HT lead connection in the cap will determine this position.

10 Slacken the distributor clamp plate pinch bolt and rotate the distributor body until the points are just opening.

11 Difficulty is sometimes experienced in determining exactly when the contact breaker points open. This can be ascertained most accurately by connection of a 12 volt bulb in parallel with the contact breaker points (one lead to earth and the other from the distributor low tension terminal). Switch on the ignition and with the distributor adjusting plate securing screw slack turn the distributor until the bulb lights up, indicating that the points have just opened. Retighten the securing screw.

12 It should be noted that to get the very best setting the final adjustment must be made on the road. The distributor can be moved slightly until the best setting is obtained. The amount of wear in the engine, quality of petrol used, and amount of carbon in the combustion chambers, all contribute to make the recommended settings no more than nominal ones. To obtain the best setting under running conditions start the engine and allow to warm up to normal temperature, and then accelerate in top gear from 30 - 50 mph, listening for heavy pinking. If this occurs, the ignition needs to be retarded slightly until just the faintest trace of pinking can be heard under these operating conditions.

13 Since the ignition advance adjustment enables the firing point to be related correctly in relation to the grade of fuel used, the fullest advantage of any change of fuel will be obtained only be re-adjustment of the ignition settings.

14 Finally, tighten the distributor body to clamp plate bolt.

7   Distributor - dismantling and inspection

1   Remove the distributor cap, rotor and contact breaker points, as described in Section 3, of this Chapter, also the vacuum capsule.

2 Remove the two securing screws from the baseplate and remove the baseplate.

3 Unscrew and remove the screw from the centre of the cam. Should this be very tight, hold the cam using a close fitting spanner and take care not to damage the high-point surfaces.

4 Using a suitable drift, drive out the pin from the drive pinion end of the shaft.

5 Withdraw the distributor drive shaft complete with the mechanical advance assembly.

6 If it is necessary to dismantle this assembly, take care not to stretch the springs during removal and to mark their respective positions; also the counter weights in relation to their pivots so that they may be refitted in their original locations.

7 With the distributor dismantled, clean all the components in paraffin and inspect for wear. Renewal of components should be limited to the advance mechanism springs. Should wear in the shaft, bushes, the counter weight pivots or holes be outside the tolerances given in Specifications, then the distributor should be renewed on an exchange basis.

8 Finally check the distributor index number aligns with the type of transmission fitted as is listed in Specifications.

8 Distributor - reassembly

1 Reassembly is a reversal of dismantlig but high melting point grease must be applied sparingly at the positions indicated in Fig. 4.2.

2 Always use a new pin to secure the pinion to the driveshaft.

3 If the mechanical advance mechanism has been dismantled then it should be reassembled in accordance with the diagram in Fig. 4.5.

4 When installing the springs and cam, make sure that the spring, (2) in Fig. 4.5 is fitted on the side adjacent to the rotor tip. In the case of the D411-61 distributor this is the shorter of the two springs.

5 The governor weight pin (3) should be fitted into the longer of the two cam slots, leaving a certain amount of clearance at the beginning and end of the centrifugal advance movement.

6 The governor weight pin at the other side is fitted into the shorter groove which does not leave a clearance at the two extremities.

9 Coil - description and polarity

1 High tension current should be negative at the spark plug terminals. To ensure this, check the LT connections to the coil are correctly made.

2 The LT wire from the distributor must connect with the (−) negative terminal on the coil.

3 The coil (+) positive terminal is connected to the ignition/starter switch.

4 An incorrect connection can cause as much as a 60% loss of spark efficiency and can cause rough idling and misfiring at speed.

5 The primary coil resistance should be 1.3 to 1.6 ohms, and the secondary 9 to 14 ohms.

10 Spark plugs and HT leads

1 The correct functioning of the spark plugs is vital for the correct running and efficiency of the engine. The plugs fitted as standard are listed on the Specification page.

2 At intervals of 5000 miles the plugs should be removed examined, cleaned and, if worn excessively, renewed. The condition of the spark plug will also tell much about the overall condition of the engine.

3 If the insulator nose of the spark plug is clean and white, with no deposits, this is indicative of a weak mixture, or too hot a plug (A hot plug transfers heat away from the electrode slowly - a cold plug transfers it away quickly).

4 If the top and insulator nose is covered with hard black looking deposits, then this is indicative that the mixture is too rich. Should the plug be black and oily, then it is likely that the engine is fairly worn, as well as the mixture being too rich.

5 If the insulator nose is covered with light tan to greyish brown deposits, then the mixture is correct and it is likely that the engine is in good condition.

6 If there are any traces of long brown tapering strains on the outside of the white portion of the plug, then the plug will have to be renewed, as this shows that there is a faulty joint between the plug body and the insulator, and compression is being allow to leak away.

7 Plugs should be cleaned by a sand blasting machine, which will free them from carbon more thoroughly than cleaning by hand. The machine will also test the condition of the plugs under compression. Any plug that fails to spark at the recommended pressure should be renewed.

8 The spark plug gap is of considerable importance, as, if it is too large or too small the size of the spark and its efficiency will be seriously impaired. The spark plug gap should be set to between 0.031 and 0.035 in (0.78 and 0.88 mm) for the best results.

9 To set it, measure the gap with a feeler gauge, and then bend open, or close, the outer plug electrode until the correct gap is achieved. The centre electrode should never be bent as this may crack the insulation and cause plug failure, if nothing worse.

10 When replacing the plugs, remember to use new plug washers and replace the leads from the distributor in the correct firing order 1,3,4,2; No 1 cylinder being the one nearest the left side of the vehicle, looking forward.

11 The plug leads require no routine attention other than being kept clean and wiped over regularly.

11 Ignition system - fault diagnosis (general)

Failure of the ignition system will either be due to faults in the HT or LT circuits. Initial checks should be made by observing the security of spark plug terminals. Lucar type terminals, coil and battery connection. More detailed investigation and the explanation and remedial action in respect of symptoms of ignition malfunction are described in the next Section.

12 Ignition system - fault diagnosis

Engine fails to start

1 If the engine fails to start and the car was running normally when it was last used, first check there is fuel in the fuel tank. If the engine turns over normally on the starter motor and the battery is evidently well charged, then the fault may be in either the high or low tension circuits. First check the HT circuit. Note: If the battery is known to be fully charged; the ignition light comes on, and the starter motor fails to turn the engine check the tightness of the leads on the battery terminals and also the secureness of the earth lead to its connection to the body. It is quite common for the leads to have worked loose, even if they look and feel secure. If one of the battery terminal posts gets very hot when trying to work the starter motor this is a sure indication of a faulty connection to that terminal.

2 One of the commonest reasons for bad starting is wet or damp spark plug leads and distributor. Remove the distributor cap. If condensation is visible internally, dry the cap with a rag and also wipe over the leads. Replace the cap.

3 If the engine still fails to start, check that current is reaching the plugs, by disconnecting each plug lead in turn at the spark plug end, and hold the end of the cable about 3/16th inch (5 mm) away from the cylinder block. Spin the engine on the starter motor.

4 Sparking between the end of the cable and the block should

be fairly strong with a regular blue spark. (Hold the lead with rubber to avoid electric shocks). If current is reaching the plugs, then remove them and clean and regap them. The engine should now start.

5 If there is no spark at the plug leads take off the HT lead from the centre of the distributor cap and hold it to the block as before. Spin the engine on the starter once more. A rapid succession of blue sparks between the end of the lead and the block indicate that the coil is in order and that the distributor cap is cracked, the rotor arm faulty, or the carbon brush in the top of the distributor cap is not making good contact with the spring on the rotor arm. Possibly the points are in bad condition. Clean and reset them as described in this Chapter.

6 If there are no sparks from the end of the lead from the coil, check the connections at the coil end of the lead. If it is in order start checking the low tension circuit.

7 Use a 12 v voltmeter or a 12 v bulb and two lengths of wire. With the ignition switch on and the points open test between the low tension wire to the coil (it is marked SW or +) and earth. No reading indicates a break in the supply from the ignition switch. Check the connections at the switch to see if any are loose. Refit them and the engine should run. A reading shows a faulty coil or condenser, or broken lead between the coil and the distributor.

8 Take the condenser wire off the points and earth. If there now is a reading, then the fault is in the condenser. Fit a new one and the fault is cleared.

9 With no reading from the moving point to earth, take a reading between earth and the CB or − terminal of the coil. A reading here shows a broken wire which will need to be replaced between the coil and distributor. No reading confirms that the coil has failed and must be replaced, after which the engine will run once more. Remember to refit the condenser wire to the points assembly. For these tests it is sufficient to separate the points with a piece of dry paper while testing with the points open.

Engine misfires

10 If the engine misfires regularly run it at a fast idling speed. Pull off each of the plug caps in turn and listen to the note of the engine. Hold the plug cap in a dry cloth or with a rubber glove as additional protection against a shock from the HT supply.

11 No differnece in engine running will be noticed when the lead from the defective circuit is removed. Removing the lead from one of the good cylinders will accentuate the misfire.

12 Remove the plug lead from the end of the defective plug and hold it about 3/16th inch away from the block. Restart the engine. If the sparking it fairly strong and regular the fault must lie in the spark plug.

13 The plug may be loose, the insulation may be cracked, or the points may have burnt away giving too wide a gap for the spark to jump. Worse still, one of the points may have broken off. Either renew the plug, or clean it, reset the gap, and then test it.

14 If there is no spark at the end of the plug lead, or if it is weak and intermittent, check the ignition lead from the distributor to the plug. If the insulation is cracked or perished, renew the lead. Check the connections at the distributor cap.

15 If there is still no spark, examine the distributor cap carefully running between two or more electrodes, or between an electrode and some other part of the distributor. These lines are paths which now conduct electicity across the cap thus letting it run to earth. The only answer is a new distributor cap.

16 Apart from the ignition timing being incorrect, other causes of misfiring have already been dealt with under the section dealing with the failure of engine to start. To recap - these are that:

    a) The coil may be faulty giving an intermittent misfire.
    b) There may be a damaged wire or loose connection in the low tension circuit.
    c) The condenser may be short ciruiting.
    d) There may be a mechanical fault in the distributor (broken driving spindle or contact breaker spring).

17 If the ignition timing is too far retarded, it should be noted that the engine will tend to overheat, and there will be a quite noticeable drop in power. If the engine is overheating and the power is down, and the ignition timing is correct, then the carburettor should be checked, as it is likely that this is where the fault lies.

Chapter 5 Clutch

Contents

Specifications

	Hydraulic clutch	Mechanical clutch
Clutch disc		
Facing size:		
Outer dia. x inside dia. x thickness	160 x 110 x 3.2 mm (6.30 x 4.33 x 0.126 in)	160 x 110 x 3.2 mm (6.30 x 4.33 x 0.126 in)
Total friction area	212 sq cm (32.9 sq in)	212 sq cm (32.9 sq in)
Thickness of disc assembly (Compressed)	7.3 to 7.7 mm (0.287 to 0.303 in)	7.3 to 7.7 mm (0.287 to 0.303 in)
No. of torsion springs	6	6
Min. allowable depth of rivet head from facing surface ...	0.3 mm (0.012 in)	0.3 mm (0.012 in)
Allowable facing run-out	0.5 mm (0.020 in)	0.5 mm (0.020 in)
Clutch pedal		
Pedal height when not depressed	167 to 173 mm (6.57 to 6.81 in)	150 to 156 mm (5.91 to 6.14 in)
Free-travel of pedal head	20 mm (0.787 in)	20 mm (0.787 in)
Master cylinder		
Master cylinder diameter	15.87 mm (5/8 in)	
Max. allowable clearance between cylinder and piston ...	0.15 mm (0.006 in)	
Operating cylinder		
Operating cylinder diameter	19.05 in (¾ in)	
Torque wrench setting	**lb f ft**	**kg f m**
Clutch assembly securing bolt	11 to 16	1.5 to 2.2

1 General description

1 All vehicles are fitted with a 6.3 inch diameter diaphragm spring, single plate clutch. The unit comprises a pressed steel cover, pressure plate and diaphragm spring.

2 The clutch disc is free to slide along the splined primary drive gear assembly, and is held in position between the cover and the pressure plate by the pressure of the pressure plate spring. Friction lining material is riveted to the clutch disc and it has a spring cushioned hub to absorb transmission shocks and to help ensure a smooth take-off.

3 The clutch disc and cover can be removed or replaced without the need to dismantle any other components, and has one or two features that distinguish it from more conventional clutches. These are: the relative assembled location of clutch cover and disc; the selection of a pushrod that operates the clutch through the primary drive gear, and, finally, the unusual type of release bearing mechanism.

4 The clutch is either actuated hydraulically (LHD vehicles) or mechanically by a cable (RHD vehicles). Where the clutch is actuated hydraulically, the pendant clutch pedal is connected to the clutch master cylinder and hydraulic fluid reservoir by a short pushrod. The master cylinder and hydraulic reservoir are mounted on the engine side of the bulkhead in front of the driver.

5 Depressing the clutch pedal moves the piston in the master

cylinder forwards, so forcing hydraulic fluid through the clutch hydraulic pipe to the slave cylinder.

6   The piston in the slave cylinder moves forward on the entry of the fluid and actuates the clutch release arm by means of a short pushrod.

7   The release arm pushes the release bearing forwards to bear against the pressure plate through a pushrod that runs through the centre of the primary drive gear assembly, so moving the centre of the diaphragm spring inwards, and disengaging the pressure plate from the clutch disc.

8   When the clutch pedal is released the diaphragm spring forces the pressure plate into contact with the high friction linings on the clutch disc. The clutch disc is not firmly sandwiched between the pressure plate and the covers so the drive is taken up.

9   As the friction linings on the clutch disc wear the pressure plate automatically moves closer to the disc to compensate. There is there no need to periodically adjust the clutch.

10 Where a cable type clutch actuating mechanism is fitted, the principle of operation is similar to that already described for the hydraulic type but correct adjustment must at all times be maintained, as described in Section 3 of this Chapter.

2   Clutch adjustment - hydraulically operated

1   Locate the clutch pedal stop on the pedal bracket and adjust it to give a floor to clutch pedal top surface dimension of 6.6 to 6.8 in (167 to 173 mm). Secure the pedal stop locknut. Now check the adjustment of the slave cylinder rod.

2   Loosen the locknut on the slave cylinder rod, then turn the adjusting nut so that it becomes further from the slave cylinder. Continue rotating the nut until the release lever is pressed against the release bearing and any free-movement has been eliminated.

3   Now turn the adjusting nut back 1¼ turns and secure it in position with the locknut. This adjustment will give the correct clearance between the release lever and the release bearing.

4   Finally, check the stroke and free-play of the pedal in accordance with the Specifications. Adjust the free play by slackening the pushrod yoke locknut and rotate the pushrod until the correct clearance exists at the clevis pin. Tighten the locknut.

3   Clutch adjustment - mechanically (cable) operated

1   Adjust the clutch pedal arm stop to provide a floor to top surface of the pedal pad dimension of between 5.91 to 6.14 in (150 to 156 mm). Secure the stop locknut.

2   Adjust the free-play of the withdrawal lever to 0.157 in (4 mm) or obtain a clearance of 0.4 in (10 mm) between the adjusting nut and ball seat (see Fig. 5.4). Note that the free-play is, in this context, really the free-play of the cable against the small spring under the adjusting nut. Tighten the locknut when the correct clearance has been btained, then make sure that the pedal travels through its full stroke of 4.53 in (115 mm).

3   The pedal should have a free-play of 0.787 in (20 mm). measured from the centre of the pedal pad.

4   Clutch pedal (hydraulic) - removal and refitting

1   Detach the return spring from the pedal arm.

2   Loosen the locknut on the master cylinder pushrod and screw the rod out of the clevis fork on the pedal arm.

3   Unscrew and remove the nut and lock washer from the pedal cross shaft and then slide the pedal arm from the shaft.

4   Refitting is a reversal of removal but always check the adjustment, as described in Section 2.

5   Clutch pedal and cable (mechanical) - removal and refitting

1   Remove the locknut and the adjusting nut and detach the

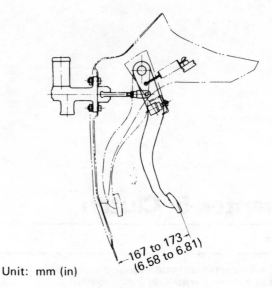

Unit: mm (in)

Fig. 5.1. Hydraulic clutch - pedal adjustment

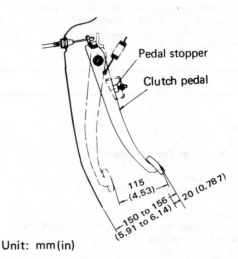

Unit: mm (in)

Fig. 5.2. Mechanical clutch - pedal adjustment

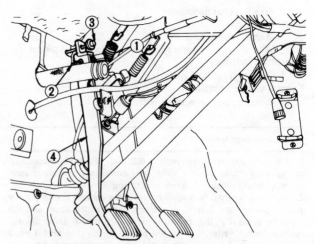

Fig. 5.3. Mechanical clutch pedal components

1 Return spring	3 Clutch cable
2 Retaining bolt	4 Clutch pedal

clutch cable from the withdrawal lever, (see Fig. 5.4). Collect the dome, spring and spring bearer from the end of the cable.

2 Refer to Fig. 5.3 and remove the pedal return spring (1). Take out the bolt (2) which secures the clutch and brake pedals. Pull the clutch cable (3) from the pedal rod and then detach the clutch pedal (4).

3 Check the pedal and associated parts for signs of deformation. Ensure that the cable has not become stretched. Unsatisfactory components should be renewed. Replacement is the reverse of removal, but re-adjustment should be carried out if a new cable is fitted.

4 When reconnecting the cable to the release lever, remember that the dome abuts the face of the lever and is tensioned by the spring on the bearer. Finally, replace the adjusting nut and the locknut.

6 Hydraulic system - bleeding

1 The need for bleeding the cylinders and fluid line arises when air gets into it. Air gets in whenever a joint or seal leaks or part

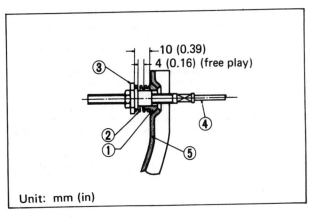

Unit: mm (in)

Fig. 5.4. Release arm adjustment

1 Ball seat   4 Clutch cable
2 Preload spring   5 Release arm
3 Adjust nut

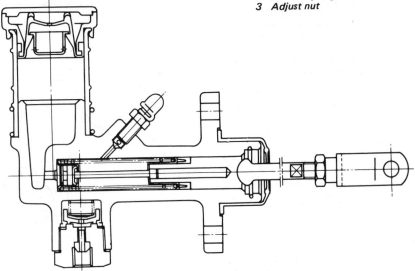

Fig. 5.5. Sectional view of master cylinder (LHD only)

has to be dismantled. Bleeding is simply the process of venting the air out again.

2 Make sure the reservoir is filled and obtain a piece of 3/16 inch (4.76 mm) bore diameter rubber tube about 2 to 3 feet long and a clean glass jar. A small quantity of fresh, clean hydraulic fluid is also necessary.

3 Detach the cap (if fitted) on the bleed nipple at the clutch slave cylinder and clean up the nipple and surrounding area. Unscrew the nipple ¾ turn and fit the tube over it. Put about ½ inch (13 mm) of fluid in the jar and put the other end of the pipe in it. The jar can be placed on the ground under the car.

4 The clutch pedal should then be depressed quickly and released slowly until no more air bubbles come from the pipe. Quick pedal action carries the air along rather than leave it behind. Keep the reservoir topped-up.

5 When the air bubbles stop tighten the nipple at the end of a down stroke.

6 Check that the operation of the clutch is satisfactory. Even though there may be no exterior leaks it is possible that the movement of the pushrod from the clutch cylinder is inadequate because fluid is leaking internally past the seals in the master cylinder. If this is the case, it is best to replace all seals in both cylinders.

7 Always use clean hydraulic fluid which has been stored in an airtight container and has remained unshaken for the preceding 24 hours.

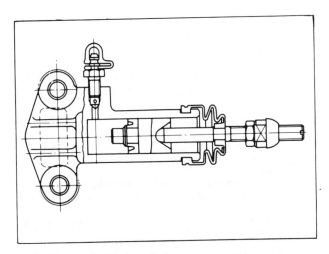

Fig. 5.6. Sectional view of slave cylinder (LHD only)

7 Master cylinder - removal, dismantling, servicing and reassembly

1   The master cylinder and fluid reservoir are a single unit and indications of something wrong with it are if the pedal travels down without operation the clutch efficiently (assuming, of course, that the system has been bled and there are no leaks).

2   To remove the unit from the car first seal the cap with a piece of film to reduce fluid wastage whilst dismantling the pipes. Alternatively, the fluid may be pumped out from the clutch cylinder bleed nipple by opening the nipple and depressing the pedal several times.

3   From inside the car remove the locknut which attaches the pushrod assembly to the clevis, and disconnect the pushrod.

4   Disconnect the fluid line which runs between the master cylinder and the slave (operating) cylinder.

5   Unscrew and remove the two bolts which secure the master cylinder to the engine rear bulkhead.

6   Withdraw the master cylinder from the bulkhead.

7   Peel back the rubber dust cover from the end of the master cylinder, remove the circlip and inlet valve stop pin.

8   The internal components may then be ejected, either by tapping the end of the cylinder on a piece of wood or by applying air pressure from a tyre pump at the fluid outlet pipe.

9   Clean all components in clean hydraulic fluid or methylated spirit. Examine the internal surfaces of the master cylinder for scoring or bright areas; also the surface of the piston. Where these are apparent, renew the complete master cylinder assembly.

10 Discard all rubber seals, making sketches if necessary before removing them from the piston so that the new seals will be fitted with their lips and chamfers the correct way round.

11 Obtain a repair kit and examine all the items supplied for damage, particularly the seals for cuts or deterioration in storage.

12 Commence reassembling by dipping the new seals in clean hydraulic fluid and fitting them to the piston, using only the fingers to manipulate them into their grooves. Ensure that they are correctly located with regard contour as originally fitted.

13 Use all the new items supplied in the repair kit and reassemble in the reverse order to dismantling, lubricating each component in clean hydraulic fluid before it is fitted into the master cylinder.

14 When all the internal components have been installed, fit a new circlip and screw in the inlet valve stop pin.

15 Bolt the master cylinder to the engine rear bulkhead. Once the master cylinder has been installed and the pushrod connected to the clutch pedal arm then the adjustment described in Section 2 must be carried out.

16 Reconnect the fluid pipe between the master and slave cylinders, fill the reservoir with clean hydraulic fluid and bleed the system. Probe the reservoir vent hole in the cap to ensure that it is not clogged.

8 Slave (operating) cylinder - removal, dismantling, servicing and reassembly

1   Disconnect the fluid pipe from the slave cylinder. To do this, uncouple the union at the master cylinder and plug the union outlet to prevent loss of fluid. Now unscrew the flexible pipe from the slave cylinder taking care not to twist the pipe and retaining the sealing washer.

2   Remove the adjustnut and locknut from the slave cylinder operating rod and then disconnect the operating rod from the clutch release lever.

3   Unscrew and remove the slave cylinder to clutch housing securing bolts and lift the cylinder away.

4   Peel back the dust cover and remove the circlip.

5   Eject the internal components of the slave cylinder either by tapping the end of the unit on a piece of wood or by applying air pressure from a tyre pump at the fluid hose connection.

6   Wash all components in clean hydraulic fluid or methylated

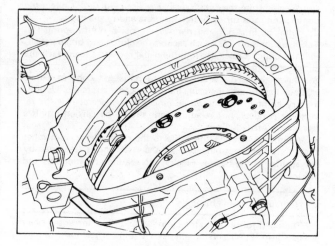

Fig. 5.7. Clutch inspection cover removed

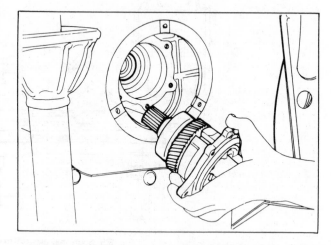

Fig. 5.8. Removing the primary drive gear through the wheel housing cut-out

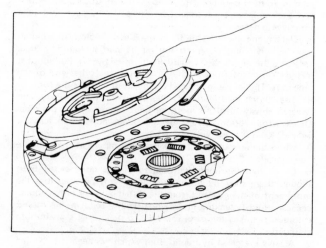

Fig. 5.9. Lifting off the pressure plate and removing   the clutch disc (driven plate)

spirit. Discard the seals and examine the piston and cylinder bore surfaces for scoring or bright areas. Where these are evident, renew the complete assembly.

7   Obtain a repair kit and examine all the items supplied for damage, particularly the seals for cuts or deterioration in storage.

8   Commence reassembling by dipping the new seals in clean hydraulic fluid and fitting them to the piston, using the fingers only to manipulate them.

9   Use all the new items supplied in the repair kit and re-assemble in reverse order to dismantling, lubricating each component in clean hydraulic fluid before it is fitted into the cylinder bore.

10 When all the internal components have been installed, fit a new circlip and the new rubber dust cover supplied with the repair kit.

11 Refit the slave cylinder to the clutch housing, reconnect the fluid supply pipe and the operating pushrod to the clutch release lever.

12 Bleed the hydraulic system, as described in Section 7.

13 Adjust the operating rod nut, as described in Section 2.

9   Clutch assembly - removal

1   Disconnect the battery leads.

2   Detach the clutch control cable, or slave cylinder operating rod, from the clutch withdrawal lever. This will depend if it is a LHD or RHD model.

3   Remove the inspection cover from the clutch housing. Remove the six bolts which secure the clutch cover. These bolts should be slackened off gradually and evenly, after first marking the relative positions of the clutch and flywheel.

4   Disconnect the clutch operating lever by first pulling off the rubber shroud, and then removing the spring clip that secures the lever pivot pin. The operation lever can be lifted away when the pin is pulled out.

5   Remove the six bolts on the bearing housing, and withdraw the primary drive gear assembly through the opening on the right-hand side wheel housing. The opening can be revealed by removing the three screws that secure the cover on the opening, from inside the wheel housing.

6   Lift the clutch cover and disc out through the inspection opening in the upper part of the clutch housing.

7   Remove the strap bolts which secure the pressure plate to the cover, and take off the clutch disc (see Fig. 5.9). Note that the relative position of pressure plate and cover are indicated on the edge of the assembly either by white paint spots or by an arrow and raised pointer.

10 Clutch - inspection and renovation

1   Since the clutch on this vehicle is so easily removed, there is no reason to delay when renewal becomes necessary. The only positive indication that something needs doing is when the clutch starts to slip or when squealing noises on engagement indicate that the friction lining has worn down to the rivets. In such instances it can only be hoped that the friction surfaces on the cover and pressure plate have not been badly worn or scored. A clutch will wear according to the way in which it is used. Much intentional slipping of the clutch while driving - rather than the correct selection of gears - will accelerate wear. It is best to assume however, that the friction disc will need renewal every 35,000 miles (56,000 km) at least and that it will be *worth* replacing it after 25,000 miles (40,000 km). The maintenance history of the car is obviously very useful in such cases.

2   Examine the surfaces of the pressure plate and cover for signs of scording. If this is only light it may be left, but if very deep the pressure plate and cover assembly will have to be replaced as a unit because they are a balanced assembly.

3   The friction plate lining surfaces should be at least 0.012 in (0.3 mm) above the rivets, otherwise the disc is not worth

9.3 Removing the six clutch cover bolts

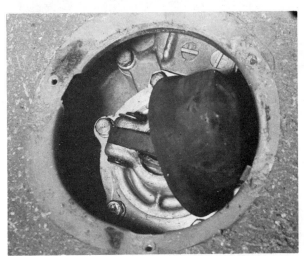
9.5A Wheel housing access hole to the primary drive gear

9:5B Primary drive gear when withdrawn

9.6 Lifting out the clutch assembly

9.7A Removing the strap bolts

9.7B Revealing the clutch disc

9.7C Relative position of pressure plate and cover shown by arrow and raised pointer

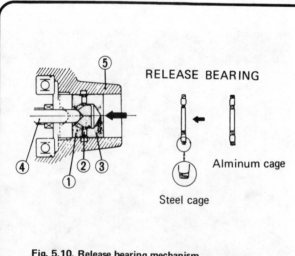

RELEASE BEARING

Aluminum cage

Steel cage

Fig. 5.10. Release bearing mechanism

1   Pushrod piece B   4   Pushrod
2   Release bearing   5   Bearing housing
3   Pushrod piece A

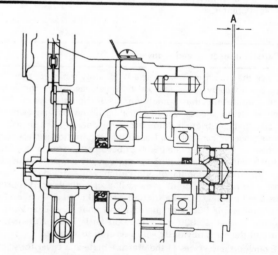

Fig. 5.11. Selecting a pushrod of the correct   length
to achieve specified distance at A

A =   0.5 to 2.5 mm (0.020 to 0.098 in.)

putting back. If the lining material shows signs of breaking up or black areas where oil contamination has occurred it should also be renewed. If facilities are readily available for obtaining and fitting new friction pads to the existing disc this may be done but the saving is relatively small compared with obtaining a complete new disc assembly which ensures that the shock absorbing springs and the splined hub are renewed also. An allowance is usually given for exchange units.

11 Pushrods and release bearing assembly - removal and replacement

1 In order to remove the pushrod and release bearing it is first necessary to remove the primary drive gear, as described in Section 9.
2 Place the primary drive gear on end, splines uppermost, with the two outer flanges supported. Using a hammer, and piece of wood on the pushrod, lightly tap the assembly out of the end of the drive gear. A drift will be needed to completely remove the pushrod.
3 Prise out the 'O' ring in the bearing housing.
4 Two types of release bearing will be found (ie; with steel or aluminium cage). They are mutually interchangeable.
5 Reassembly is the reverse of dismantling, but the following points should be noted:
    a) If a steel cage release bearing is to be used be sure to insert it in the direction of the arrow mark in Fig. 5.10. That is, with the lip of the cage away from the pushrod, otherwise the 'O' ring will be damaged.
    b) Insert the pushrod, the release bearing carrier, the release bearing and its outer section in the housing as an assembled unit.
    c) Grease the release mechanism as indicated in Fig. 5.13.

12 Pushrod - selection

1 If any parts of the clutch or release mechanism are replaced, it will be necessary to check the pushrod clearance and renew the pushrod if necessary.
2 With the primary drive gear, and the release mechanism, in position and bolted up, gently press the release bearing, and thus the pushrod, until movement is arrested by the pressure plate. Then measure the depth 'A' as shown in Fig. 5.11. Select a pushrod from the table below to keep the clearance at A to the specified valve of 0.0020 to 0.098 in (0.5 to 2.5 mm).

Length of notch on rod	Length of push rod
6.0 mm. (0.236 in.)	114.95 to 115.15 mm. (4.5256 to 4.5335 in.)
None	113.89 to 114.09 mm. (4.4838 to 4.4917 in.)
3.5 mm. (0.138 in.)	112.83 to 113.03 mm. (4.4421 to 4.4500 in.)

3 As shown in Fig. 5.12, each pushrod is marked with a notch of a specified length which indicates the pushrod overall length.

13 Clutch - refitting

1 Insert the clutch disc between the clutch cover and pressure plate and, before securing the assembly, ensure that the two marks on the cover and pressure plate are aligned. Note that the raised centre of the clutch disc faces towards the clutch cover (ie; away from the flywheel).
2 Offer up the clutch assembly to the flywheel aligning the

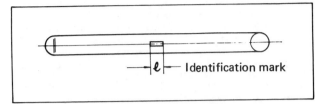

Fig. 5.12. Pushrod identification mark

Length of Notch	Length of Pushrod
6.0 mm (0.236 in.)	114.95 - 115.15 mm (4.5256 - 4.535 in.)
No notch	113.89 - 114.09 mm (4.4838 - 4.4917 in.)
3.5 mm (0.138 in.)	112.83 - 113.03 mm (4.4421 - 4.450 in.)

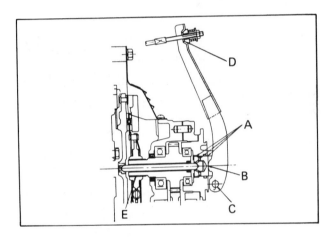

Fig. 5.13. Release bearing lubrication points

Points A to D	Multi-purpose grease
Point E	Molybdenum disulphide grease

Apply a light coating of grease to the primary gear splines.
Never apply grease to the clutch disc splines.
Do not lubricate the pressure plate at the bushing location.

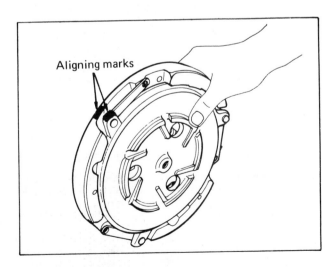

Fig. 5.14. Assembling clutch cover, disc and pressure plate

marks made prior to dismantling and insert the retaining bolts finger tight. Where a new clutch assembly is being fitted, locate it to the flywheel in a similar relative position to the original by reference to the index marking and dowel positions.

3 Insert a guide tool through the splined hub of the driven plate so that the end of the tool locates in the pressure plate. This action of the guide tool will centralise the driven plate by causing it to move in a sideways direction.

4 Insert and remove the guide tool two or three times to ensure that the driven plate is fully centralised and then tighten the securing bolts a turn at a time and in a diametrically opposite sequence, to a torque of 16 lb/ft (2.21 kg/m) to prevent distortion of the pressure plate cover. If a guide tool is not available it is acceptable to insert the clutch assembly and then replace the primary drive gear assembly, before bolting the clutch assembly to the flywheel. This will have the effect of centralising the clutch disc.

5 The remainder of clutch refitting is the reverse of dismantling.

6 Adjust the clutch free-movement, according to type, as described in Section 2 or 3.

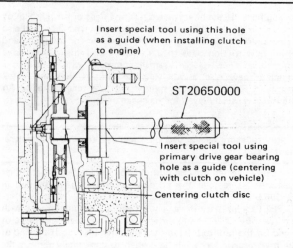

Fig. 5.15. Aligning the clutch assembly using a special Datsun tool

Note: A similar tool can be made up locally or the primary drive gear used. (Refer to Section 13, paragraph 4).

14 Fault diagnosis - Clutch

Symptom	Reason/s	Remedy
Judder when taking up drive	Loose engine or gearbox mountings	Tighten and inspect rubber insulators for deterioration.
	Badly worn friction surfaces or contaminated with oil	Renew driven plate and rectify oil leakage, probably crankshaft rear oil seal or input shaft oil seal.
	Worn splines on primary drive gear input shaft or driven plate hub	Renew component.
Clutch spin (failure to disengage) so that gears cannot be meshed	Incorrect release bearing clearance	Adjust according to type, see Sections 2 or 3.
	Incorrect pushrod	Select another pushrod
	Driven plate sticking on input shaft splines due to rust. May occur after vehicle standing idle for long period	As temporary remedy, engage top gear, apply handbrake, depress clutch and start engine. If driven plate badly stuck, engine will not turn. When engine running, rev up and slip clutch until normal clutch disengagement is possible. Renew driven plate at earliest opportunity.
	Damaged or misaligned pressure plate assembly	Renew pressure plate assembly.
Clutch slip (increase in engine speed does not result in increase in vehicle road speed - particularly on gradients)	Incorrect release bearing clearance	Adjust clearance according to type, see Sections 2 or 3.
	Friction surfaces worn out or oil contaminated	Renew driven plate and rectify oil leakage.
	Incorrect pushrod	Sleect another pushrod
Noise evident on depressing clutch pedal	Dry, worn or damaged release bearing	Renew bearing.
	Insufficient pedal free travel	Adjust according to type see Sections 2 or 3.
	Weak or broken pedal return spring	Renew.
	Weak or broken clutch release lever return spring.	Renew.
	Excessive play between driven plate hub splines and input shaft splines	Renew both components.
Noise evident as clutch pedal released	Distorted driven plate	Renew.
	Broken or weak driven plate cushion coil springs	Renew driven plate as an assembly.
	Insufficient pedal free travel	Adjust according to type, see Section 2 or 3.
	Weak or broken clutch pedal return spring	Renew.
	Weak or broken release lever return spring	Renew.
	Distorted or worn input primary gear shaft splines	Renew primary gear and driven plate if necessary.
	Release bearing loose on retainer hub	Renew hub and bearing.

Chapter 6 Gearbox

Contents

Specifications

Type	Combined gearbox and final drive assembly
No. of speeds	4-forward, 1 reverse
Gear ratios	
First	3.673
Second	2.217
Third	1.448
Fourth	1.000
Reverse	4.093
Operation	Floor change
Synchronising	Warner synchro
Final drive gear ratio	4.286 (60/14)
Oil capacity	4½ Imp pints, 2.3/8 U.S. qts., 2.3 litres
Backlash in gears	
Primary gear train	0.05 to 0.14mm (0.0020 to 0.0055 in)
Main drive gear 1st, 2nd, 3rd gear	0.05 to 0.15mm (0.0020 to 0.0059in)
Reverse idler gear	
Final gear	0.05 to 0.15mm (0.0020 to 0.0059 in)
Transmission gear standard end play	0.2 to 0.3mm (0.0079 to 0.0118 in)
Clearance in baulking and cone:	
Standard value	1.2mm (0.0472 in)
Replacement standard	0.5mm (0.0197 in)
Side gear endplay (differential)	0.10 to 0.20mm (0.0039 to 0.0079 in)
Side gear thrust washer (selected):	

No.	Thickness mm (in)
1	0.7 (0.0276)
2	0.8 (0.0315)
3	0.9 (0.0354)
4	1.0 (0.0394)
5	1.1 (0.0433)

Torque wrench settings

	lb f ft	kg f m
Main drive gear nut	43 to 58	6.0 to 8.0
Reverse idler shaft lock nut	72 to 87	10.0 to 12.0
Main shaft lock nut	36 to 43	5.0 to 6.0
Differential side flange lock nuts	87 to 101	12.0 to 14.0
Final gear lock nuts	43 to 51	6.0 to 7.0
Reverse lamp switch	14 to 22	2.0 to 3.0
Interlock plugs	8.0 to 12	1.1 to 1.6

1 General description

The engine drive is carried through the clutch and primary drive gear, through the primary idler gear to the main drive input gear, and subsequently to the mainshaft in the gearbox.

The gearbox is fairly standard having a 4-speed mainshaft and a layshaft (countershaft). The mainshaft also provides the drive to the final drive and differential unit which shares the same housing with the gearbox. A common lubrication system is shared by the two assemblies.

The final gear used in the final drive is a helical gear which is of the same design as that used in the transmission, requiring no adjustment for gear contact pattern.

The transmission gearchange is of a remote control floor shift type. It consists essentially of a hand lever, a linkage which connects the hand lever to the transmission, and a radius link assembly which supports the linkage at the location between the control rod and the transmission.

The reverse stop mechanism is incorporated in the socket located at the lower end of the hand lever.

2 Transmission - removal

The gearbox and differential assembly are removed from the vehicle together with the engine. Details of this operation are contained in Chapter 1. In this Chapter we are assuming the complete assembly has been removed from the vehicle in accordance with the operations described in Chapter 1, and the dismantling sequence commences at this point.

3 Transmission - dismantling (general)

1 Before the gearbox or differential assembly can be dismantled it is necessary to separate the transmission from the engine.

2 Ensure that an exceptionally clean area is available for the dismantling, and that a good supply of clean fluff-free rags is available, together with various jars and containers in which to store items.

3 It is sound policy to replace bolts, after a component has been dismantled, to aid replacement. Failing this identify them in some other way.

4 As a general aid it is a good policy to have the following tools at hand:

    a) Good quality circlip pliers; 2 pairs, 1 expanding and 1 contracting.

    b) Copper head mallet, at least 2 lbs.
    c) Drifts, steel 3/8 inch and brass 3/8 inch.
    d) Small containers for needle rollers.
    e) Engineer's vice mounted on firm bench.

5 Any attempt to dismantle the gearbox without the foregoing is not necessarily impossible, but will certainly be very difficult and inconvenient resulting in possible injury or damage.

6 Take care not to let the synchromesh hub assemblies come apart before you want them to. It accelerates wear if the splines of hub and sleeve are changed in relation to each other. As a precaution it is advisable to make a line up mark with a dab of paint.

7 Before finally going ahead with dismantling first ascertain the availability of spare parts. If several major components need replacing, work out the total cost. It could well be that a reconditioned unit is cheaper in the long run.

4 Engine and transmission - separation

1 Disconnect the clutch operating lever by first pulling off the protective boot, then removing the clip that secures the lever pivot pin. Drift the pin out and remove the lever.

2 Remove the bolts that secure the clutch thrust bearing housing and the primary drive gear. Withdraw the assembly.

3 Remove the bolts that secure the primary gear cover and remove the cover by tapping it with a soft hammer. This might be a little difficult due to the bearings in the cover. **Do not** prise it off with a screwdriver. It will be noted that some bolts either have a white or green protective resin on the threads, in order to prevent oil leakage. When replacing any bolts of this type a protective coating of golden loctite should be applied to the threads.

4 Detach bottom cover from transmission case by removing the 12 bolts that retain it. Mesh reverse gear and 1st (or 2nd) gear at the same time by operating the gearchange levers. Loosen main drive gear nut, and remove main drive input bearing, using a puller, then the gear. Collect the lock-washer and thrust washer under the nut.

5 Remove the primary idler bearing and gear, preferably by using a sliding hammer type of puller; if this is not available, an ordinary three-legged puller is equally acceptable.

6 Remove the clutch housing bolts, both to the transmission and the engine. These will be of various sizes so note which is which to aid replacement. Lift away the clutch housing.

7 Disconnect the nut and bolt that passes through the flange on the transmission are now completely separated. Lift the transmission assembly away to a separate, extremely clean area, ready for dismantling.

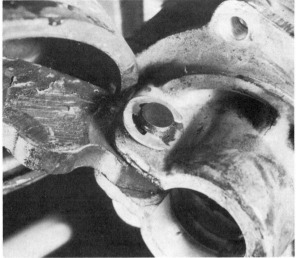
4.1A Clip securing pivot pin

4.1B Removing the pin

4.2 Removing the primary drive gear ...

4.3 ... and then the cover

4.5A Using a puller to remove the idler bearing ...

4.5B ... and then the idler gear

4.6 Lifting away the clutch housing

4.7 The nut and bolt that must be removed to separate the transmission from the engine

5 Transmission - dismantling

1 Support the assembly on a stand or on a bench. Remember that the housing is of aluminium alloy which should be handled with reasonable care. Where the exterior of the unit is only lightly covered with oil or road dirt then it should be cleaned with paraffin. Heavy deposits of oil and dirt should be removed using a proprietary solvent such as 'Gunk'

2 Remove the nuts securing the flanges (one each side) to the differential, and remove the flanges. The driving flange can normally be locked in place with a couple of steel rods jammed against the casing. If the flange cannot be locked in position using the steel rods then you might have to use the technique shown in the associated photograph, where a socket spanner and bar are put on the opposite nut. Be sure to put a piece of wood under the bar or damage to the casing may result. It may be necessary to use a puller to remove the flanges if tapping with a block of wood and hammer does not suffice.

3 Remove the bolts securing the transmission case cover and remove the cover. It will probably be necessary to separate the cover from the case by using a hammer and a block of wood. Note the bolts with resin on the threads.

4 Remove the speedometer pinion and lift out the final gear and differential case as a unit.

5 Remove the detent plugs and take out locking springs and steel balls. **Note: The locking spring used on the reverse fork shaft is distinguished from those on 1st and 2nd or 3rd and 4th shafts by a white color coating. It is longer than the others.**

6 Remove the taper plug by unscrewing it. This will give you access to drive out the roll pin on the gearchange fork.

7 Using a suitable drift, drive out the roll pin that secures the gearchange fork to the fork shaft, then remove the shaft and fork.

8 Remove the bolts that retain the reverse gear fork and bracket. Separate the bracket from the fork by unclipping the pivot pin and lifting the fork.

9 Remove the bolts and flanged nut that secures the main shaft bearing retainer and remove the retainer.

10 Remove the reverse idler gear and its shaft.

11 The next step can be a little tricky. In order to remove the counter shaft (layshaft) it is necessary to drive it out using either a special Datsun tool or a piece of rod of the same diameter as the shaft and the same length as the distance between the two faces of the gearbox casing. One could argue that the tool, or rod, is more important when replacing the layshaft (in order to retain the needle bearings in position) but it is just as well to use it at this stage to ensure that it fits and no needle bearings are lost.

12 Drive out the countershaft, using the tool described above,
then remove the countershaft and gear cluster, and collect the thrust washers from the ends of the countershaft.

13 Using a suitable drift, remove the roll pins from each of the remaining selector forks and pull each selector shaft out through the casing, complete with the attached dogs. Collect the selector forks and store in a safe place. The interlock plungers can now be removed from their housing in the casing between the selector shafts.

14 Lift the gear main shaft assembly and the main drive input gear out of the casing through the final drive side. Collect the needle bearing from the main shaft nose.

15 Measure the endplay present in each gear of the mainshaft, as shown in Figure 6.3. If the specified limit of 0.0079 to 0.0118 in (0.2 to 0.3 mm) is exceeded new parts will have to be fitted.

6 Mainshaft - dismantling, inspection and reassembly

1 Place the mainshaft in a vice, but ensure that some form of padding is used so as not to damage the gears.

2 Remove the locknut from the end of the mainshaft. **The lock nut is staked, so when it is removed be sure to clean the threaded portion of the main shaft until all the metal chips are removed. The lock nut should be discarded and should not be reused.**

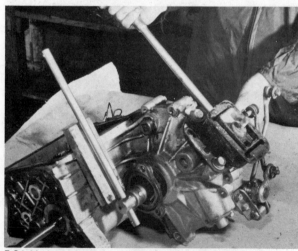

5.2A Method of removing the nuts securing the flanges ...

5.2B ... and then using a puller to remove the flange

5.3A Removing the mounting

5.3B Separating the casing

5.4 Lifting out the differential assembly

5.5A & B Removing the detent plugs, springs and balls

5.8A Removing reverse gear fork and shaft bolts ...

5.8B ... unclipping the pivot pin ...

5.8C ... and removing the bracket

5.9 Removing the bearing retainer

5.10 Removing the reverse gear and shaft

5.12A Inserting the dummy layshaft and pressing out the original one

5.12B Flanged thrust washer at each end of layshaft

5.12C Lifting out the laygear

5.13 Removing the selector shafts

5.14A Separating the mainshaft and input gears ...

5.14B ... lifting out the mainshaft ...

5.14C ... and then the input gear

5.14D Collecting the needle bearing

6.2 Removing the mainshaft locknut

6.3A Remove the 3rd/4th gear synchroniser ...

6.3B ... 3rd gear with bushing ...

6.3C ... spacer ...

6.3D ... 2nd gear with bushing ...

6.3E ... 1st/2nd synchroniser ...

6.3F ... and first gear with its bushing

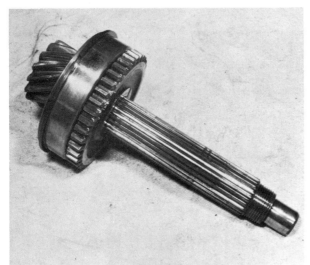

6.3G The reverse gear can now be removed followed by the bearing which will need to be pressed off

8.1 Dismantled laygear assembly

8.3 Inserting the spacer

8.4A Smearing grease around the layshaft

3   Remove the 3rd and 4th synchronizer, 3rd gear, main gear bushing, main gear spacer, 2nd gear, main gear bushing, 1st and 2nd synchronixer, 1st and main gear bushing from main shaft in the order enumerated.

4   Press out the bearing from the mainshaft. This can be done by resting the outer face of the bearing on the vice, and with a piece of wood interposed, lightly tapping the shaft down through the bearing. Leave the circlip on the bearing outer face.

7   Final drive and differential - dismantling and reassembly

1   Place the final drive assembly in a vice, using padded jaws, and pull off the differential side bearings using a puller.

2   Remove the bolts that secure the final gear to the differential.

3   Detach the differential case. Withdraw the differential pinion, by using a drift and hammer, from the mainshaft, and then remove the differential side gears and pinion.

4   Reassembly is the reverse of dismantling; critical adjustments taking place at a later stage in the rebuild.

8   Countershaft - dismantling

1   Place the countershaft (layshaft) in a vice with padded jaws. Although the actual shaft is out of the gear assembly at this stage, it is now necessary to drive out the dummy shaft, remove the needle roller bearings, and then drive out the spacer and locating washers. Do this using a suitable piece of rod, and taking care not to damage the needle bearings or score the shaft.

2   Reassembly is the reverse of dismantling, but the following points are important.

3   First install the spacer in the laygear. This should be pushed in until it is roughly central. Then position a locating washer either side of the spacer.

4   Next, insert the layshaft until it is protuding at one end of the laygear. Smear the end with grease and place the needle bearings around the layshaft.

5   Press the needle bearings down into the laygear with another locating washer. This should be done at either end of the laygear.

6   Finally, replace the layshaft with the dummy layshaft. The assembly is now ready for insertion in the gearbox during reassembly.

9   Primary drive gear and idler gear - dismantling and reassembly

1   The primary drive gear can be dismantled by first using a piece of bar and lightly tapping the pushrod through the assembly so that the thrust bearing and its two-piece carrier block emerges. Then tap the pushrod right through.

2   The front section of the drive gear can now be removed by using a suitable drift and driving it out.

3   The bearings on the drive gear and idler gear can be pressed out in a vice, always ensuring that soft jaws are used and that suitably spaced blocks of wood carry the pressure.

4   Replacement is the reverse of dismantling, but if any clutch components have been renewed it is most important that the length of the pushrod is selected as covered in Chapter 5.

10 Transmission components - inspection and overhaul

1   Thoroughly clean all parts in cleaning solvent, and blow dry with compressed air. Check each part for wear, damage, or other defective conditions.

2   Inspect the primary gear cover, clutch housing, transmission case and transmission case cover. Repair or replace parts if burrs, pitting or damage is apparent on their mating surfaces.

3   Repair or replace a dowel pin if it is distorted or other damage is apparent.

4   Make sure that each bearing is thoroughly cleaned and free from dirt.

5   Check ball bearings to insure that they roll freely and are free

8.4B Positioning the needle bearings

8.5 Pressing down the bearings with a washer

8.6 Replacing the layshaft with a dummy shaft

9.1 Thrust bearing and its two-piece carrier block

9.2 Splitting the drive gear

from cracked, pitted, or worn balls. Also check outer, inner races and balls for indications of bearing creepage. Replace if any of the above conditions are apparent.

6   Replace needle roller bearing, if worn or damaged.

7   Check all the gears for wear, damaged or chipped teeth. Where such damage is evident, the driven and driving gears should be renewed as a set. Where the gearbox has covered a substantial period of service it will be appropriate to test for backlash and endfloat with the gear train assembled on the main-shaft and countershaft and installed in the gearbox. Use a dial gauge to check for backlash, turning each gearwheel as far as it will go whilst holding the mainshaft perfectly still. The permitted backlash tolerance is given below. Use a feeler gauge to check for endplay. The correct tolerance is 0.0079 to 0.0118 in (0.2 to 0.3 mm).

8   Where the backlash or endplay is greater than that specified, consideration should be given to purchasing a reconditioned gearbox as the cost of a complete set of gears and other internal components will probably prove uneconomical by comparison.

Standard backlash

Primary driver gear	0.05 to 0.14 mm
Primary idler gear	(0.0020 to 0.0055 in)
Main drive input gear	
Main drive gears, 1st, 2nd,	
3rd gears, reverse idler gear	0.05 to 0.15 mm
Final gear	(0.0020 to 0.0059 in)

11.13 Mating the mainshaft and the main drive input gear

9   Check baulk rings for evidence of wear, pitting, crack, or damage. If any of the above conditions is apparent, replace with a new one.

10   Measure the clearance between baulk ring end and cone (Figure 6.5). The standard clearance is 0.0472 in (1.2 mm). If it is less than 0.0197 in (0.5 mm) replace baulk ring with a new one.

11   Replace all gaskets and oil seals.

11 Transmission - reassembly

1   Ensure that all parts are thoroughly cleaned and dipped in light oil before reassembly. Ensure that each paper gasket is free from moisture. Do not use any liquid sealants between the mating faces of the relative units.

2   Press the differential side bearings into the differential case. If a proper press is not available use a hammer and block of wood to spread the load over the face of the bearing. Tap the bearing home gently.

3   The next stage is slightly more complex and involves the use of a dial gauge. Fit the final drive assembly on a testing tool like

11.14A Inserting the bottom selector shaft ...

that shown in Figure 6.6. If you cannot obtain the official Datsun tool there should be no problem in making one up locally. Using the dial gauge adjust each side gear endplay to obtain a figure of 0.004 to 0.008 in (0.1 to 0.2 mm) by selective thrust washers. Sizes of thrust washers available are given in the Specifications.

4 Fit the final drive gear on the differential assembly. Apply loctite to the bolts and tighten them to a torque of 43 to 51 ft/lb. (6.0 to 7.0 kg/m).

5 Ensure that the sliding surfaces of the mainshaft bushes are lubricated with oil before assembly.

6 Press the ball bearing onto the mainshaft and install the reverse gear. Slide the bush into position on the mainshaft, so that the oil holes are aligned. Fit the first gear, baulk ring and synchronizer hub. Make sure that the insert is correctly seated in the groove of the baulk ring.

7 Fit the second gear bush so that its oil hole is aligned with the hole in the mainshaft and then install the second gear.

8 Fit the main gear spacer followed by the bush and third gear. Install the baulk ring and synchronizer hub.

9 Place the mainshaft in a vice equipped with soft jaws.

10 Replace the locknut and tighten to a torque of 36 to 43 lb/ft (5.0 to 6.0 kg/m). Before staking the locknut to the shaft it is obviously important to ensure that endplay is still within tolerance.

11 Using a suitable drift, lightly tap the distance piece into the laygear into an approximate central position. Insert a spacer either side of the distance piece. Next, drift the dummy layshaft, used on dismantling, through the laygear. Insert twenty-one needle rollers at either end, after ensuring they are well greased. Now fit the remaining two spacers. The laygear is now ready for installation, but should not be fitted at this point.

12 Lubricate the lip of the differential side flange oil seal with multi-purpose grease, and press it into position using a block of wood between the faces of a vice. Note that the lip should be innermost.

13 Ensure the main drive gear bearing is in position in the casing, then ease the main drive gear through the bearing and into position. Fit a needle bearing on the nose of the mainshaft and mate it with the main drive gear in the transmission case.

14 Insert the bottom selector shaft, slide the fork over it and engage the fork with the nearest coupling sleeve on the mainshaft. Secure in position with a roll pin. Insert the interlock plunger through the bore in centre selector shaft housing.

15 Insert the centre selector shaft, slide the fork over it and engage the fork with the end coupling sleeve on the mainshaft. Secure in position with a roll pin. Insert the interlock plunger.

16 Hold the laygear in position in the transmission case. Insert the layshaft (countershaft) into the gear and then drive out the special tool. Don't forget to fit the thrust washers at either end of the layshaft and locate their tabs in the casing slots.

17 Insert the reverse idler gear, position the bearing retainer and secure the two components with the flanged nut. Fit the remaining retainer nuts. Tighten the flanged nut to a torque of 72 - 87 ft/lb (9.95 - 12 kg/m).

18 Insert the reverse fork shaft, and slide the reverse fork pivot over the shaft and secure with a roll pin.

19 Insert the reverse fork bracket and secure with two bolts. Place the reverse fork on the pivot and secure to the bracket with a clevis pin and clip.

20 Replace the steel balls, locking springs and retaining plugs. A longer and white coated locking spring is used for the reverse fork rod. Manipulate the selector shafts manually to ensure that all gears can be selected.

21 Install the final drive assembly and transmission cover. Apply Loctite sealer to the threads of the differential side flanges, then install and tighten to a torque reading of 87 to 101 lb/ft (12.0 to 14.0 kg/m). Then insert the reversing lamp switch in its housing in the cover.

22 Install the clutch housing. New bolts should be used if the resin coating has come off the threads of the original bolts, although a coating of Golden Loctite is considered satisfactory. Use a new gasket.

23 Lightly tap the primary idler gear into the clutch housing wiht a wooden mallet, making sure that the mark on the gear is towards the primary gear cover.

24 Fit the main drive input gear and bearing by lightly tapping them over the mainshaft splines with a wooden mallet. Next assemble the thrust washer, lock washer, and main drive gear nut, in the order given. The nut for the main drive gear must be installed with its chamfered side facing the lock washer.

25 Mesh two sets of gears to prevent the main drive gear from turning, then tighten the nut to a torque reading of 43 to 58 lb/ft (6.0 to 8.0 kg/m), and bend over the lock washer to lock the nut.

26 Install the primary gear cover, and the bottom cover. Replace the taper plug.

27 Do not fit the bearing housing assembly and primary drive gear at this stage because of the problem of lining up with the flywheel and clutch assembly.

28 Refit the clutch operating lever and secure in position with a pivot pin through the primary drive gear flange. Fit a locking clip over the pin. Replace the protective rubber boot.

29 Reconnect the transmission to the engine, first by the single belt through the transmission flange and engine stay rod, then by the bolts through the clutch housing to the engine endplate. The clutch should still be in position on the flywheel.

30 Now replace the primary drive gear and bearing assembly. If the clutch has been removed it is most likely that you will have to use some form of centering tool to line-up the clutch with the primary drive gear splines. Another way of tackling it is to loosen the clutch bolts, insert the primary drive gear, and adjust the clutch position until the two are correctly mated. Then tighten the bolts.

31 Replace the clutch inspection cover. The assembly is now ready for replacing in the car. Refer to Chapter 1 for these details.

12 Gearchange linkage - removal, inspection and replacement

1 Remove the bolts which secure the gear lever to its mounting bracket. Take out the split pin and remove the snap ring which secures the control rod to the gear lever.

2 Remove the bolts which secure the radius link assembly to the transmission case cover, then remove the snap ring to free the radius link assembly from the subframe.

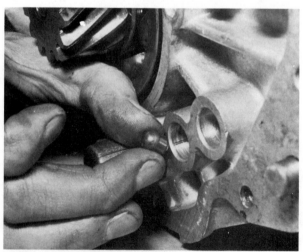

11.14B ... then the interlock plunger

11.14C Securing the fork with a roll pin

11.15A Inserting the centre selector shaft ...

11.15B ... then the interlock plunger

11.15C Securing the selector fork with a roll pin

11.16A Inserting the laygear ...

11.16B ... then the layshaft, driving out the dummy shaft

11.17A Inserting the reverse idler gear ...

11.17B ... positioning the bearing retainer ...

11.17C ... and securing with retaining nuts

11.18 The selector dogs should now look like this

11.19A Reverse fork secured to the bracket ...

11.19B ... and the bracket retained by two bolts

11.20A Replacing the detent balls, ...

11.20B ... springs and ...

11.20C ... retaining plugs

11.21A Installing the final drive assembly ...

11.21B ... and the cover

11.21C Fitting a differential side flange ...

11.21D ... and securing with a nut

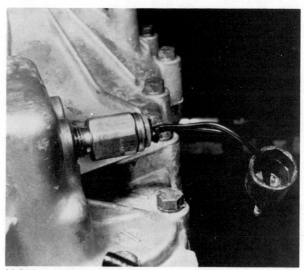

11.21E Assembling the reversing lamp switch

11.22A Fitting the clutch housing gasket ...

11.22B ... and then the housing

11.23 Replacing the primary idler gear

11.24A Assembling the main drive input gear and bearing ...

11.24B ... and securing with a thrust washer, lockwasher and nut

11.26A Installing the primary gear cover

11.26B Showing the position of the two long retaining bolts

11.26C Fitting a new gasket and replacing the bottom cover

3 Remove the bolts that secure the select lever to the transmission case cover and detach the selector lever from the transmission case cover. Take out the pin that secures the shift rod to the lever and detach the shift rod from the lever. Withdraw the control linkage from the vehicle.
4 Each linkage is securely retained with various fasteners such as washers and snap-rings. Special care should be taken so that they may be reinstaled in exactly the same location when reconnecting the linkage.
5 Inspect all of the linkage components for general wear, corrosion or distortion. If general sloppiness is apparent in the linkage it is recommended that all of the snap-rings, springs and clips are replaced as a matter of course.
6 Installation of the linkage is a reversal of the removal procedures, noting the followig points:
7 'O' rings are fitted between the shift lever and radius link assembly and between gear lever and control rod.
    The 'O' rings and radius link bosses should be lubricated with

multi-purpose grease.
8 The shift lever and selector lever should also be greased.

13 Gear linkage - adjustment

1 The gearchange linkage can be adjusted as follows:
2 Refer to Fig. 6.8. Set hand lever to neutral position and loosen adjusting nut fully. This will involve cutting the wire locking. Under this condition, measure transmission case cover-to-protector clearance. Adjustment is correct if there exists an "A" + 0.315 in (8 mm) of clearance between them. The "A" refers to the clearance between protector and transmission case cover when shift lever is moved all the way in the direction of "P". Turn the adjusting nuts until correct clearance is obtained. Finally, tighten the nuts to a torque of 7.2 to 10.0 lb/ft (1 to 1.38 kg/m) and replace the wire locking.

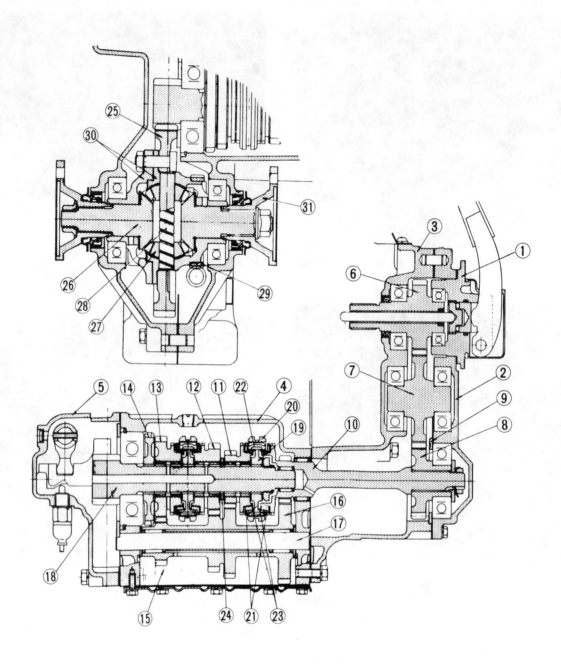

Fig. 6.1. Cross-section through the transmission

1	Bearing housing
2	Primary gear cover
3	Clutch housing
4	Transmission case
5	Transmission case cover
6	Primary drive gear
7	Primary idler gear
8	Main drive input gear
9	Bearing retainer
10	Main drive gear
11	3rd gear
12	2nd gear
13	1st gear
14	Reverse gear
15	Reverse idler gear
16	Counter gear
17	Counter gear shaft
18	Mainshaft
19	Synchronizer hub
20	Coupling sleeve
21	Baulk ring
22	Shifting insert
23	Spread ring
24	Main gear spacer
25	Final gear
26	Differential side gear
27	Pinion gear
28	Differential pinion shaft
29	Speedometer drive gear
30	Differential case
31	Differential side flange

97

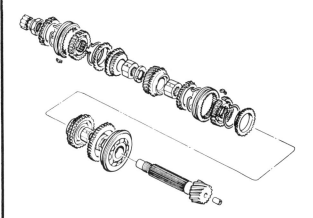

Fig. 6.2. Exploded view of mainshaft

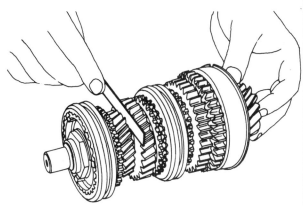

Fig. 6.3. Measuring endplay in the mainshaft

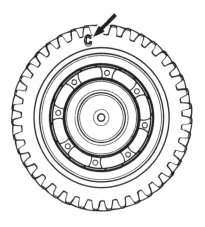

Fig. 6.4. Location of mark on primary idler gear

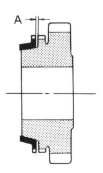

Fig. 6.5. Baulkring-to-cone clearance

A = 1.2 mm (0.0472 in.)

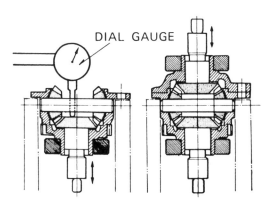

Fig. 6.6. Measuring side-gear endplay using a dial gauge

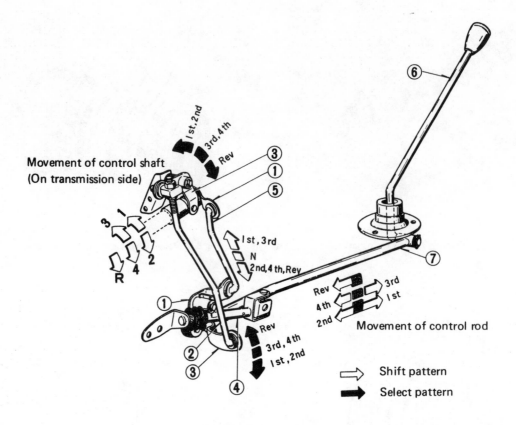

Fig. 6.7. Gearlever mechanism

1 Shift lever   5 Shift rod
2 Select rod   6 Hand lever
3 Select lever   7 Control rod
4 Radius link

Movement of control shaft
(On transmission side)

Movement of control rod

Shift pattern

Select pattern

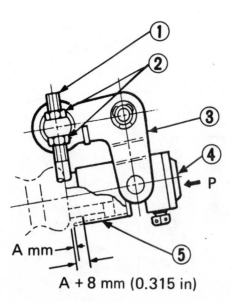

A mm

A + 8 mm (0.315 in)

Fig. 6.8. Gear linkage adjustment

1 Select rod
2 Adjusting nut
3 Select lever
4 Shift lever
5 Protector

Fault diagnosis - transmission

Symptom	Reason/s	Remedy
Gearbox		
Obstructive gearchange	*When difficulty in changing gear is encountered, it is necessary to determine whether the transmission or the remote control system is causing the trouble.*	
	If this condition is accompanied by a dragging clutch, trouble may be due to failure of clutch to disengage. Under such conditions, check to insure that it couples or uncouples the engine and transmission properly. If upon inspection the clutch is in good condition, then check the cause of trouble to determine whether the transmission or the remote control system is causing trouble.	
	Control linkage out of adjustment or lack of lubrication to balljoint.	Re-adjust or lubricate.
	Failure of parts to reach their full measurement due to worn sliding contact surfaces or excessive free-play.	Check and, if necessary, repair or replace worn parts.
	Improper contact pattern of baulk ring-to-gear cone or worn parts.	Replace worn parts
	Worn or deformed insert.	Replace.
Jumping out of gear	*Jumping out of gear is often experienced when wear occurs to the interlock plunger, steel ball, locking spring, etc., or when the control linkage is out of adjustment.*	
	Interlock plunger worn.	Replace.
	Steel ball worn, or locking spring fatigued or broken.	Replace faulty parts.
	Worn groove in shift rod.	Replace.
	Gear tip worn or damaged.	Replace gear.
	Busing worn.	Replace.
	Excessive end play.	Replace faulty parts.
	Main shaft mounting nut loose.	Re-tighten.
Excessive noise	*Noise in the transmission indicates a fault if it is heard when engine is running at idling speed or when gears are shifted from one speed position to another, and if it ceases when the clutch is disengaged. To determine whether the transmission (included primary gear) or the differential is producing the noise, run the vehicle with top gear selected. Under this condition, if noise ceases, it is produced in the transmission.*	
	Lack of lubricating oil or use of improper oil.	Lubricate or use recommended lubricant.
	Bearing worn (humming at a high speed travel).	Replace.
	Bearing damaged (rattling noise at a low speed travel).	Replace.
	Worn splines.	Replace worn shaft or gear.
	Gear contact surfaces damaged.	Replace damaged gears.
	Oil leakage or insufficient oil due to damaged oil seal or gasket, or clogged breather.	Clean or replace.
Gearchange linkage		
Failure of gears to mesh or hard to mesh gears.	Control linkage out of adjustment (or lack of lubricating oil to ball joint).	Re-adjust or lubricate.

	Excessive free-play due to worn control linkage.	Check and correct.
Jumping out of gear.	Control linkage out of adjustment.	Re-adjust.
	Excessive free play - due to worn control linkage.	Repair or replace faulty parts.
Gearlever drag or failure of gearlever to respond quickly.	Control rod deformed or bent.	Repair or replace.
	Lack of oil to sliding contacts or sliding resistance excessive due to deformed parts.	Lubricate, repair, or replace, as required.
Shifting noise	Worn bearing or excessive free-play in linkage.	Repair or replace.
	Interference of lever, link, etc, with adjacent parts.	Repair.

Final drive

Damage to final drive	*Replace any damaged parts. Also check every possible parts for condition.*	
	Improper backlash in final gear.	Replace final gear.
	Excessive backlash in differential gear.	Replace differential gear or thrust washer.
	Final gear mounting bolt loose.	Re-tighten.
	Damage due to overloading.	Replace damaged parts.
Abnormal noise when steering	Differential gear damaged.	Replace.
	Thrust washer worn excessively or damaged.	Replace.
	Pinion main shaft damaged.	Replace.
	Side bearing seized or damaged.	Replace.

Excessive gear noise	*To clearly determine whether noise is produced in transmission gears (incl. primary gear), engine, wheel bearings, tires, or body, check and locate cause of noise in the following manner:*	

a) *Run vehicle at a creeping speed and then at a constant speed, accelerating engine as necessary.*
b) *Jack-up front portion of vehicle, and run engine with top gear selected. After cause of trouble is located, use a systematic procedure to repair or replace defective parts.*

	Improper backlash in final gear.	Replace final gear.
	Final gear tooth tip damaged.	Replace final gear.
	Side bearing seized, broken or damaged.	Replace.
	Oil leakage (or lack of oil) due to defective oil seal or gasket.	Replace faulty parts.

Chapter 7 Driveshafts

Contents

Specifications

Driveshafts

Double offset joint maximum swing arc	20°	
Double offset joint maximum lateral movement	17 mm (0.669 in.)	
Birfield joint maximum swing arc	42°	
Birfield joint maximum lateral movement	0°	

Torque wrench settings

	lb f ft	kg f m
Wheel bearing locknut	72 to 87	10.0 to 12.0
Driveshaft installation nut (hub side)	51 to 83	7.0 to 11.5
Driveshaft installation bolt (differential)	29 to 36	4.0 to 5.0

1 General description

1 Power is transmitted to the front wheels by two driveshafts which are carried by knuckle arms attached to the lower ends of the struts. Each driveshaft is supported on two ball bearings mounted back to back, and is splined to the wheel hub.

2 Constant velocity joints are incorporated at each end of the driveshafts. The joint at the wheel end of the shaft provides a forty-two degree swivel movement, while the double offset type of joint at the other end of the shaft allows for a movement of twenty degrees.

3 The outer universal joints are of the Birfield constant velocity type. The driveshaft fits inside the circular outer C.V. joint which is also the driven shaft. Drive is transmitted from the driveshaft to the driven shaft by six steel balls which are located in curved grooves machined in line with the axis of the shaft on the inside of the driven shaft and outside of the driveshaft. This allows the driven shaft to hinge freely on the driveshaft, but at the same time keeps them together. Enclosing the C.V. joint is a rubber boot.

2 Routine maintenance

At intervals of 3,000 miles inspect the rubber boots which protect the universal joints. If they are torn, split, or damaged

they should be replaced as soon as possible. When the boot splits the C.V. joint is subjected to a bombardment of water, road dust, and grit, which leads to rapid deterioration of the bearings in the joint.

Wear in the joints is detected by a regular knocking when the front wheels are turned on full lock. In very severe cases it is only necessary to turn the wheels slightly for the noise to begin.

3 Driveshaft removal

1 Remove the wheel trim from the wheel from which the driveshaft is to be removed.

2 Place the car in gear and apply the handbrake firmly. Extract the split pin from the hub nut, and undo and remove the nut and thrust washer.

3 Loosen the front roadwheel securing nuts and jack-up the car on the same side.

4 As it will be necessary to work underneath the car, supplement the jack with a stand or support blocks. This will minimise the danger should the jack collapse.

5 Remove the roadwheel.

6 Remove the bolts which secure the driveshaft to the final drive assembly, then use the subframe to support the detached driveshaft.

7 It will now be possible to partially free the end of the driveshaft from the centre of the hub. With a soft drift and hammer tap the end of the shaft until it is seen to move inwards slightly.

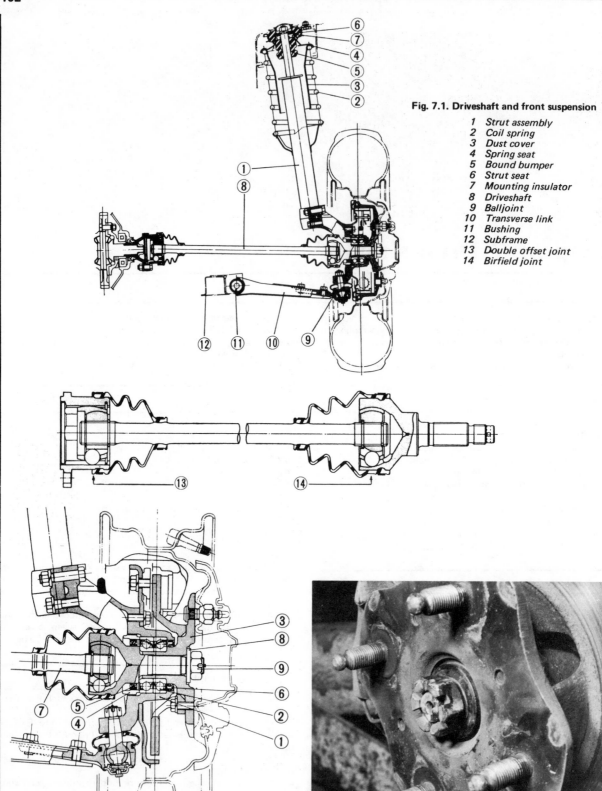

Fig. 7.1. Driveshaft and front suspension

1 Strut assembly
2 Coil spring
3 Dust cover
4 Spring seat
5 Bound bumper
6 Strut seat
7 Mounting insulator
8 Driveshaft
9 Balljoint
10 Transverse link
11 Bushing
12 Subframe
13 Double offset joint
14 Birfield joint

Fig. 7.2. Driveshaft and disc brake front hub - sectional view

1	Knuckle	4	Bearing locknut	7	Driveshaft
2	Wheel bearing	5	Oil seal (inner)	8	Washer
3	Wheel hub	6	Oil seal (outer)	9	Nut

3.2 Split pin removed prior to removing hub nut

3.6A Driveshaft inner securing bolts

3.6B Bolts removed and shaft resting on the subframe

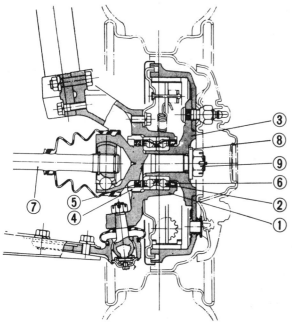

Fig. 7.3. Driveshaft and drum brake front hub - sectional view

1	Knuckle	4	Bearing locknut	7	Driveshaft
2	Wheel bearing	5	Oil seal (inner)	8	Washer
3	Wheel hub	6	Oil seal (outer)	9	Nut

Sometimes the shaft can be completely removed this way, but great care must be taken or the splines, bearings or oil seals will be damaged. If the resistance to the initial taps is significant, it is better to obtain a special tool from your Datsun agent (ST35100000).

8   Place the special removal tool 'ST35100000' on the hub and secure it with the wheel nuts. The driveshaft can now be removed by screwing in the removal tool, but take care not to damage the oil seals.

9   Inspect the driveshaft for distortion, corrosion or cracks. Replace if necessary.

4   Constant velocity joint (inner) - dismantling

1   The double offset type of constant velocity joint used at the final drive end of the driveshaft can be dismantled if defective

3.7 Splined end of shaft nearly out of the hub

parts are to be renewed.

2   Place the driveshaft in a vice equipped with soft jaws. Expand and remove the band which secures the rubber boot, and remove the boot from the joint.

3   Use a screwdriver to prise off the retaining ring and withdraw the flanged outer ring of the joint (Fig. 7.5). You will also need to remove the sealing plate from the other end of the joint.

4   Wipe grease from the ball cage and take out the ball bearings. Rotate the cage by approximately half a turn, and detach it from the inner ring.

5   Take off the retaining ring, using a pair of circlip pliers, and withdraw the inner ring of the joint by lightly tapping it with a soft-faced mallet.

6   Finally, withdraw the flanged outer ring and the rubber boot.

5   Constant velocity joint (inner) - examination and reassembly

1   Thoroughly clean all the component parts of the joint by washing in paraffin.

2   Examine each ball in turn for cracks, flat spots, or signs of surface pitting.

3   The cage which fits between the inner and outer races must be examined for wear in the ball cage windows and for cracks

4.3 Withdrawing the outer ring

4.5A Removing the circlip ...

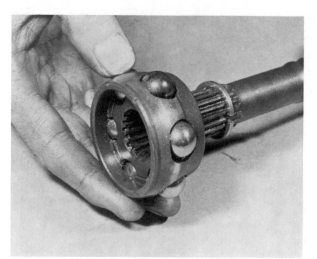

4.5B ... and withdraw the inner ring

4.6A Removing the flanged outer ring

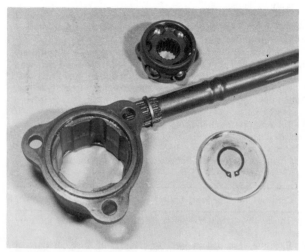

4.6B Inner constant velocity joint components

which are especially likely to develop across the narrower portions between the outer rims and the holes for the balls.

4   Wear is most likely to be found in the ball tracks on the inner and outer races. If the tracks have widened the balls will no longer be a tight fit and, together with excessive wear in the ball cage windows, will lead to the characteristic 'knocking' on full lock described previously.

5   If wear is excessive then all the parts must be renewed as a matched set.

6   Examine the rubber boot and replace if there is evidence of splits, wear or deformation. It is sound policy to replace it anyway since it could save another strip later on.

7   Reassembly is the reverse of the dismantling operations in Section 4.

6   Constant velocity joints (outer) - removal and replacement

1   If it is necessary to simply replace a complete outer C.V. joint, because of lack of facilities or spares, then use the following technique (overhaul is covered in Section 7):

2   Remove the driveshaft, as described in Section 3.

3   The next task is to remove the joint from the driveshaft. First remove the boot by expanding the clips and then easing it back from the joint. Remove the joint by tapping the outer edge of

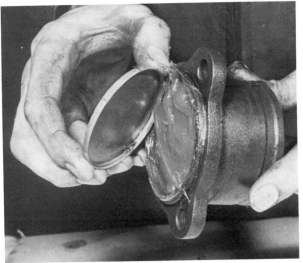

5.7A Replacing the sealing plate after packing with grease

5.7B Driveshaft with boot fitted and secured

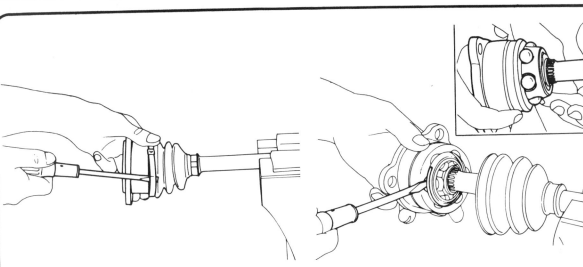

Fig. 7.4. Prising off the boot retaining band

Fig. 7.5. Removing the outer circlip and pulling off the outer casing

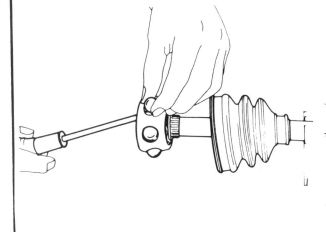

Fig. 7.6. Prising out the balls

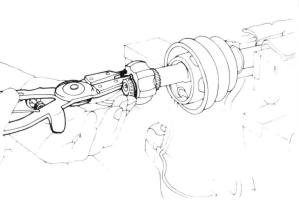

Fig. 7.7. Removing the inner circlip

the C.V. joint with a hide or plastic headed hammer. The C.V. joint is held to the shaft by an internal circular section circlip and tapping the joint in the manner described forces the circlip to contract into a groove so allowing the joint to slide off. Remove the boot.

4   At this stage it is just as well to fit a new boot, since it might well save a major operation later on. Slide the boot over the shaft and do not secure at this stage. Obtain a new C.V. joint and ensure that it is packed with the correct molybdenum disulphide compound grease.

5   Fit the C.V. joint onto the shaft the correct way round and with the joint pressing against the circlip. Contract the circlip right into its groove in the shaft with the aid of two screwdrivers, so the inner race of the C.V. joint will slide over it. It may be necessary to tap the outside end of the joint smartly with a soft faced hammer in order to close the circlip completely. Tap the joint till it is fully home with the inner race resting against the large retaining clip. The circular section circlip should now have expanded inside the joint.

6   Secure the rubber boot, and refit the driveshaft to the car, as described in Section 7.

7   Constant velocity joint (outer) - dismantling, inspection and reassembly

There is little point in dismantling the outer constant velocity joints if they are known to be badly worn. In this case it is better to remove the old joint from the shaft and fit a new unit. To remove and then dismantle the constant velocity joint proceed as follows:

1   Remove the driveshaft from the car, as described in Section 3.

2   Thoroughly clean the exterior of the driveshaft and rubber gaiter, preferably not using a liquid cleaner.

3   Mount the driveshaft vertically in between soft faces in a vice, with the constant velocity joint facing downwards. Using a screwdriver, prise off the large diameter aluminium gaiter retaining ring towards the stub axle. Prise off the small diameter aluminium ring again using a screwdriver. Turn back the gaiter and, if it is to be renewed, cut it off and throw away.

4   Before the joint can be dismantled it must be removed from the driveshaft. This is easily done by firmly tapping the outer edge of the constant velocity joint with a hide or plastic headed hammer. Alternatively, use a copper drift located on the inner

member and give the drift a sharp blow. Whichever method is used, the inner spring ring will be contracted so releasing the joint from the shaft.

5   Ease off the round section spring kit and, when reassembling, use the new one supplied in the service kit.

6   Mark the position of the inner and outer races with a dab of paint, or with a file, so that upon reassembly the mated parts can be correctly replaced.

7   Tilt the inner race until one ball bearing is released. Repeat this operation, easing out each ball bearing in turn, using a small screwdriver.

8   Manipulate the cage until the special elongated slot coincides with the lands of the bellhousing. Drop one of the lands into the slot and lift out the cage and race assembly.

9   Turn the inner race at right angles to the cage and in line with the elongated slot. Drop one land into the slot and withdraw the inner race.

10 Thoroughly clean all component parts of the joint by washing in paraffin.

11 Examine each ball bearing in turn for cracks, flat spots or signs of the surface pitting. Check the inner and outer tracks for widening which will cause the ball bearings to be a loose fit. This, together with excessive wear in the ball cage, will lead to the characteristic 'knocking' on full lock. The cage which fits between the inner and outer races must be examined for wear in the ball cage windows, and for cracks which are likely to develop across the narrower portions between the outer rims and the holes for the ball bearings. If wear is excessive, then all parts must be renewed as a matched set.

12 To reassemble, first ensure that all parts are very clean and then lubricate with the special Datsun grease that is mixed with molybdenum disulphide. Do not under any circumstances use any other grease. Provided that all parts have been cleaned and well lubricated, they should fit together easily without force.

13 Refit the inner race into the cage by manipulating one of the lands into the elongated slot in the cage. Insert the cage and inner race assembly into the balljoint by fitting one of the elongated slots over one of the lands in the outer race. Rotate the inner race to line up with the bellhousing in its original previously marked position.

14 Taking care not to lose the position, tilt the cage until one ball bearing can be inserted into a slot. Repeat this procedure until all six ball bearings are in their correct positions. Ensure that the inner race moves freely in the bellhousing throughout its

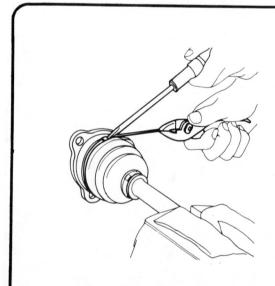

Fig. 7.8. Tightening the boot retaining band

Fig. 7.9. Locking the band with a punch

movement range, taking care that the ball bearings do not fall out.

15 Using the remainder of the special grease, pack the joint evenly. Smear the inside of a new rubber boot with Datsun grease and fit the rubber boot and a new circlip to the end of the shaft.

16 Hold the shaft in a vice and locate the inner race on the splines. By pressing the constant velocity joint against the circlip, position the ring centrally and contract it in the chamber in the inner race leading edge with two screwdrivers. Using a soft faced hammer, sharply tap the end of the stub shaft to compress the ring and then tap the complete assembly onto the driveshaft. Double check that the shaft is fully engaged and the circlip fully locked against the inner race.

17 Ease the rubber boot over the constant velocity joint and ensure the moulded edges of the boot are seating correctly in the retaining groove of the shaft and bellhousing. Secure in position with the large and small clips, as described in Section 8.

8 Driveshaft - reassembly and installation

1 Assembly is a reversal of the dismantling procedures. Tie the band twice round the rubber boot before tightening it with screwdriver and pliers, as shown in Fig. 7.8. A punch should be used to lock the clip to the band and then the band should be secured by bending it over. The width of the band should be used as a guide to determine how much to bend over. Exercise great care in securing the band, not to scratch the boot. When renewing grease, take great care to prevent the ingress of dirt or other foreign matter into the joint.

2 When installing the driveshafts make sure that the lips of the oil seals are lubricated with multi-purpose grease and are not damaged on installation. The driveshaft can be tapped into position with a hammer until the threads are sufficiently exposed, but the flange of the shaft should be protected with a soft pad so that the seal plate does not suffer damage.

3 Tighten the bolts at the hub side of the shaft to a torque reading of 7.0 to 11.5 kgm. (57 to 83 lb ft.), and the bolts at the final drive side to 4.0 to 5.0 kgm. (29 to 36 lb ft.).

Chapter 8 Steering mechanism

Contents

Specifications

Type	Rack and pinion type
Steering gear ratio	17.95 : 1
Turns of steering wheel (lock-to-lock)	3.22
Turning angle of front wheel	
Inside	37° 30' to 40° 30'
Outside	31° 30' to 34° 30'
Minimum turning radius	4.6 m (15 ft)
Steering wheel diameter	390 mm (15.4 in)
Steering wheel free-play	0 to 35 mm (0 to 1.378 in)
Rack stroke	66 mm (2.598 in)
Lubrication interval	50,000 km (30,000 miles)
Retainer spring	
Free-length	22.3 mm (0.838 in)
Load x length	40 kg (88 lb) x 16.5 mm (0.650 in)
Inner socket spring	
Free-length	20.0 mm (0.787 in)
Load x length	24.4 kg (54 lb) x 18 mm (0.709 in)
Trackrod inner ball joint	
Swing torque (max)	5.0 kg/cm (4.3 lb/in)
Play (max)	0.1 mm (0.0039 in)
Trackrod outer ball joint	
Swing torque	2 to 30 kg/cm (1.7 to 26 lb/in)
Play	0.1 to 1.0 mm (0.0039 to 0.0394 in)
Pinion rotary torque	10 to 15 kg/cm (8.7 to 13 lb/in)
Pinion axial play	0.3 mm (0.1181 in)
Rack force to pull	10 to 28 kg (22 to 62 lb)

Pinion snap-ring oversize

Thickness (rack side)	1.20 to 1.24 mm (0.0472 to 0.0488 in)
Thickness (yoke side)	1.05 to 1.09 mm (0.0413 to 0.0429 in)
	1.10 to 1.14 mm (0.0433 to 0.0449 in)
	1.15 to 1.19 mm (0.0453 to 0.0469 in)
	1.20 to 1.24 mm (0.0472 to 0.0488 in)
Pinion bearing-to-gear housing snap-ring oversize	1.25 to 1.29 mm (0.0492 to 0.0508 in)
	1.30 to 1.34 mm (0.0512 to 0.0528 in)
	1.56 to 1.60 mm (0.0614 to 0.0630 in)
	1.61 to 1.65 mm (0.0634 to 0.0650 in)
	1.66 to 1.70 mm (0.0654 to 0.0669 in)
	1.71 to 1.75 mm (0.0673 to 0.0689 in)

Torque wrench settings

	lb f ft	kg f m
Steering wheel mounting nut	14 to 18	2 to 2.5
Column clamp mounting bolt	6.5 to 10	0.9 to 1.4
Rubber coupling mounting bolt	7.2 to 11	1.0 to 1.5
Coupling yoke mounting nut	14 to 18	2 to 2.5
Retainer locknut	29 to 43	4 to 6
Trackrod inner socket locknut	58 to 72	8 to 10
Trackrod locknut	27 to 34	3.8 to 4.7
Clamp mounting bolt	11 to 17	1.5 to 2.4
Trackrod socket assembly-to-knuckle arm stud	40 to 47	5.5 to 6.5
Coupling yoke-to-steering column assembly mounting nut ...	7.2 to 11	1.0 to 1.5

1 General description

1 All models in the Cherry range utilize a rack and pinion steering system. The steering wheel is splined to the upper inner column which in turn is connected, via a flexible coupling, to the steering gearbox pinion. The pinion teeth mesh with those machined in the rack so that rotation of the pinion moves the rack from one side of the housing to the other. Located at either end of the rack are tie-rods and balljoints which are attached to the steering arms.

2 All of the 120A Coupe models and most of the 100A models are fitted with a collapsible steering column.

3 One other point is that, unlike so many contemporary vehicles, it is possible to lubricate the balljoints at the end of the trackrods.

2 Steering wheel and column - removal

1 Disconnect the cable to the horn button (black wire).

2 Depress the horn bar and simultaneously turn it counter-clockwise. You should now be able to lift it away.

3 Remove the steering wheel retaining nut and then bump the wheel off the shaft splines.

4 Loosen and remove the five screws that retain the column shrouds. Detach the two halves of the shrouds.

5 Remove the two screws that secure the multi switch assembly to the steering column; then remove the assembly.

6 Remove the two bolts that retain the steering column clamp and remove the clamp.

7 Remove the five screws that secure the rubber boot at the base of the steering column. Pull the boot up the shaft and away from the coupling flange.

8 Release the four nuts that secure the shaft to the coupling yoke. It should now be possible to lift out the steering column.

9 If difficulty is experienced in removing the steering column, prise off the circlip holding the gearchange control rod and ease the rod to one side.

10 Remove the bolts connecting the rubber coupling to the shaft. Take care to collect the coupling plates, two for each bolt, also the earthing cable.

3 Steering column and coupling - inspection

1 Inspect the column shaft and casing for evidence of distortion, corrosion or cracks.

2.2A Removing the horn bar retaining screws ...

2.2B ... and lifting away the bar to reveal the steering wheel retaining nut

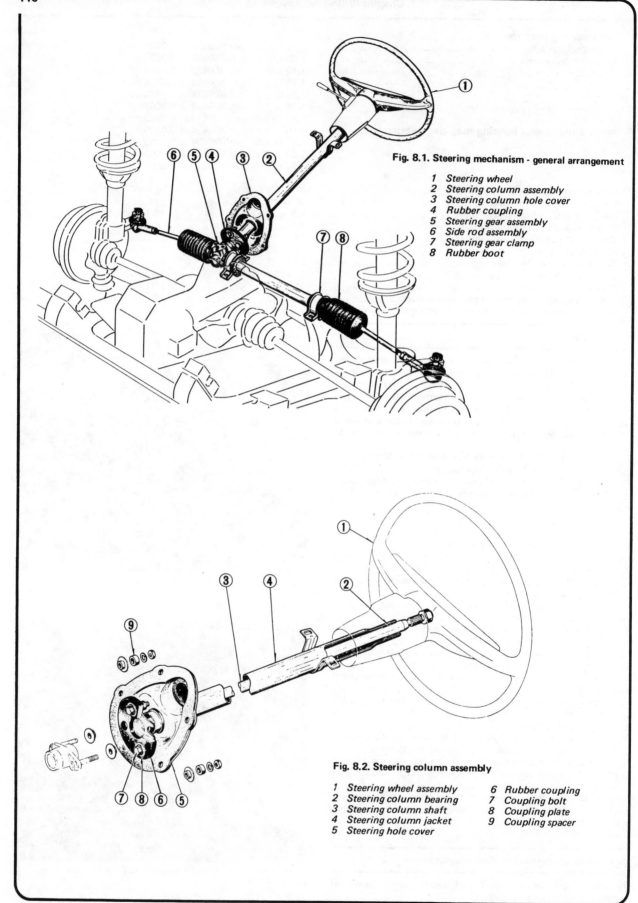

Fig. 8.1. Steering mechanism - general arrangement

1 Steering wheel
2 Steering column assembly
3 Steering column hole cover
4 Rubber coupling
5 Steering gear assembly
6 Side rod assembly
7 Steering gear clamp
8 Rubber boot

Fig. 8.2. Steering column assembly

1 Steering wheel assembly
2 Steering column bearing
3 Steering column shaft
4 Steering column jacket
5 Steering hole cover
6 Rubber coupling
7 Coupling bolt
8 Coupling plate
9 Coupling spacer

2 Prise the top and bottom bearings out of the casing and check them for wear, corrosion and free-running. Some models are fitted with nylon bushes instead of bearings and it is advisable to renew these.
3 Check the rubber coupling for deterioration, splits or other damage.
4 On some models, particularly the 120A Coupe sports model, a collapsible steering column is fitted. If, on inspection, any damage to the collapsible section is noticed, it is recommended that the complete assembly is replaced.

4 Steering wheel, column and coupling - replacement

1 Replacement is essentially the reversal of the removal instructions, but note the following points.
2 The earth wire must always be connected to the shaft coupling and looped from a bolt on the yoke to a bolt on the flange. It must also be ensured that the earth wire does not protrude outside the rubber coupling.
3 Replace any coupling plates that are distorted. Always ensure that the uncoated face of the coupling flange faces upwards.
4 When the column is clamped in position, adjust the distance between the end of the casing and the start of the shaft taper to the specified value of 0.57 in. (14.5 mm), as indicated in Fig. 8.10. Adjustment is by using the elongated mounting hole in the clamp. Failure to achieve this will result in the horn not sounding and incorrect clearance between the boot on the floor panel and the steering wheel.
5 Tighten all nuts to the correct torque figures: as defined in the Specifications. Don't forget to reconnect the horn cable.

5 Steering tie-rods outer balljoints - removal and replacement

1 The removal of the balljoints is necessary if they are to be renewed, or if the rubber boots on the steering gear are being renewed.
2 It is not necessary to jack-up the car but the increase in height above ground level may make it more convenient to do so.
3 Slacken the nut after removing the split pin; completely remove it to clear the threads, and replace it after oiling them until the head of the nut is level with the end of the stud. This will protect the threads in subsequent operations if the same joint is being replaced.
4 If a claw clamp is being used to 'break' the taper of the joint pin from the steering arm, the joint may be disconnected without further ado.
5 If no claw clamp is available and it is necessary to strike the pin out, it is essential to provide a really firm support under the steering arm first. A firm tap with a normal weight hammer is all that is then necessary to move the pin out of the steering arm. Another way is to strike one side of the arm whilst holding the head of another hammer against the opposite side. This tends to 'squeeze' the taper pin out.
6 If the nut now turns the pin when trying to remove it, (despite the precaution taken in paragraph 3) jam the pin back into the arm with the jack to hold it whilst the nut is removed. If difficulty is experienced with a joint being renewed then cut it off.
7 Once the balljoint is clear, slacken the locknut on the rod but leave it at its original position. The joint may then be removed and a new one fitted by screwing it up as far as the locknut. The pin should point upwards and then be fitted into the steering arm.
8 Replace the castellated locknut and secure with a split pin. See Specifications for the correct torque. Tighten the locknut on the tie-rod.
9 It is advisable to have the front wheel alignment checked as soon as possible.

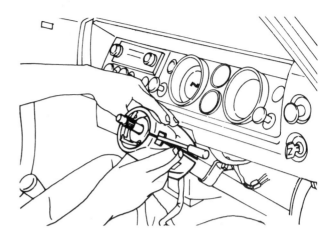
Fig. 8.3. Removing the column shrouds

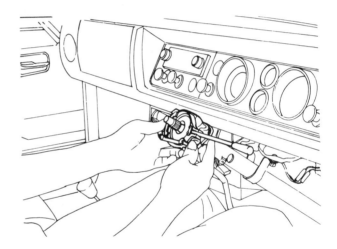
Fig. 8.4. Removing the switch assembly

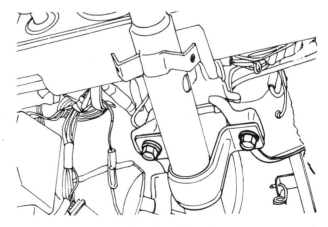
Fig. 8.5. Steering column clamp

6 Steering mechanism - inspection

1   The steering mechanism is uncomplicated and easy to check. As the statutory test for vehicles more than three years old pays particular attention to it, the owner can save himself a lot of trouble by regular examination, apart from, of course, keeping a check on his own safety.

2   Assuming that the suspension joints and bushes and front wheel bearings have been checked and found in order the steering check involves tracing the amount of lost motion between the rim of steering wheel and the roadwheels. If the rim of the steering wheel can be moved more than 2 inches (50 mm) at its periphery with no sign of movement at either or both of the front wheels it may be assumed that there is wear at some point. If there are signs of lost motion, jack-up the car at the front and support it under the front crossmember so that both wheels hang free.

3   Grip each wheel in turn and rock it in the direction it would move when steering. It will be possible to feel any play. Check first for any sign of lateral play in the balljoints which connect the tie-rods from the steering gear to the steering arms on the wheel hubs. This is the more common area for wear to occur and if any is apparent the balljoint(s) must be renewed. The joints are spring loaded up and down so they can move in this plane, but not without considerable pressure. If the socket moves easily then the joint needs renewal.

4   Having checked the balljoints, next grip the tie-rod and get someone to move the steering wheel. Do this with the bonnet open and if there is any play still apparent look first to see whether the coupling in the steering column shaft is causing the trouble. If it is it should be renewed.

5   Finally, if play still exists it must be in the steering gear itself. This is more serious (and expensive!). If either of the rubber boots at each end of the gear housing is damaged, resulting in loss of oil from the unit then various bearings and teeth on the rack and pinion may have been severely worn. In such cases renewal of the complete steering gear assembly may be necessary. Certainly adjustments will be required.

7 Rack and pinion unit - removal and replacement

1   Before starting this job set the front wheels in the straight ahead position. Then jack up the front of the car and place blocks under the wheels; lower the car slightly on the jack so that the trackrods are in a near horizontal position.

2   Remove the steering coupling nuts, as described in Section 2.

3   Working on the front subframe, remove the two bolts that secure each steering gear clamp.

4   Remove the split pins and castellated nuts from the ends of each trackrod where they join the steering arms. Separate the trackrods from the steering arms and lower the steering gear downwards out of the car.

5   Before replacing the steering gear make sure that the wheels have remained in the straight ahead position. Also check the condition of the mounting rubbers round the housing and if they appear worn or damaged renew them.

6   Check that the steering gear is also in the straight ahead position. This can be done by ensuring that the distances between the ends of both trackrods and the steering gear housing on both sides are the same.

7   Place the steering gear in its location on the subframe and at the same time mate up the splines on the pinion with the splines in the yoke on the steering column flexible coupling.

8   Ensure the subframe bracket is aligned with the mount on the side of the gearbox by turning and/or moving the mount as necessary.

9   Install and tighten the U-clamps.

10   The yellow clamp is 0.126 in. (3.2 mm) in thickness and used on the gear housing, while the white one is 0.079 in. (2.0 mm) and used on the rubber mount.

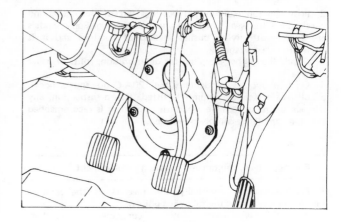

Fig. 8.6. Rubber boot at base of column

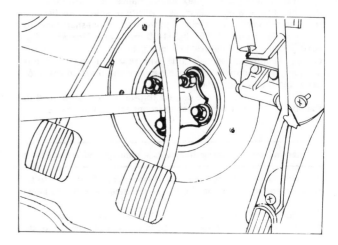

Fig. 8.7. Column coupling bolts

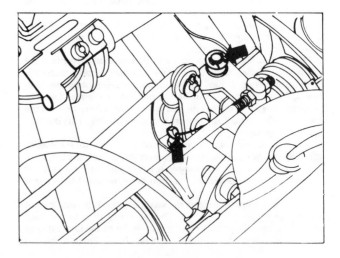

Fig. 8.8. Disconnection points for control rod

11 Reconnect the tie-rods to the steering arm.
12 Reconnect the steering column and gear, as described in Section 4.
13 Finally, recheck the toe-in specifications and adjust as necessary.

8   Rack and pinion unit - dismantling

1   Wash the outside of the rack and pinion assembly in paraffin or Gunk and wipe dry with a non-fluffy rag.
2   Slacken off the two tie-rod end locknuts and unscrew the two tie-rod ends as complete assemblies.
3   Unscrew and remove the two locknuts from the ends of the tie-rods.
4   Take off the boot clamps and ease the boot off the socket. Loosen the locknut on the inner socket and detach the tie-rod from the rack.
5   Remove the inner socket spring from each end of the rack, then loosen the locknut and separate the inner socket from the tie-rod socket.
6   Remove the locknut and take out the retainer adjusting screw. Withdraw the steering gear retainer. Remove the nut, coupling yoke and oil seal.
7   Take out the circlip, using circlip pliers, and withdraw the steering pinion, then prise off the circlip to release the pinion yoke.
8   Press the bearing out of the pinion shaft, withdraw the rack from the gear housing, then take off the circlip and ease out the rack bushing.

9   Rack and pinion unit components

1   Clean all parts in paraffin, thoroughly, and then either let dry naturally or, if available, use compressed air. Check each part for evidence of deterioration, (ie; burrs, cracks, chipped rack or pinion). If damaged, the rack and pinion must be replaced as a matching pair.
2   Check the tie-rod inner and outer balljoints for excess axial play. Use an ordinary spring balance to check the torque necessary to move the balljoints axially. Limits are detailed in the Specifications.
3   Visually inspect the bearing for cracked, pitted or worn balls and races. Ensure that it runs freely. Renew if at all doubtful. The oil seal should be renewed as a matter of policy, since they are reasonably inexpensive.
4   Compare the spring dimensions with the Specifications and renew if necessary.
5   Replace the rack bushing if it is scored, cracked or excessively worn.

10   Rack and pinion unit and tie-rods - assembly and adjustment

1   Using a suitable drift and hammer, drive the bushing into the rack and secure with a circlip (snap-ring).
2   Fit the rubber mounting on the end of the tube ensuring that the cut-out in the mounting is lined up with the hole in the tube. Ensure that the ventilation hole is free from grease. (Fig. 8.21).
3   Press the bearing over the pinion and secure it with snap-rings, ensuring that the snap-rings are located in the correct grooves. Snap-ring sizes are selected from the table below. Item (2) in Fig. 8.22 will always be (d) in the table, while item (1) must be chosen to give an axial play of less than 0.1 mm (0.0039 in.).

Snap ring (circlip) sizes

a)   1.05 to 1.09 mm   (0.0413 to 0.0429 in.)
b)   1.10 to 1.14 mm   (0.0433 to 0.0449 in.)
c)   1.15 to 1.19 mm   (0.0453 to 0.0469 in.)
d)   1.20 to 1.24 mm   (0.0472 to 0.0488 in.)

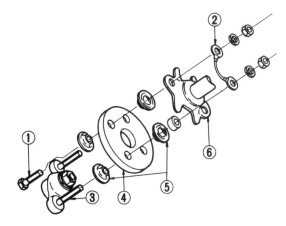

Fig. 8.9. Coupling details

1   Coupling bolt   4   Coupling rubber
2   Earth wire   5   Coupling plate
3   Coupling yoke   6   Coupling flange

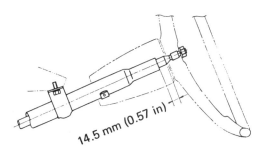

Fig. 8.10. Critical distance when replacing column

14.5 mm (0.57 in.)

e)   1.25 to 1.29 mm   (0.0492 to 0.0508 in.)
f)   1.30 to 1.34 mm   (0.0512 to 0.0528 in.)

4   Place the housing in a vice; then lightly grease all the mating surfaces and teeth. Insert the rack from the housing side, mesh the pinion with the rack and secure with a snap-ring selected from the following table:

Pinion to housing snap ring sizes

a)   1.56 to 1.60 mm   (0.0614 to 0.0630 in.)
b)   1.61 to 1.65 mm   (0.0634 to 0.0650 in.)
c)   1.66 to 1.70 mm   (0.0654 to 0.0669 in.)
d)   1.71 to 1.75 mm   (0.0673 to 0.0689 in.)

5   Insert the oil seal, with the lipped face towards the outside, over the pinion stem and onto the snap-ring. Pack the seal with grease.
6   Measure the axial play of the pinion: it should be less than 0.0118 in. (0.3 mm).
7   Adjust the position of the rack until there is a distance of 1.831 in. (46.5 mm) between the housing endface and the stopper. Then, ensuring that the yoke and rack are parallel, install the coupling yoke. Exercise caution or the oil seal can be damaged.
8   Insert the retainer and spring in the gear housing; then fit the locknut. Rotate the adjusting screw until the retainer is tight and then back it off by 20 to 30 degrees. Apply a coat of Loctite to the adjusting screw and tighten the locknut to the specified torque.

9 When assembly is completed, check the torques necessary to keep the rack and pinion in motion:

   a) *Using a spring balance on a pinion stud, the rotary torque should be 8.7 to 13 in/lb (10 to 15 kg/cm).*
   b) *Using a spring balance on the end of the rack, the force to keep the rack in motion should be 42 to 62 lb (19 to 28 kg).*

Tighten or slacken the adjusting screw, as necessary, to achieve these figures.
10 Connect the outer sockets to the side rods (tie-rods). Adjust the exposed length of each tie-rod to be 5.2 in. (132 mm).

Tighten the locknut temporarily.
11 Fit the rubber boot, first greasing the groove in the tie-rod where the boot is secured. This will facilitate rotation of the boot if it twists in subsequent adjustment of the tie-rod.
12 Connect the toe-rod to the inner socket, first installing the inner socket spring. Screw in the inner socket as far as it will go. Then apply Loctite to the locknut threads and tighten to the prescribed torque.
13 Mate the boot with the groove in the gear housing and ensure that the boot is not distorted before securing.
14 Re-check the tie-rod exposed length is 5.20 in. (132 mm) and tighten the locknuts to the prescribed torque. Assemble the gear to the vehicle, as described in Section 7.

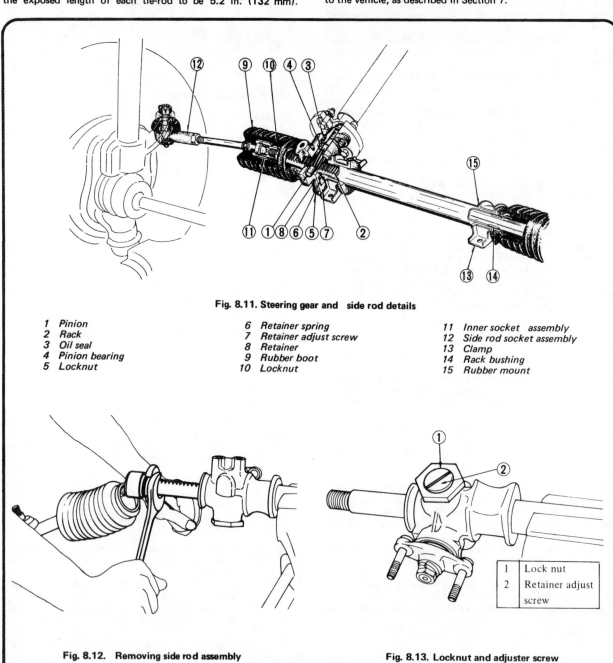

Fig. 8.11. Steering gear and side rod details

1 Pinion	6 Retainer spring	11 Inner socket assembly
2 Rack	7 Retainer adjust screw	12 Side rod socket assembly
3 Oil seal	8 Retainer	13 Clamp
4 Pinion bearing	9 Rubber boot	14 Rack bushing
5 Locknut	10 Locknut	15 Rubber mount

1	Lock nut
2	Retainer adjust screw

Fig. 8.12.   Removing side rod assembly

Fig. 8.13. Locknut and adjuster screw

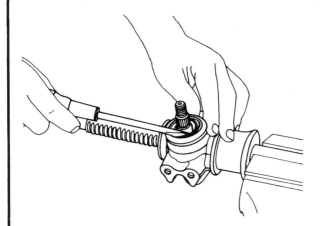

Fig. 8.14. Prising out oil seal

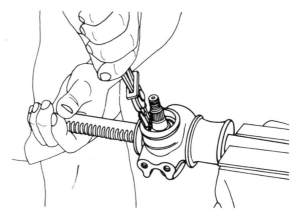

Fig. 8.15. Removing snap-ring from top of bearing

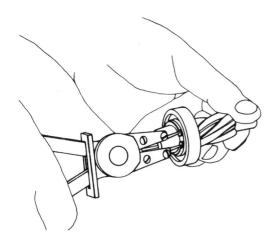

Fig. 8.16.   Removing bottom snap-ring having lifted out the pinion

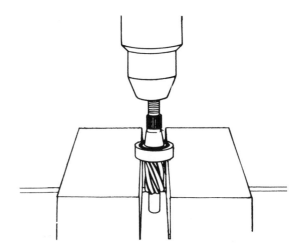

Fig. 8.17. Pressing out the pinion bearing

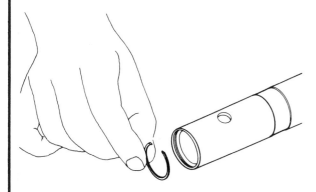

Fig. 8.18. Removing rack bush snap-ring

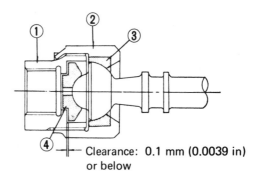

Clearance: 0.1 mm (0.0039 in) or below

Fig. 8.19. Cross-section of inner balljoint

1   Inner socket B   3   Ball seat B
2   Inner socket A   4   Ball seat A

116

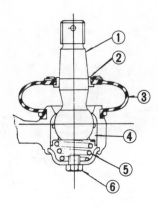

Fig. 8.20. Cross-section of outer balljoint

1 Ball stud   4 Ball seat
2 Retainer   5 Spring
3 Dust cover   6 Plug

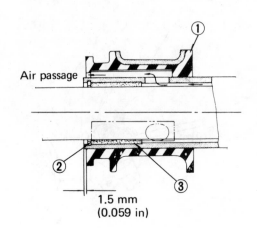

Fig. 8.21. Section through the rubber mounting and bushing

1 Rubber mount   3 Rack bushing
2 Snap-ring

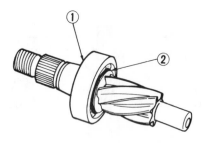

Fig. 8.22. Pinion bearing and snap-rings
(Refer to Section   10, paragraph 3)

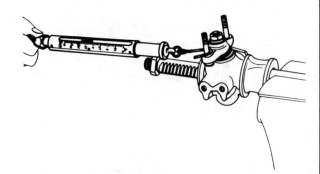

Fig. 8.23. Measuring pinion rotary torque

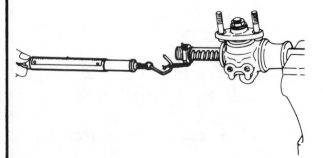

Fig. 8.24. Measuring force to pull the rack

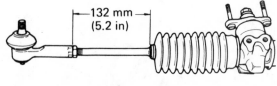

Fig. 8.25. Temporary side rod adjustment figure

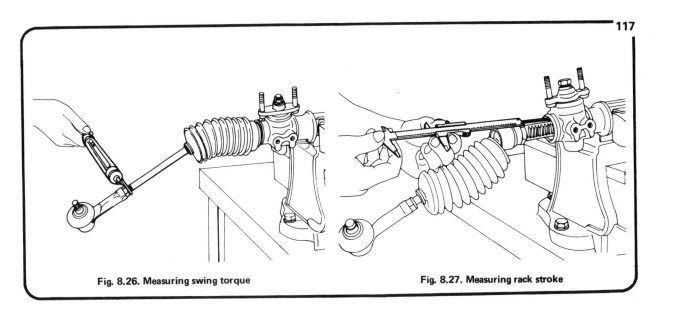

Fig. 8.26. Measuring swing torque   Fig. 8.27. Measuring rack stroke

Chapter 9 Braking system

Contents

Specifications

Brake type

Front ...	Two-leading shoe drum type or disc brake
Rear ...	Leading-trailing shoe drum type
Handbrake ...	Mechanical, operating on rear wheels only

Brake drum inner diameter

Front ...	203 mm (8.0 in.)
Rear ...	180 mm (7.09 in.)

Disc brake

Outer diameter x thickness ...	200 x 10 mm (7.87 x 0.394 in.)

Brake lining and pad (disc)

Width x thickness x length

Front drum ...	35 x 5 x 195 mm (1.378 x 0.1969 x 7.68 in.)
Front disc ...	37 x 9 x 109 mm (1.457 x 0.3543 x 4.29 in.)
Rear ...	30 x 4 x 173 mm (1.181 x 0.1575 x 6.81 in.)

Wheel cylinder

Front drum ...	22.2 mm (7/8 in.)
Front disc ...	47.63 mm (1 7/8 in.)
Rear ...	17.46 mm (11/16 in.)

Master cylinder inner diameter

Tandem ...	17.46 mm (11/16 in.)
Single ...	17.46 mm (11/16 in.)

Brake pedal height

R.H. drive ...	150 to 156 mm (5.91 to 6.14 in.)
L.H. drive ...	167 to 173 mm (6.57 to 6.81 in.)

Master cylinder pushrod
Axial play at brake pedal pad ... ... 2 to 7 mm (0.0787 to 0.276 in.)
Available shims thickness ... ... 1.6, 0.8, 0.6 mm, (0.063, 0.031, 0.024 in.)

Master cylinder
Allowable maximum clearance between cylinder and piston ... 0.15 mm (0.0059 in.)

Brake drum
Allowable maximum out-of-round of drum ... ... 0.03 mm (0.0012 in.)
Allowable maximum inside diameter of rebored drum:
Front ... ... 204.5 mm (8.051 in.)
Rear ... ... 181 mm (7.13 in.)

Disc
Allowable run-out ... ... 0.15 mm (0.0059 in.)
Allowable maximum out-of-parallel ... ... 0.07 mm (0.0028 in.)
Allowable minimum thickness ... ... 9.0 mm (0.3543 in.)

Brake lining and pad (disc)
Allowable minimum thickness ... ... 1.0 mm (0.0394 in.)

Brake shoe clearance
Front ... ... 4 to 8 notches
Rear ... ... 11 to 12 notches

Handbrake
Normal stroke ... ... 3 to 4 notches = 69 to 92 mm (2.717 to 3.622 in.)
Allowable maximum stroke ... ... 8 to 9 notches = 180 to 200 mm (7.09 to 7.87 in.)

Torque wrench settings

	lb f ft	kg f m
Fulcrum pin (holding brake pedal lever to bracket)	14 to 20	2.0 to 2.7
Proportioning valve	2.9 to 4.3	0.4 to 0.6
4-way connector	2.9 to 4.3	0.4 to 0.6
3-way connector	2.9 to 4.3	0.4 to 0.6
Front brake:		
Wheel cylinder	12 to 15	1.6 to 2.1
Brake plate	18 to 25	2.5 to 3.4
Rear brake:		
Wheel cylinder	12 to 15	1.6 to 2.1
Brake plate	18 to 25	2.5 to 3.4
All brake line connections	11 to 13	1.5 to 1.8

1 General description

According to model either disc or drum brakes are fitted to the front wheels while all models have single leading shoe drum brakes at the rear. The mechanically operated handbrake works on the rear wheels only.

Where front drum brakes are fitted these are of the two leading shoe type with a separate cylinder for each shoe. Two adjusters are provided on each front wheel so that wear can be taken up on the brake linings. One adjuster is provided on each rear wheel for the same purpose. It is unusual to have to adjust the handbrake system as the efficiency of this system is largely dependent on the condition of the rear brake linings and the adjustment of the brake shoes. The handbrake can however be adjusted separately to the footbrake operated hydraulic system.

The hydraulic brake system on drum brakes operates in the following manner: On application of the brake pedal, hydraulic fluid under pressure is pushed from the master cylinder to the brake operating cylinders in each wheel by means of a union, steel pipe lines and flexible hoses.

The hydraulic fluid moves the pistons out of the wheel cylinders so pushing the brake shoes into contact with the brake drums. This provides an equal degree of retardation on all four wheels in direct proportion to the brake pedal pressure. Return springs draw the shoes together again when the brake pedal is released.

The front disc brakes fitted to certain models (see specifications) are of the rotating disc and floating caliper type, with one caliper per disc. The caliper is positioned to act on the trailing edge of the disc. Each caliper contains two piston operated friction pads, which on application of the footbrake pinch the disc between them.

Application of the footbrake creates hydraulic pressure in the master cylinder and fluid from the cylinder travels via steel and flexible pipes to the cylinder in each caliper, thus pushing the pistons, to which are attached the friction pads, into contact with either side of the disc.

Two seals are fitted to the operating cylinder; the outer seal prevents moisture and dirt entering the cylinder, while the inner seal which is retained in a groove inside the cylinder, prevents fluid leakage.

As the friction pads wear so the pistons move further out of the cylinder due to the elasticity of the seals and the level of the fluid in the hydraulic reservoir drops. Disc pads wear is therefore taken up automatically and eliminates the need for periodic adjustment by the owner.

The handbrake lever on all models is located between the front seats. A single cable runs from the lever to an equaliser bracket on the left of the rear axle. The cable runs through the equaliser bracket and operates the right hand rear brake. At the same time the bracket is deflected and the cable attached to it operates the left-hand rear brake.

On certain models, a dual braking system is fitted providing separate hydraulic circuits for the front and rear brakes. Should one circuit fail the other circuit is unaffected and the car can still be stopped. A warning light is fitted on the facia which illuminates should either circuit fail. Some models are fitted with a

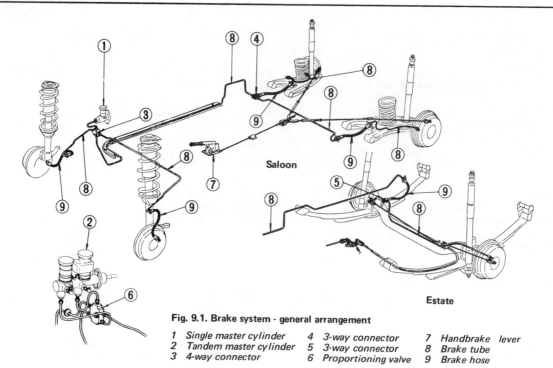

Fig. 9.1. Brake system - general arrangement

1	Single master cylinder	4	3-way connector	7	Handbrake lever
2	Tandem master cylinder	5	3-way connector	8	Brake tube
3	4-way connector	6	Proportioning valve	9	Brake hose

proportioning valve that prevents the rear brakes locking before the front brakes.

2 Routine maintenance

1 Every 3,000 miles (4,800 km) or more frequently if necessary, carefully clean the top of the brake master cylinder reservoir, remove the cap, and inspect the level of the fluid which should be ¼ in. (6.35 mm) below the bottom of the filler neck. Check that the breathing holes in the cap are clear.

2 If the fluid is below this level, top-up the reservoir with any hydraulic fluid conforming to specification. It is vital that no other type of brake fluid is used. Use of a non-suitable fluid will result in brake failure caused by the perishing of special seals in the master and brake cylinders. If topping-up becomes frequent then check the metal piping and flexible hoses for leaks, and check for worn brake or master cylinders which will also cause loss of fluid.

3 At intervals of 3,000 miles (4,800 km), or more frequently if pedal travel becomes excessive, adjust the brake shoes to compensate for wear of the brake linings. On models with disc brakes on the front it will only be necessary to adjust the rear brakes.

4 Every 6,000 miles (9,650 km) in the case of drum brakes, remove the drums, inspect the linings for wear and renew them as necessary. At the same time thoroughly clean out all dust from the drums. With disc brakes, remove the pads and examine them for wear. If they are worn down to 1/8 inch (3.175 mm) or less (the distance being measured between the contact face of the pad and the face of the brake pad support plate) then they should be renewed.

5 Every 36,000 miles (58,000 km) or three years whichever comes sooner, it is advisable to change the fluid in the braking system and at the same time renew all hydraulic seals and flexible hoses.

3 Bleeding the hydraulic system

1 Removal of all the air from the hydraulic system is essential to the correct working of the braking system, and before undertaking this examine the fluid reservoir cap to ensure that both

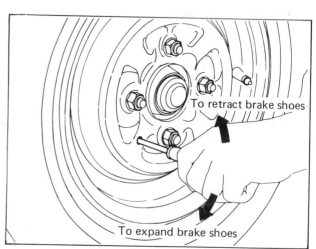

Fig. 9.2. Adjusting the brakes (drum type)

vent holes, one on top and the second underneath but not in line, are clear; check the level of fluid and top-up if required.

2 Check all brake line unions and connections for possible seepage, and at the same time check the condition of the rubber hoses, which may be perished.

3 If the condition of the wheel cylinders is in doubt, check for possible signs of fluid leakage.

4 If there is any possibility of incorrect fluid having been put into the system, drain all the fluid out and flush through with methylated spirit. Renew all piston seals and cups since these will be affected and could possibly fail under pressure.

5 Gather together a clean jam jar, a 9 inch (230 mm) length of tubing which fits tightly over the bleed nipples, and a tin of the correct brake fluid.

6 To bleed the system clean the areas around the bleed valves, and start by removing the rubber cup over the bleed valve, if fitted, and fitting a rubber tube in position.

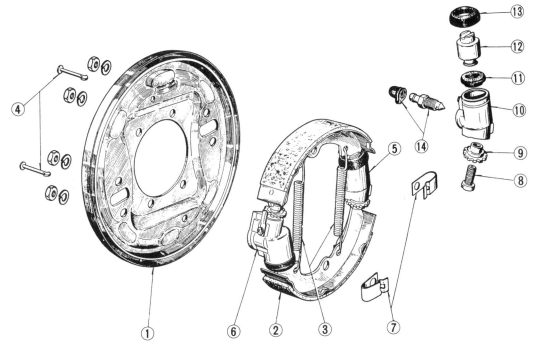

Fig. 9.3. Exploded view of front drum brake

1	Brake plate	6	Wheel cylinder (after)	11	Piston cup
2	Brake shoe assembly	7	Spring (fixing shoe)	12	Piston
3	Brake shoe return spring	8	Adjusting screw	13	Dust cover
4	Pin (fixing shoe)	9	Adjusting nut	14	Bleed screw and cap
5	Wheel cylinder (fore)	10	Wheel cylinder body		

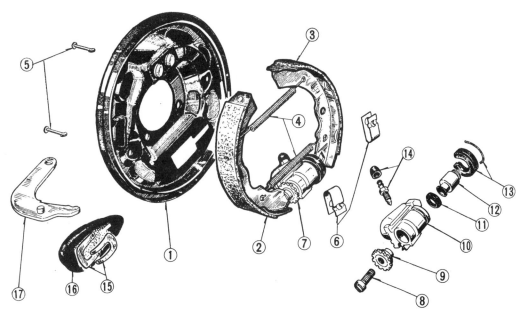

Fig. 9.4. Exploded view of rear drum brake

1	Brake plate	7	Wheel cylinder assembly	13	Dust cover
2	Brake shoe assembly	8	Adjust screw	14	Bleeder screw
3	Brake shoe assembly	9	Adjust nut	15	Adjust plate, stopper plate
4	Brake shoe return spring	10	Wheel cylinder body	16	Dust cover
5	Pin (fixing shoe)	11	Piston cup	17	Lever
6	Spring (fixing shoe)	12	Piston		

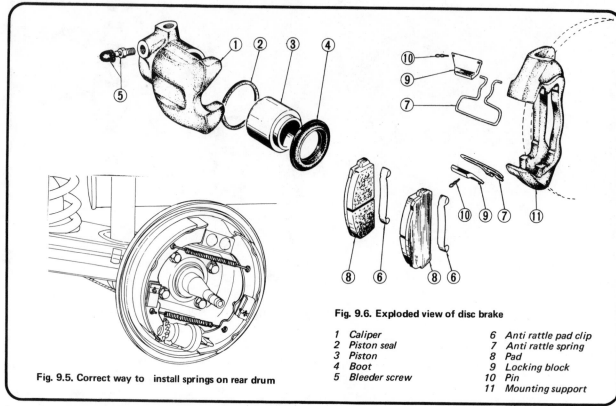

Fig. 9.5. Correct way to   install springs on rear drum

Fig. 9.6. Exploded view of disc brake

1	Caliper	6	Anti rattle pad clip
2	Piston seal	7	Anti rattle spring
3	Piston	8	Pad
4	Boot	9	Locking block
5	Bleeder screw	10	Pin
		11	Mounting support

7 Place the end of the tube in a clean glass jar containing sufficient fluid to keep the end of the tube submerged during the operation.

8 Open the bleed valve with a spanner and quickly press down the brake pedal. After slowly releasing the pedal, pause for a moment to allow the fluid to recoup in the master cylinder and then depress again. This will force air from the system. Continue until no more air bubbles can be seen coming from the tube. At intervals make certain that the reservoir is kept topped up, otherwise air will enter at this point again.

9 Bleeding should be carried out at each of the six bleed valves fitted to the system, in the following order: 1 and 2, master cylinder; 3, left rear; 4, right rear; 5, left front; 6, right front.

10 Tighten the bleed screws when the pedal is still in the fully depressed position.

11 Use only clean hydraulic fluid for topping up.

4 Front drum brake adjustment

1 Chock the rear wheels apply the handbrake, jack up the front of the car and support on firmly based axle stands.

2 Depress the brake pedal several times to centralise the shoes.

3 Insert a screwdriver through the adjusting hole at the rear of the wheel, and then turn the adjuster wheel downwards until the wheel is locked. Now turn the adjuster back until the wheel is free to rotate. Four to eight notches should suffice.

4 Spin the wheel and apply the brakes hard to centralise the shoes. Re-check that it is not possible to turn the adjuster further without locking the wheel.

5 **Note:** A rubbing noise when the wheel is spun is usually due to dust on the brake drum and shoe lining. If there is no obvious slowing down of the wheel due to brake binding there is no need to slacken off the adjusters until the noise disappears. It is far better to remove the drum and clean, taking care not to inhale any dust.

6 Repeat this process for the other adjuster and then on the other drum.

5 Rear drum brake adjustment

1 The principle of adjustment is identical to that for the front brakes. Only one adjuster is fitted and is located at the bottom of the backplate. Do not forget to release the handbrake before commencing. Normally adjustment of the rear brakes will also adjust excessive movement of the handbrake except where the cables have stretched. In this instance it will be necessary to adjust the linkage, as described later in this Chapter.

2 A rear brake shoe adjusting nut and screw should never be interchanged from one rear wheel to the other. The silvery nut and screw should always be on the left side of the vehicle, and the yellow nut and screw should be to the right side of the vehicle.

3 Some models have no rear adjusters provided. Adjustment is automatic when the handbrake is applied.

6 Front brake shoes - inspection, removal and refitting

1 After high mileages it will be necessary to fit replacement brake shoes with new linings. Refitting new brake linings to old shoes is not always satisfactory, but if the services of a local garage or workshop with brake lining equipment is available, then there is no reason why your own shoes should not be successfully relined.

2 Remove the hub trim, slacken off the wheel nuts, securely jack-up the car and remove the roadwheel.

3 Slacken the brake shoe adjusters.

4 Withdraw the brake drum; if necessary, use two bolts in the special drum threads to force the drum away from the hub.

5 Brush any accumulated dust from the brake shoes and internal components.

6 The brake linings should be renewed if they are so worn that

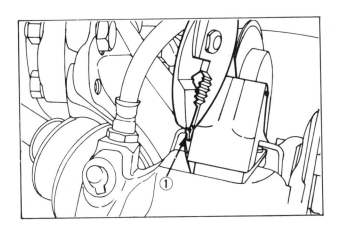

Fig. 9.7. Removing spring clip

1   Spring clip

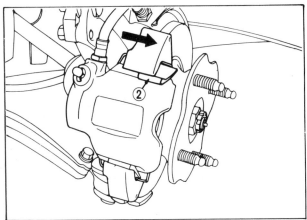

Fig. 9.8. Sliding out the locking block

2   Locking block

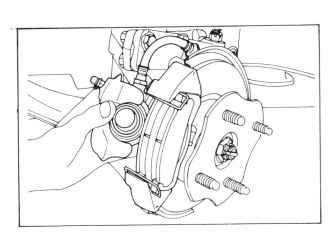

Fig. 9.9. Removing the caliper assembly

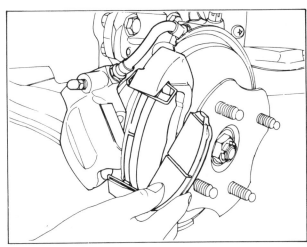

Fig. 9.10. Removing pad

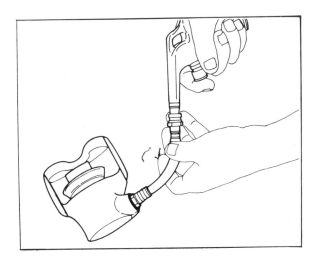

Fig. 9.11. Blowing out the piston using an air-line

the rivet heads are flush with the surface of the lining. If bonded linings are fitted they must be removed when the material has worn down to 1/32 inch (0.8 mm) at its thinnest point. If the shoes are being removed to give access to the wheel cylinders, then cover the linings with masking tape to prevent any possibility of their becoming contaminated with grease or oil.

7   Before removing the shoes, note and sketch if necessary the location of the shoes with regard to their leading and trailing edges and the position of the shoe return springs.

8   Using a pair of pliers, unhook the return springs from the elongated holes in the shoe webs.

9   Again using pliers, grip the edges of the shoe steady spring retaining plates. Depress the plates and turn them through 90° so that they can be released from the retaining Tee posts. Withdraw the steady springs.

10 Remove the brake shoes and use rubber bands to retain the wheel cylinder pistons in their cylinders. **On no account depress the footbrake pedal while the drum and brake shoes are removed.**

11 Slacken the shoe adjusters completely and then fit the new shoes taking particular care to see that they are the correct way round and that the return springs are correctly located.

12 Check the condition of the friction surface of the drum. If it

6.2 Removing the trim

7.1A Removing the hubcap ...

7.1B ... then the split pin

7.1C Removing the brake drum. Note the thumb keeping the bearing in place

7.1D Rear brake shoes

is scored, it must be skimmed professionally or renewed.
13 Refit the brake drum and adjust the brakes, as described in Section 4 of this Chapter.
14 Refit the roadwheel and lower the jack.

7   Rear brake shoes - inspection, removal and refitting

1   The servicing of the rear brake shoes is similar to that described for the front shoes except that only one adjuster is fitted. The rear hub/brake drum should be removed and refitted as described in Chapter 11, Section 8.
2   It is most important that the springs are replaced correctly: the upper spring from outside the shoe with the hooked ends inside, and the lower springs from inside the shoe with the

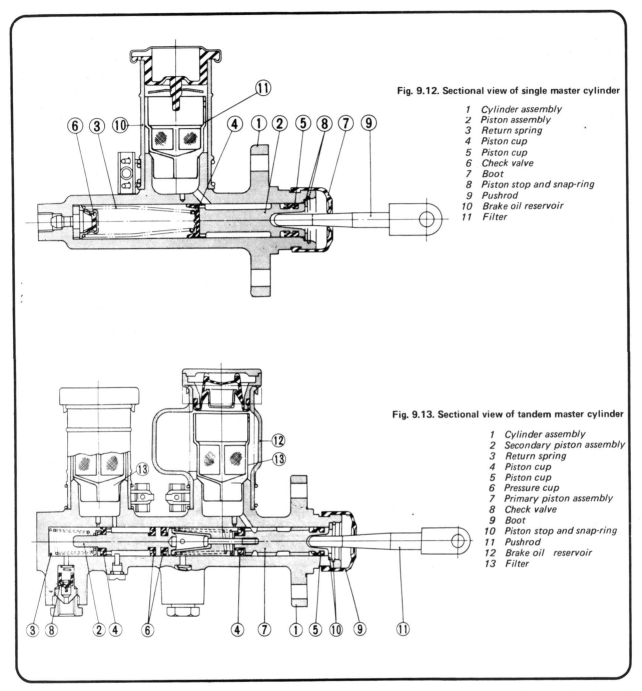

Fig. 9.12. Sectional view of single master cylinder

1   Cylinder assembly
2   Piston assembly
3   Return spring
4   Piston cup
5   Piston cup
6   Check valve
7   Boot
8   Piston stop and snap-ring
9   Pushrod
10 Brake oil reservoir
11 Filter

Fig. 9.13. Sectional view of tandem master cylinder

1   Cylinder assembly
2   Secondary piston assembly
3   Return spring
4   Piston cup
5   Piston cup
6   Pressure cup
7   Primary piston assembly
8   Check valve
9   Boot
10 Piston stop and snap-ring
11 Pushrod
12 Brake oil   reservoir
13 Filter

hooked ends outside. (Refer to Fig. 9.5).

8   Flexible hoses - inspection, removal and refitting

1   Inspect the condition of the flexible hydraulic hoses leading from under the front wings to the wheel connections, and also the hoses on the rear wheels. If they are swollen, damaged or chafed, they must be renewed.
2   Undo the locknuts at both ends of the flexible hoses and then holding the hexagon nut on the flexible hose steady undo the other union nut and remove the flexible hose and washer.
3   Replacement is a reversal of the removal procedure, but carefully check all the securing brackets are in a sound condition and that the locknuts are tight. Bleed the hydraulic system.

4   After a brake hose has been replaced, ensure there is enough clearance between the hose and surrounding part:

a) Hose to driveshaft boot:
    30 to 40 mm (1.2 to 1.6 in.)
b) Hose to steering side rod:
    40 to 50 mm (1.6 to 2.0 in.)
c) Hose to driveshaft:
    50 to 60 mm (2.0 to 2.4 in.)

9   Rigid brake lines - inspection, removal and refitting

1   At regular intervals wipe the steel brake pipes clean and examine them for signs of rust or denting caused by flying

stones.

2 Examine the securing clips which are plastic coated to prevent wear to the pipe surface. Bend the tongues of the clips if necessary to ensure that they hold the brake pipes securely without letting them rattle or vibrate.

3 Check that the pipes are not touching any adjacent components or rubbing against any part of the vehicle. Where this is observed, bend the pipe gently away to clear.

4 Any section of pipe which is rusty or chafed should be renewed. Brake pipes are available to the correct length and fitted with end unions from most Datsun dealers and can be made to pattern by many accessory suppliers. When installing the new pipes use the old pipes as a guide to bending and do not make any bends sharper than is necessary.

5 The system will of course have to be bled when the circuit has been reconnected.

6 The brake lines should clear adjacent parts as follows:

   a) *Rear lines to suspension arm:*
      More than 10 mm (0.4 in.)
   b) *Front lines to subframe:*
      More than 20 mm (0.8 in.)

---

10 Drum brake wheel cylinder seals - renewal

If hydraulic fluid is leaking from one of the brake cylinders it will be necessary to dismantle the cylinder and replace the dust cover and piston sealing rubber. If brake fluid is found running down the side of the wheel, or it is noticed that a pool of liquid forms alongside one wheel and the level in the master cylinder has dropped, and the hoses are in good order proceed as follows:

1 Remove the offending brake drum and shoes, as described in Sections 6 or 7.

2 Gently pull off the rubber dust cover.

3 Take the piston complete with its seal out of the cylinder bore. Should the piston and seal prove difficult to remove, gentle pressure on the brake pedal will push it out of the bore. If this method is used place a quantity of rag under the brake backplate to catch the hydraulic fluid as it pours out of the cylinder.

4 Inspect the cylinder bore for score marks caused by impurities in the hydraulic fluid. If any are found the cylinder and piston will require renewal together as an exchange unit.

5 If the cylinder bore is sound, thoroughly clean it out with fresh hydraulic fluid.

6 The old rubber seal will probably be visibly worn or swollen. Detach it from the piston, smear a new rubber seal with hydraulic fluid and assemble it to the piston with the flat face of the seal next to the piston rear shoulder.

7 Reassembly is a direct reversal of the above procedure. If the rubber dust cap appears to be worn or damaged this should also be renewed.

8 Replenish the hydraulic fluid, replace the brake shoes and drum and bleed the braking system.

---

11 Front wheel cylinders - removal and refitting

1 Remove the brake drum and shoes, as described in Section 5.

2 Unscrew the flexible hose from the wheel cylinder. Plug the end of the flexible hose.

3 Unscrew the unions from the interconnecting pipe which joins the two wheel operating cylinders.

4 Unscrew and remove the two securing nuts from the wheel cylinders and withdraw the cylinder assemblies from the brake backplate.

5 Refitting the wheel cylinders is a reversal of removal but a smear of high melting grease must be applied to the brake backplate upon which the wheel cylinders slide and the raised shoe contact points.

6 Tighten the wheel cylinder securing nuts to a torque of between 12 and 15 lb ft. only.

7 When reassembly is complete, bleed the brakes (Section 3).

---

12 Rear wheel cylinders - removal and refitting

1 Remove the drum and shoes as described in Section 7.

2 Disconnect the handbrake clevis from the wheel cylinder operating arm and unscrew the brake pipe union from the wheel cylinder. Plug the brake pipe.

3 Peel back and remove the rubber dust cover from the wheel cylinder aperture and then slide out the adjustment shims and plates, noting carefully their sequence and exact location.

4 Refitting is a reversal of removal but smear the raised sliding surfaces of the backplate with high melting point grease.

5 Smear the wheel cylinder shims and plate surfaces with grease and locate the cylinder assembly on the backplate. Using a spring balance check that the wheel cylinder will slide in its elongated aperture with a pull of between 5 and 15 lbs (2.26 and 6.8 kg). If it moves too stiffly or too freely, check for rust or burrs or renew the forked shims.

6 When reassembly is complete, bleed the system (Section 3).

---

13 Disc brake pad - removal, inspection and refitting

1 Apply the handbrake. Chock the rear wheels, jack-up the front of the car and place on firmly based axle stands. Remove the roadwheels.

2 Using a pair of pliers, extract the two spring wire clips from the caliper locking blocks.

3 Using a parallel pin punch, carefully remove the two caliper locking blocks.

4 Lift away the caliper from its mounting bracket and allow to hang suspended by a piece of wire or string. Do not allow it to hang by the flexible hose.

5 Release the lining springs and lift away the two pads from the caliper support bracket. Mark them so that they may be refitted in their original positions if they are not too worn.

6 Measure the thickness of the linings and if they are less than 0.079 inch (2 mm) new linings must be fitted.

7 Before fitting either new linings or the original ones, wipe the top of the brake hydraulic fluid reservoir and unscrew the cap. Place some absorbent cloth around the filler neck to catch any fluid that may overflow during the operation described in the next paragraph.

8 Using a 'G' clamp or other suitable tool, push the piston to the bottom of the caliper cylinder bore.

9 Smear a little Castrol PH Grease on the back of the pad to prevent subsequent possible seizure and refit the pads and caliper, this being the reverse sequence to removal.

10 Check the level of hydraulic fluid in the reservoir and top-up if necessary.

11 Road test the car and operate the brakes several times to adjust the pad to disc clearance.

---

14 Caliper unit - removal and refitting

1 Remove the friction pads, as described in the preceding Section.

2 Unscrew the fluid pipe union at the caliper body, slightly loosen the rigid pipe union at the bracket and swing the hydraulic pipe out of the way.

3 Unscrew and remove the caliper unit securing bolts. Withdraw the caliper.

4 Refitting the caliper unit is a reversal of removal, tighten the caliper securing bolts to a torque of between 33 and 44 lb ft. (4.56 and 6.08 kgm).

5 Bleed the hydraulic system when the caliper and friction pads have been refitted.

13.1 Roadwheel removed

13.2 Extracting the spring clips ...

13.3 ... then the locking blocks

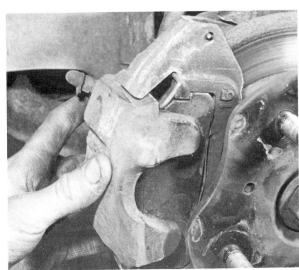
13.4 Lifting away the caliper ...

13.5 ... and removing the pads

Fig. 9.14. Primary piston assembly

15 Disc brake caliper - dismantling, overhaul and reassembly

1   Thoroughly clean the caliper free of dust and dirt before dismantling.
2   Before overhaul commences it should be noted that the only possible repairs are confined to renewal of the piston seals or the piston. No other component parts are available as spares.
3   Using a non-metal pointed rod, ease the piston rubber boot from the caliper body and piston.
4   To remove the piston from the caliper, apply an air line to the caliper and blow the piston out.
5   Carefully ease the 'O' ring seal from the inside of the cylinder using a non-metal pointed rod. Great care must be taken so as not to score the walls of the cylinder.
6   Inspect the cylinder bore and the piston for signs of scoring and, if evident a complete new caliper assembly must be obtained.
7   To reassemble, first wet the cylinder 'O' ring seal with fresh hydraulic fluid, and carefully insert it into its bore in the cylinder.
8   Next wet the piston and place it in the cylinder bore.
9   Push the piston down the cylinder bore until the piston rubber boot can be fitted to the piston and caliper body.
10 Reassembly is now the reverse sequence to dismantling.
11 To make easier bleeding the hydraulic system, the caliper should be filled with fresh hydraulic fluid by removing the bleed nipple and pouring the fluid with the caliper in a tilted position. Refit the bleed nipple.

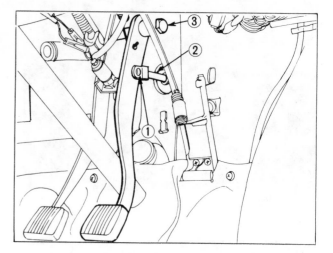

Fig. 9.15. Removing the brake pedal

1   Snap pin   2   Pushrod   3   Retaining bolt

16 Front brake disc - removal and refitting

1   When the friction pads are inspected also check the condition of the discs themselves. If they are badly scored then they may be skimmed professionally but the minimum disc thickness which must be maintained is 0.354 in. (9 mm). Where skimming will produce a disc thinner than this, then the disc must be renewed.
2   The maximum run-out (out of true) is limited to a maximum of 0.003 in. (0.07 mm). Where this is exceeded, the disc must either be re-machined or renewed.
3   To remove the disc, first remove the pads (Section 13) and the caliper unit (Section 14).
4   Tap off the cap from the end of the hub, remove the split pin and castellated nut from the end of the driveshaft.
5   Remove the driveshaft, as described in Chapter 7. Then drive out the hub, as described in Chapter 11.
6   The disc can be separated from the hub by removing the four securing bolts.
7   Refitting is a reversal of removal. Tighten the hub/disc bolts to a torque of 32 to 43 lb ft. (4.42 to 5.94 kg m).

17 Master cylinder (single braking circuit) - removal and refitting

1   Disconnect the brake pedal arm from the master cylinder operating pushrod.
2   Unscrew the hydraulic fluid outlet pipe from the master cylinder. Plug the pipe to prevent the ingress of dirt.
3   Unscrew and remove the two bolts which secure the master cylinder to the ending rear bulkhead and withdraw the unit complete with any adjustment shims.
4   Refitting is a reversal of removal. Always refit the shims which were retained on removal and check the pedal adjustment. Bleed the hydraulic system.

18 Master cylinder (dual braking circuit) - removal and refitting

1   The removal and refitting of the tandem master cylinder used on dual braking circuits is similar to that described in the

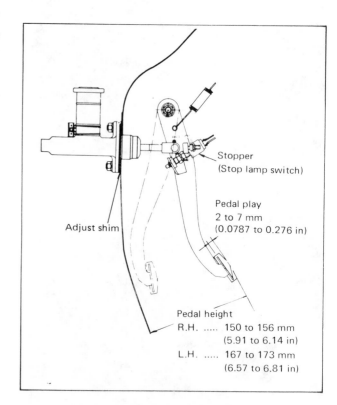

Stopper
(Stop lamp switch)

Pedal play
2 to 7 mm
(0.0787 to 0.276 in)

Adjust shim

Pedal height
R.H. ..... 150 to 156 mm
(5.91 to 6.14 in)
L.H. ..... 167 to 173 mm
(6.57 to 6.81 in)

Fig. 9.16. Adjusting the brake pedal height

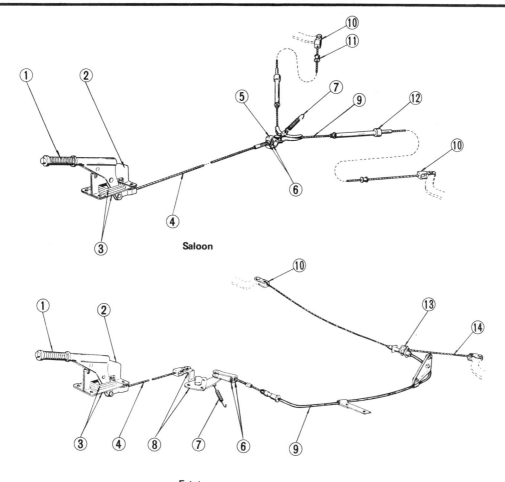

Saloon

Estate

Fig. 9.17. Handbrake systems - Saloon and Estate

1	Hand lever	6	Adjuster nut and locknut	11	Clip
2	Hand lever bracket	7	Return spring	12	Guide
3	Dust seal and plate	8	Counter lever & support	13	Equalizer
4	Front cable	9	Rear cable	14	Rear cable LH
5	Equalizer	10	Clevis		

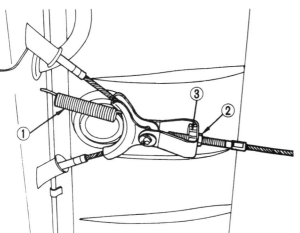

Fig. 9.18. Front brake cable (Saloon) - adjustment

1   Spring   2   Locknut   3   Adjuster

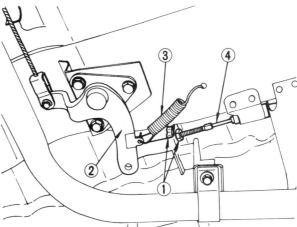

Fig. 9.19. Rear brake cable (Estate) - adjustment

1   Locknut and adjuster nut   3   Spring
2   Counter lever   4   Rear cable

preceding Section for single master cylinders.

2   Note that there are two fluid outlet unions and pipes, one to supply the rear hydraulic circuit and one to supply the front circuit.

19 Master cylinders - dismantling, servicing and reassembly

1   The procedure for dismantling, servicing and reassembly of both the single and tandem type master cylinders is similar. Both types of unit will be described in this Section and the operations will generally apply if reference is made to the appropriate illustration for the location of internal seals and components. There are two types of single master cylinders: NABCO and TOKIKO. Parts are not interchangeable between these types.

2   Drain the hydraulic fluid from the reservoir and expel the fluid remaining in the cylinder bodies by actuating the pushrod.

3   Unscrew and remove the stop bolt from the base of the cylinder body (tandem type only).

4   Peel bath the rubber dust cover from the end of the cylinder body, extract the now exposed circlip and withdraw the stop washer and pushrod assembly.

5   With tandem master cylinders, remove the primary piston assembly, the secondary piston assembly and the return spring. If these components are difficult to extract from the cylinder body, either tap the unit on a piece of wood or apply pressure from a tyre pump to one of the fluid outlet ports (holding the other closed with the finger).

6   Remove the valve caps and valve assemblies.

7   With single type master cylinders, removal of the internal components is similar to that described for tandem units but only one piston assembly is used.

8   Clean all components in methylated spirit or hydraulic fluid. Examine the cylinder bores for scoring or bright wear areas. If these are evident, renew the master cylinder complete.

9   Obtain the appropriate repair kit. It is essential that the correct kit for the make of cylinder is obtained, either NABCO or TOKIKO. They are not interchangeable. If the piston seals have deteriorated, do not attempt to remove them but renew the piston as an assembly.

10 Do not remove the fluid reservoirs unless essential.

11 Assemble the internal components into the master cylinder body in the reverse order to dismantling. Dip each part in clean hydraulic fluid before assembly and use only the fingers to manipulate the rubber seals and cups into the cylinder bore. With tandem type master cylinders, tighten the valve caps to between 18 and 25 lb ft. (2.5 and 3.4 kg m), tightening torque and the stop bolt to 2 lb ft. (0.27 kg m).

20 Dual circuit pressure differential switch

1   With dual circuit hydraulic braking systems, a switch is fitted to the engine rear bulkhead to monitor any drop in pressure in either of the circuits. It also serves as a handbrake 'ON' warning device.

2   The switch is essentially a piston which is kept in balance when the pressure in the front and rear hydraulic circuits is equal. Should a leak occur in either circuit then the piston is displaced by the greater pressure existing in the non-leaking circuit and makes an electrical contact to illuminate a warning lamp on the vehicle facia.

3   In the event of the warning lamp coming on, check immediately to establish the source of fluid leakage. This may be in the rigid or flexible pipes or more likely, at the wheel operating cylinders, master cylinder or caliper units.

4   When the faulty component has been repaired or renewed, bleed the brakes as described in Section 3 of this Chapter when the pressure differential switch piston will automatically return to its 'in balance' position.

5   In the event of a fault developing in the switch itself, renew it as an assembly.

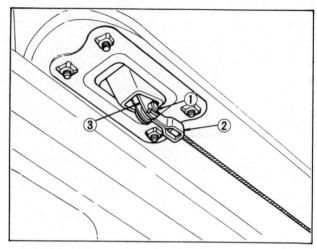

Fig. 9.20. Handbrake front cable - connection to handbrake lever

1   Clevis pin   3   Handbrake lever
2   Clevis

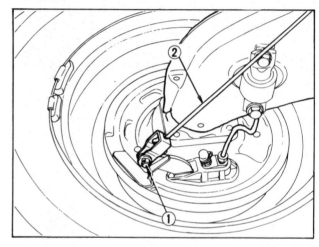

Fig. 9.21. Handbrake   cable to rear wheel connection

1   Clevis pin   2   Cable

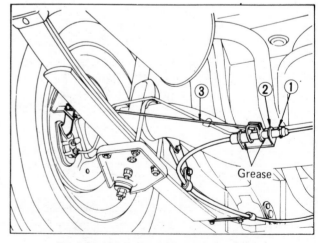

Fig. 9.22. Handbrake cable equalizer - Estate

1   Circlip   2   Bracket   3   Cable

21 Footbrake pedal and stop lamp switch - removal, adjustment and replacement

1 The footbrake pedal is attached to a common cross-shaft with the clutch pedal. Removal and refitting of the clutch pedal is described in Chapter 5.
2 Unhook the pedal return spring.
3 Remove the snap pin from the master cylinder pushrod and separate the brake pedal lever from the pushrod.
4 Loosen the nut holding the brake pedal lever to the bracket. Remove the bolt and then the pedal lever.
5 Check all sliding surfaces for excessive wear; the pedal lever for cracks or warping, and the nylon bush for evidence of deterioration. Replace any relevant parts, grease all moving parts and then replace in the reverse order to removal.
6 The height of the brake pedal must be checked and adjusted if necessary whenever the master cylinder or pedal assembly have been removed and refitted.
7 Loosen the locknut on the pedal arm stop bolt and screw the bolt free from contact with the pedal arm.
8 Measure the distance between the inclined slope of the floor and the top surface of the pedal pad. This should be 5.91 to 6.14 in. (150.11 to 155.96 mm) for RHD vehicles, and 6.57 to 6.81 in. (166.88 to 172.97 mm) for LHD vehicles.
9 Next, check that there is 0.050 to 0.17 in. (2 to 7 mm) of free pedal play; this is to achieve clearance between the pushrod and piston.
10 If the dimension varies from this, add or remove shims between the master cylinder mounting face and the engine rear bulkhead. Ensure that the upper and lower half shim packs are of equal thickness. Availability - 0.063, 0.031 and 0.024 in. (1.60, 0.78 and 0.60 mm).
11 The stoplamp switch is located on the reverse side of the pedal arm stop bolt bracket. It is operated by a spring loaded plunger operating immediately the footbrake pedal is depressed. Any fine adjustment which may be required is carried out by loosening the locknut and moving the switch body nearer or further from the bracket as necessary.

22 Handbrake - adjustment

1 The handbrake is adjusted automatically whenever the rear brake shoes are adjusted. However, due to cable stretch, additional adjustment may be required when the handbrake lever can be pulled more than six notches (clicks) to the full-on position.
2 Carry out the adjustment by slackening the locknut on the equaliser (saloon) and on the counter lever (estate). Rotate the knurled adjusting nut sufficiently to bring the handbrake lever movement within that specified and tighten the locknut.
3 Jack-up the rear roadwheels and check that the rear brake shoes do not bind when the handbrake is fully off.

23 Handbrake cable - replacement

1 *Front cable (Saloon):* Disconnect the return spring, then remove the locknut and adjustment nut (knurled) on the equalizer.
2 Remove the pin securing the clevis to the handbrake lever; the front cable should now be free to lift away.
3 *Front cable (Estate):* Disconnect the return spring, then loosen the locknut and adjusting nut on the counter lever.
4 Remove the clevis pin securing the front cable clevis to the counter lever, then the clevis pin securing the cable to the handbrake lever. Remove the cable.

5 *Rear cable (Saloon):* Remove the clevis pin securing the rear brake cable to the rear brake lever. Disconnect the cable clamp at the rear suspension arm.
6 Ease the rear cable out through the cable guide and equalizer.
7 *Rear cable (Estate):* Remove the clevis pin securing the rear brake cable to the rear brake lever. Disconnect the return spring, adjusting nut and locknut at the counter lever. Ease the front end of the rear cable out through the bracket and hole in the chassis.
8 Remove the brackets on the left rear spring and on the axle tube.
9 Remove the circlip from the sliding section of the bracket. Pull out the rear cable assembly, towards the left rear spring, through the guide bracket. Finally, disconnect the left-hand rear cable from the equalizer.
10 Check the cables for chafing or corrosion and the handbrake lever ratchet for wear. Renew as necessary.
11 Reassembly is a reversal of dismantling. Apply a small quantity of grease to the handbrake lever ratchet and to the threads of the adjusters to prevent corrosion. Use new split pins in the clevises which connect the cable end fittings to the wheel cylinder operating levers and apply a drop of oil to the clevis pins.
12 When installation is complete, adjust the handbrake as described in Section 24.

24 Proportioning valve (general)

1 The valve is an optional fitting together with the tandem master cylinder. It is integral with the connector and enables the front brakes to operate normally even when the rear brake line has developed a serious leak. Also should there be a leak in the front brake line the rear brake will still function.
2 It is recommended that every 24,000 miles (40,000 km) valve operation be checked for correct operation. Remove all luggage and then drive the car to a dry concrete road. With the car travelling at 30 mph (50 km h) apply the brakes suddenly.
3 The valve is functioning normally when the rear wheels lock simultaneously with the front wheels or when the front wheels lock before the rear wheels.
4 Should the rear wheels lock before the front wheels then it is probable that the valve has developed an internal fault and it should be renewed.

25 Fault diagnosis - braking system

Brake grab
   Brake shoe linings or pads not bedded-in
   Contaminated with oil or grease
   Scored drums or discs

Brake drag
   Master cylinder faulty
   Brake foot pedal return impeded
   Blocked filler cap vent
   Seized wheel caliper or cylinder
   Incorrect adjustment of handbrake
   Weak or broken shoe return springs
   Crushed or blocked pipelines

Brake pedal feels hard
   Friction surfaces contaminated with oil or grease
   Glazed friction material surfaces
   Rusty disc surfaces
   Seized caliper or wheel cylinder

Excessive pedal travel
    Low fluid level in reservoir
    Excessive disc run-out
    Worn front wheel bearings
    System requires bleeding
    Worn pads or linings

Pedal creep during sustained application
    Fluid leak
    Faulty master cylinder

Pedal spongy or springy
    System requires bleeding
    Perished flexible hose
    Loose master cylinder
    Cracked brake drum
    Linings not bedded-in
    Faulty master cylinder

Fall in master cylinder fluid level
    Normal disc pad wear
    Leak

Chapter 10 Electrical system

Contents

Specifications

Electrical system (general)

Battery type	Hitachi
Voltage	12
Capacity at 20 hour rate	60 amp/hr
Earth	negative

Alternator

	Hitachi LT125-06	Hitachi LT133-05
Make and type	12 volts/25 amps	12 volts/33 amps
Nominal output	Negative earth	Negative earth
Pole	1,050 to 13,500 rpm	1,000 to 13,500 rpm
Revolution	Less than 1,050 rpm	Less than 1,000 rpm
No-load minimum revolution	More than 18 amps (14 volts at 2,500 rpm)	More than 24 amps (14 volts at 2,500 rpm)
Output current	More than 25 amps (14 volts at 5,000 rpm)	More than 33 amps (14 volts at 5,000 rpm)
Weight	3.4 kg (7.5 lb)	3.4 kg (7.5 lb)
Applied regulator	TLIZ-37	TLIZ-37
Stator coil - resistance per phase	0.17 Ω at 20°C (68°F)	0.15 Ω at 20°C (68°F)
Rotor coil - resistance	4.4 Ω at 20°C (68°F)	4.5 Ω at 20°C (68°F)
Brushes:		
length	14.5 mm (0.571 in)	
Wear limit	7 mm (0.2756 in)	
Spring pressure	0.25 to 0.35 kg (0.55 to 0.77 lb)	
Slip ring:		
Outer diameter	31 mm (1.220 in)	
Reduction limit	1 mm (0.0394 in)	
Repair limit	0.3 mm (0.0118 in)	
Repair accuracy	0.05 mm (0.0197 in)	

Voltage regulator

Type ...	Hitachi TLIZ - 37 or TLIZ - 57
Regulating voltage ...	14.3 to 15.3 volts at 68°F (20°C)
Core gap ...	0.024 to 0.040 in (0.60 to 1 mm)
Point gap ...	0.012 to 0.016 in (0.30 to 0.40 mm)

Cut-out

Release voltage ...	4.2 to 5.2 at 'N' terminal
Core gap ...	0.032 to 0.040 in (0.81 to 1 mm)
Point gap ...	0.016 to 0.024 in (0.40 to 0.60 mm)

Fusebox

Type ...	cartridge
Number of fuses ...	4 (some models have an eight-way fusebox. When this is so, fusible links are not fitted).
Rating ...	3 x 15 amp 1 x 10 amp

Fusible links ...

3 (headlamps two, starting circuit one).

Starter motor (early models)

	S114-155 (A10 engine)	Hitachi S114-87M (A12 engine)
Make and type ...	S114-155 (A10 engine)	Hitachi S114-87M (A12 engine)
Nominal output ...	1.0 kw	1.0 kw
Rating ...	30 seconds	30 seconds
System voltage ...	12 volts	12 volts
Weight ...	4.7 kg (10.3 lb)	4.6 kg (10.1 lb)
No load:		
Terminal voltage ...	12 volts	12 volts
Current ...	less than 60 amps	less than 60 amps
Revolution ...	more than 7,000 rpm	more than 7,000 rpm
Load:		
Terminal voltage ...	6.3 volts	6.3 volts
Current ...	less than 420 amps	less than 420 amps
Torque ...	more than 0.9 kg/m 6.5 lb/ft)	more than 0.9 kg/m (6.5 lb/ft)
Pinion drive out voltage ...	less than 8 volts	less than 8 volts
Brush length:		
Standard height ...	16 mm (0.630 in)	16 mm (0.630 in)
Wear limit ...	6.5 mm (0.256 in)	6.5 mm (0.256 in)
Brush spring tension (standard pressure) ...	1.6 kg (3.5 lb)	0.8 kg (1.8 lb)
Commutator:		
Outer diameter:		
Standard OD ...	33 mm (1.299 in)	33 mm (1.299 in)
Wear limit ...	1 mm (0.0394 in)	2 mm (0.0787 in)
Difference between maximum and minimum diameters:		
Repair limit ...	0.4 mm (0.0157 in)	0.4 mm (0.0157 in)
Repair accuracy ...	0.05 mm (0.0020 in)	0.05 mm (0.0020 in)
Depth of mica:		
Repair limit ...	0.2 mm (0.0079 in)	0.2 mm (0.0079 in)
Repair accuracy ...	0.5 to 0.8 mm (0.0197 to 0.0315 in)	0.5 to 0.8 mm (0.0197 to 0.0315 in)
Clearance between armature shaft and bushing:		
Repair limit ...	0.2 mm (0.0079 in)	0.2 mm (0.0079 in)
Repair accuracy ...	0.03 to 0.1 mm (0.0012 to 0.0039 in)	0.03 to 0.1 mm (0.0012 to 0.0039 in)
Armature shaft:		
Outer diameter:		
Pinion side ...	12.5 mm (0.492 in)	13 mm (0.512 in)
Rear end ...	11.5 mm (0.453 in)	11.5 mm (0.453 in)
Wear limit ...	0.1 mm (0.0039 in)	0.1 mm (0.0039 in)
Bend limit ...	0.08 mm (0.003 in)	0.08 mm (0.0031 in)
Gap between the pinion front edge and the pinion stopper ...	0.3 to 1.5 mm (0.0118 to 0.0591 in)	0.3 to 1.5 mm (0.0118 to 0.0591 in)
Magnetic switch:		
Coil resistance:		
Series coil ...	0.3 Ω at 20°C (68°F)	0.3 Ω at 20°C (68°F)
Shunt coil ...	0.9 Ω at 20°C (68°F)	0.9 Ω at 20°C (68°F)
Plunger "L" dimension ...	31.7 to 32.3 mm (1.248 to 1.272 in)	31.7 to 32.3 mm (1.248 to 1.272 in)

Starter motor (later models - A10 and A12

Make and type	...	...	...	...	...	...	...	Hitachi S114 - 161
Brush length	...	...	...	...	...	...	...	More than 0.47 in (12 mm)
Brush spring tension	...	...	...	...	...	...	...	3.1 to 4 lb (1.4 to 1.8 kg)

Windscreen wiper motor

Rated voltage	...	...	...	...	...	...	...	12V
Test voltage	...	...	...	...	...	...	...	13.5V
Starting voltage	...	...	...	...	...	...	...	Less than 8V
Voltage range	...	...	...	...	...	...	...	10 to 15V
Unloaded speed	...	...	...	...	...	...	...	Low: 46 to 58 rpm; High: 67 to 83 rpm
Unloaded current	...	...	...	...	...	...	...	Low: Less than 1.5A; High: Less than 2.0A
Locking torque	...	...	...	...	...	...	...	80 kg/m (176 ft/lb) or greater
Wiping system	...	...	...	...	...	...	...	Parallel interlock (tandem type)
Wiping angle	...	...	...	...	...	...	...	88°30' (Driver side), 103° (Left side)
Blade length	...	...	...	...	...	...	...	380 mm (15.0 in) (Right), 330 mm (13.0 in) (Left)
Type of blade	...	...	...	...	...	...	...	5-point support for curved glass
Arm installation method	...	...	...	...	...	...	...	Tapered serration
Locking torque	...	...	...	...	...	...	...	80 kg/m (176 ft/lb) or more

Bulbs

								Wattage	Number
Headlamp	...	...	...	...	...	...	...	12V-50/40W	2
Front turn signal lamp	...	...	...	...	...	...	...	12V-23W	2
Front parking lamp	...	...	...	...	...	...	...	12V-7.5W	2
Side turn signal lamp	...	...	...	...	...	...	...	12V-3.4W	2
Licence plate lamp	...	...	...	...	...	...	...	12V-10W	1
Rear turn signal lamp	...	...	...	...	...	...	...	12V-23W	2
Stop and tail lamp	...	...	...	...	...	...	...	12V-8/23W	2
Reverse lamp	...	...	...	...	...	...	...	12V-12W	2
Interior lamp	...	...	...	...	...	...	...	12V-6W	1
High beam indicator lamp	...	...	...	...	...	...	...	12V-3.4W	1
Oil pressure warning lamp	...	...	...	...	...	...	...	12V-3.4W	1
Meter illumination lamp	...	...	...	...	...	...	...	12V-3.4W	2
Turn signal indicator lamp	...	...	...	...	...	...	...	12V-3.4W	2

1 General description

The electrical system is of the 12 volt negative earth type and the major components comprise a 12 volt battery of which the negative terminal is earthed, an alternator which is driven from the crankshaft pulley and a starter motor.

The battery supplies a steady amount of current for the ignition, lighting, and other electrical circuits and provides a reserve of electricity when the current consumed by the electrical equipment exceeds that being produced by the alternator.

The alternator has its own regulator which ensures a high output if the battery is in a low state of charge or the demand from the electrical equipment is high, and a low output if the battery is fully charged and there is little demand for the electrical equipment.

When fitting electrical accessories to cars with a negative earth system it is important, if they contain silicone diodes or transistors, that they are connected correctly, otherwise serious damage may result to the components concerned. Items such as radios, tape players, electronic ignition systems, automatic headlight dipping etc., should all be checked for correct polarity.

It is important that the battery positive lead is always disconnected if the battery is to be boost charged. Also if body repairs are to be carried out using electric arc welding equipment, the alternator must be disconnected otherwise serious damage can be caused to the more delicate instruments. Whenever the battery has to be disconnected it must always be reconnected with the negative terminal earthed.

2 Battery - removal and replacement

1 The battery should be removed once every three months for cleaning and testing. Disconnect the negative lead first, followed by the positive lead, from the battery terminals by slackening the clamp bolts and lifting away the clamps.

2 Undo and remove the nuts securing the clamps. Lift away the clamps. Carefully lift the battery from its carrier and hold it vertically to ensure that none of the electrolyte is spilled.

3 Replacement is a direct reversal of the removal procedure. Smear the terminals and clamps with vaseline to prevent corrosion. **Never** use an ordinary grease.

2.1 Removing the battery

3 Battery - maintenance and inspection

1 Normal weekly battery maintenance consists of checking the electrolyte level of each cell to ensure that the separators are covered by ¼ inch (6.35 mm) of electrolyte. If the level has fallen top-up the battery using distilled water only. Do not overfill. If a battery is overfilled or any electrolyte spilled, immediately wipe away the excess as electrolyte attacks and corrodes very rapidly any metal it comes into contact with.
2 As well as keeping the terminals clean and covered with petroleum jelly (vaseline), the top of the battery, and especially the top of the cells, should be kept clean and dry. This helps to prevent corrosion and ensures that the battery does not become partially discharged by leakage through dampness and dirt.
3 Once every three months remove the battery and inspect the clamp nuts, clamps, tray and battery leads for corrosion (white fluffy deposits on the metal which are brittle to the touch). If any corrosion is found, clean off the deposits with ammonia and

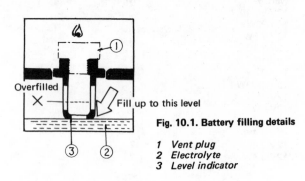

Fig. 10.1. Battery filling details

1 Vent plug
2 Electrolyte
3 Level indicator

5 If topping up the battery becomes excessive and the case has been inspected for cracks that could cause leakage, but none are found, the battery is being overcharged and the alternator control unit will have to be checked and reset.
6 With the battery on the bench, at the three monthly interval check, measure its specific gravity with a hydrometer to determine the state of the charge and condition of the electrolyte. There should be very little variation between the different cells and, if variation in excess of 0.025 is present, it will be due to either:

a) Loss of electrolyte from the battery caused by spillage or a leak resulting in a drop in the specific gravity of the electrolyte, when the deficiency was replaced with distilled water instead of fresh electrolyte.
b) An internal short circuit caused by a buckled plate or a similar malady pointing to the likelihood of total battery failure in the near future.

7 The specific gravity of the electrolyte from fully charged conditions at the electrolyte temperature indicated is listed in Table A. The specific gravity of a fully discharged battery at different temperatures of the electrolyte is given in Table B.
8 Specific gravity is measured by drawing up into the body of a hydrometer sufficient electrolyte to allow the indicator to float freely. The level at which the indicator floats shows the specific gravity.

Table A
Specific gravity - battery fully charged

1.268 at 100°F or 38°C electrolyte temperature
1.272 at 90°F or 32°C electrolyte temperature
1.276 at 80°F or 27°C electrolyte temperature

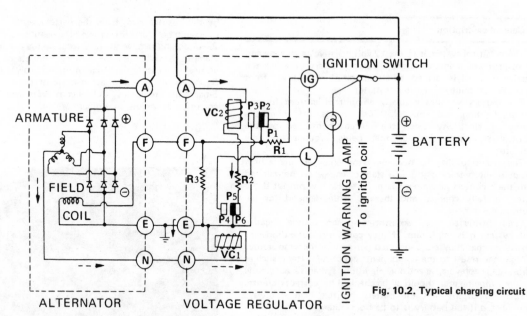

Fig. 10.2. Typical charging circuit

paint over the clean metal with an anti-rust/anti-acid paint.
4 At the same time inspect the battery case for cracks. If a crack is found, clean and plug it with one of the proprietary compounds marketed. If leakage through the crack has been excessive it will be necessary to refill the appropriate cell with fresh electrolyte as detailed later. Cracks are frequently caused to the top of a battery case by pouring in distilled water in the middle of winter *after,* instead of *before,* a run. This gives the water no chance to mix with the electrolyte and so the former freezes and splits the battery case.

1.280 at 70°F or 21°C electrolyte temperature
1.284 at 60°F or 16°C electrolyte temperature
1.288 at 50°F or 10°C electrolyte temperature
1.292 at 40°F or   4°C electrolyte temperature
1.296 at 30°F or -1.5°C electrolyte temperature

Table B
Specific gravity - battery fully discharged
1.098 at 100°F or 38°C electrolyte temperature
1.102 at 90°F or 32°C electrolyte temperature

1.106 *at* 80°*F or* 27°*C electrolyte temperature*
1.110 *at* 70°*F or* 21°*C electrolyte temperature*
1.114 *at* 60°*F or* 16°*C electrolyte temperature*
1.118 *at* 50°*F or* 10°*C electrolyte temperature*
1.122 *at* 40°*F or* 4°*C electrolyte temperature*
1.126 *at* 30°*F or* -1.5°*C electrolyte temperature*

4 Electrolyte replenishment

1 If the battery is in a fully charged state and one of the cells maintains a specific gravity reading which is 0.025 or lower than the others and a check of each cell has been made with a voltage meter to check for short circuits (a four to seven second test should give a steady reading of between 1.2 and 1.8 volts), then it is likely that electrolyte has been lost from the cell with the low reading at some time.
2 Top-up the cell with a solution of 1 part sulphuric acid to 2.5 parts of water. If the cell is already fully topped-up draw some electrolyte out of it with a pipette.
3 When mixing the sulphuric acid and water **never add water to sulphuric acid** - always pour the acid slowly onto the water in a glass container. **If water is added to sulphuric acid it will explode.**
4 Continue to top-up the cell with the freshly made electrolyte and to recharge the battery and check the hydrometer readings.

5 Battery charging

1 In winter time when a heavy demand is placed on the battery, such as when starting from cold, and much electrical equipment is continually in use, it is a good idea to occasionally have the battery fully charged from an external source at a rate of 3.5 to 4 amps.
2 Continue to charge the battery at this rate until no further rise in specific gravity is noted over a four hour period.

3 Alternatively, a trickle charger, charging at the rate of 1.5 amps can be safely used overnight.
4 Special rapid 'boost' charges which are claimed to restore the power of the battery in 1 to 2 hours are most dangerous unless they are thermostatically controlled as they can cause serious damage to the battery plates through overheating.
5 While charging the battery note that the temperature of the electrolyte should never exceed 100°F (37.8°C).

6 Alternator - general description

The main advantage of the alternator over a dynamo lies in its ability to provide a high charge at low revolutions.
An important feature of the alternator system is its ouput control, this being based on thick film hybrid integrated minor circuit techniques.
The alternator is of the rotating field, ventilated design. It comprises principally, a laminated stator on which is wound a star connected 3 phase output; and an 8 pole rotor carrying the field windings. The front and rear ends of the rotor shaft run in ball races each of which is lubricated for life, and natural finish die cast end brackets incorporating the mounting lugs.
The rotor is belt driven from the engine through a pulley keyed to the rotor shaft and a pressed steel fan adjacent to the pulley draws cooling air through the machine. This fan forms an integral part of the alternator specifications. It has been designed to provide adequate air flow with a minimum of noise and to withstand the high stresses associated with maximum speed.
The brush gear of the field system is mounted in the slip ring end brackets. Two carbon brushes bear against a pair of concentric brass slip rings carried on a moulded disc attached to the end of the rotor. Also attached to the slip ring end bracket are six silicone diodes connected in a three phase bridge to rectify the generated alternating current for use in charging the battery and supplying power to the electrical system.

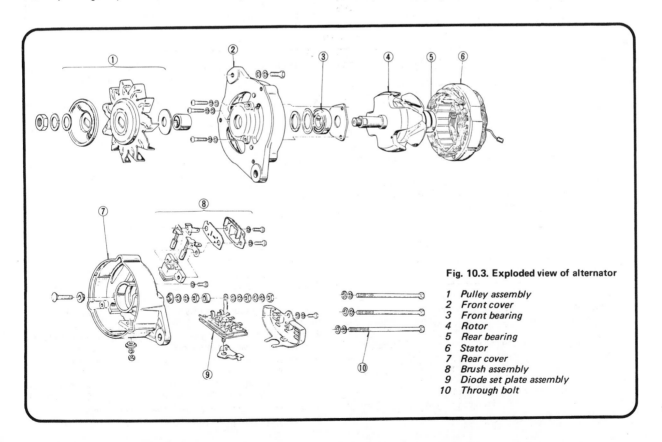

Fig. 10.3. Exploded view of alternator

1 *Pulley assembly*
2 *Front cover*
3 *Front bearing*
4 *Rotor*
5 *Rear bearing*
6 *Stator*
7 *Rear cover*
8 *Brush assembly*
9 *Diode set plate assembly*
10 *Through bolt*

Fig. 10.4. Alternator with pulley removed

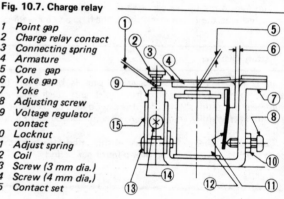

Fig. 10.5. Charge relay (right) and voltage regulator (left)

Fig. 10.6. Voltage regulator

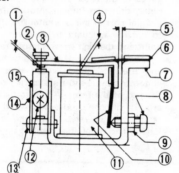

1 Point gap
2 Lower contact
3 Armature
4 Core gap
5 Yoke gap
6 Connecting spring
7 Yoke
8 Adjusting screw
9 Locknut
10 Adjust spring
11 Coil
12 Screw (3 mm) dia.
13 Screw (4 mm) dia.
14 Contact set
15 Upper contact

Fig. 10.7. Charge relay

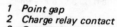

1 Point gap
2 Charge relay contact
3 Connecting spring
4 Armature
5 Core gap
6 Yoke gap
7 Yoke
8 Adjusting screw
9 Voltage regulator contact
10 Locknut
11 Adjust spring
12 Coil
13 Screw (3 mm dia.)
14 Screw (4 mm dia,)
15 Contact set

7 Alternator - maintenance

1 The equipment has been designed for the minimum amount of maintenance in service, the only items being subject to wear are the brushes and bearings.
2 Brushes should be examined after about 75,000 miles (120,000 km) and renewed if necessary. The bearings are pre-packed with grease for life and should not require further attention.
3 Check the 'V' belt drive regularly for correct adjustment which should be 0.394 - 0.590 in. (10 - 15 mm). Depress with the finger and thumb between the alternator and water pump pulleys.

8 Alternator - special procedures

Whenever the electrical system of the car is being attended to or an external means of starting the engine is used there are certain precautions that must be taken otherwise serious and expensive damage can result.
1 Always make sure that the negative terminal of the battery is earthed. If the terminal connections are accidentally reversed or if the battery has been reverse charged the alternator will burn out.
2 The output terminal of the alternator must never be earthed but should always be connected directly to the positive terminal of the battery.

3 Whenever the alternator is to be removed, or when disconnecting the terminals of the alternator circuit, always disconnect the battery first.
4 The alternator must never be operated without the battery to alternator cable connected.
5 If the battery is to be charged by external means always disconnect both battery cables before the external charger is connected.
6 Should it be necessary to use a booster charger or booster battery to start the engine always double check that the negative cables are connected to negative terminals and positive cables to positive terminals.

9 Alternator - removal and refitting

1 Disconnect both battery leads.
2 Make a note of the terminal connections at the rear of the alternator and disconnect the cables and terminal connector.
3 Undo and remove the alternator adjustment arm bolt, slacken the alternator mounting bolts and remove the 'V' drive belt from the pulley.
4 Remove the remaining two mounting bolts and carefully lift the alternator away from the car.
5 Take care not to knock or drop the alternator; this can cause irreparable damage.
6 Refitting the alternator is the reverse sequence to removal. Adjust the 'V' drive belt so that it has 0.394 - 0.590 in. (10 - 15 mm) maximum deflection between the alternator and water pump pulleys.

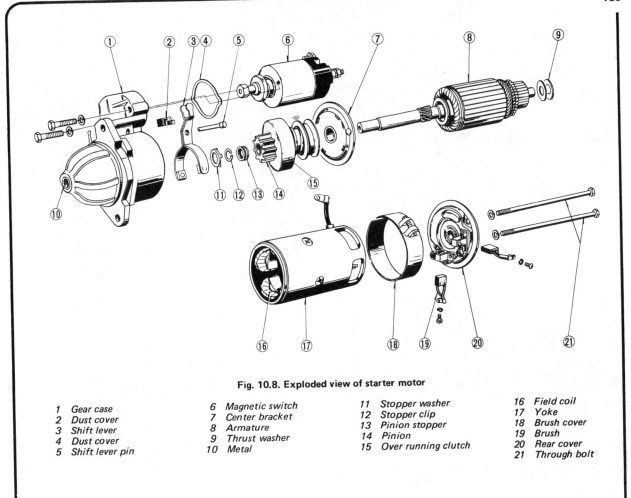

Fig. 10.8. Exploded view of starter motor

1	Gear case	6	Magnetic switch	11	Stopper washer	16	Field coil
2	Dust cover	7	Center bracket	12	Stopper clip	17	Yoke
3	Shift lever	8	Armature	13	Pinion stopper	18	Brush cover
4	Dust cover	9	Thrust washer	14	Pinion	19	Brush
5	Shift lever pin	10	Metal	15	Over running clutch	20	Rear cover
						21	Through bolt

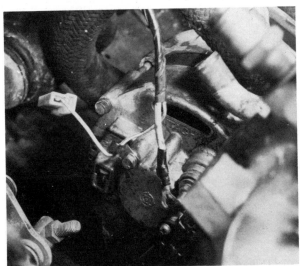

9.2 Disconnect the electrical leads

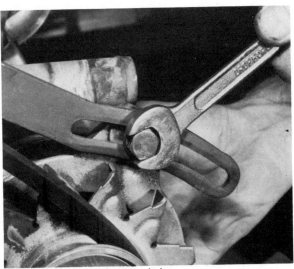

9.3A Removing the adjustment bolt ...

9.3B ... then the drivebelt

9.4A Remove the remaining bolts ...

9.4B ... then lift the alternator away

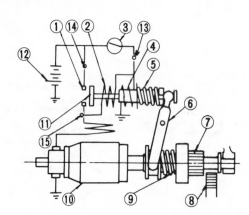

Fig. 10.9. Starter motor circuit

1	Stationary contact	6	Shift lever	11	Moving contact
2	Series coil	7	Pinion	12	Battery
3	Starting switch	8	Ring gear	13	'S' terminal
4	Shunt coil	9	Pinion sleeve spring	14	'B' terminal
5	Return spring	10	Armature	15	'M' terminal

Fig. 10.10. Removing the brush cover

Fig. 10.11. Removing the magnetic switch assembly

Fig. 10.12. Removing the brush cover and yoke

Fig. 10.13. Removing the armature assembly and shift lever

Fig. 10.14. Removing the clutch over-run assembly

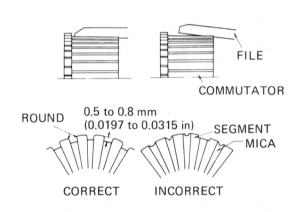

Fig. 10.15. Commutator under-cutting details

PLUNGER "L" DIMENSION
31.7 to 32.3mm (1.248 to 1.272 in)

Fig. 10.16. Measuring the plunger dimension

1   Adjusting nut   2   Plunger adjuster

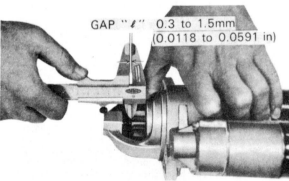

GAP "ℓ" 0.3 to 1.5mm
(0.0118 to 0.0591 in)

Fig. 10.17. Measuring plunger movement

10 Alternator - fault diagnosis and repair

Due to the specialist knowledge and equipment required to test and service an alternator it is recommended that if the performance is suspect, the car be taken to an automobile electrician who will have the facilities for such work. Because of this recommendation no further detailed service information is given.

11 Voltage regulator - general description

The regulator basically comprises a voltage regulator and a charge relay. The voltage regulator has two sets of contact points, lower and upper sets to control the alternator voltage. An armature plate placed between the two sets of contacts, moves upward, downward or vibrates. When closed the lower contacts complete the field circuit direct to earth, and the upper contacts when closed, complete the field circuit to earth through a field coil resistance and thereby regulates the alternator output.

The charge relay is basically similar to that of the voltage regulator. When the upper contacts are closed the ignition warning light extinguishes. The construction of the voltage regulator is basically identical to the charge relay. If the regulator performance is suspect the services of a reputable auto electrician should be sought.

12 Starter motor - general description

The starter motor comprises a solenoid, a lever, starter drive gear and the motor. The solenoid is fitted to the top of the motor. The plunger inside the solenoid is connected to a centre pivoting lever the other end of which is in contact with the drive sleeve and drive gear.

When the ignition switch is operated, current from the battery flows through the series and shunt solenoid coils thereby magnetizing the solenoid. The plunger is drawn into the solenoid so that it operates the lever and moves the drive pinion into the starter ring gear. The solenoid switch contacts close after the drive pinion is partially with the ring gear.

13 Starter motor - testing on engine

1 If the starter motor fails to operate then check the condition of the battery by turning on the headlights. If they glow brightly for several seconds and then gradually dim, the battery is in an undercharged condition.
2 If the headlights continue to glow brightly and it is obvious that the battery is in good condition, then check the tightness of the earth lead from the battery terminal to its connection on the body frame. Also check the positive battery lead connections. Check the tightness of the connections at the rear of the solenoid. If available check the wiring with a voltmeter or test light for breaks or short circuits.
3 If the wiring is in order check the starter motor for continuity using a voltmeter.
4 If the battery is fully charged, the wiring is in order and the motor electrical circuit continuous and it still fails to operate, then it will have to be removed from the engine for examination. Before this is done, however, make sure that the pinion has not jammed in mesh with the ring gear due either to a broken solenoid spring or dirty pinion gear splines. To release the pinion, engage a low gear (not automatic) and with the ignition switched off, rock the car backwards and forwards which should release the pinion from mesh with the ring gear, if the pinion still remains jammed the starter motor must be removed.

14 Starter motor - removal and refitting

1 Disconnect the cable from the battery negative terminal.

2 Disconnect the black and yellow wire from the 'S' terminal on the solenoid and the black cable from the 'B' terminal also on the end cover of the solenoid. Also disconnect the earthing cable from under one of the mounting bolts.
3 Unscrew and remove the two starter motor securing bolts, pull the starter forward, tilt it slightly to clear the motor shaft support from the flywheel ring gear and withdraw it.
4 Refitting is a reversal of removal.

15 Starter motor - dismantling, servicing and reassembly

1 Servicing operations should be limited to renewal of brushes, renewal of the solenoid, the overhaul of the starter drive gear and cleaning the commutator.
2 The major components of the starter should normally last the life of the unit and in the event of failure, a factory exchange replacement should be obtained.
3 The starter fitted to vehicles with automatic transmission is of heavy duty type but the descriptions given in this Section apply to both types.
4 Access to the brushes is obtained by slipping back the cover band. Unscrew and remove the screws which retain the brush lead tags. With an 'L' shaped roll pull aside the brush tension springs and pull the brushes from their holders.
5 Measure the overall length of each of the two brushes and where they are worn below the minimum recommended (see Specifications) renew them.
6 Ensure that each brush slides freely in its holder. If necessary, rub with a fine file and clean any accumulated carbon dust or grease from the holder with a fuel moistened rag.
7 Disconnect the cable which runs from the starter motor to the 'M' terminal on the solenoid cover. Withdraw the split pin and cotter pin from the shift fork and the two solenoid securing bolts. Remove the solenoid rearwards from the starter motor front housing.
8 Refitting a solenoid is a reversal of removal but the length of the plunger must be checked and adjusted if necessary. To do this, depress the plunger fully against a hard surface and measure the distance between the end of the plunger and the face of the solenoid body ('L' in Fig. 10.16).
9 Carry out any adjustment by slackening the nut (1) and rotating the pillar nut (2). Retighten the locknut when adjustment is complete.
10 Normally, the commutator may be cleaned by holding a piece of non-fluffy rag moistened with fuel against it as it is rotated by hand. If on inspection, the mica separators are level with the copper segments then they must be undercut by between 0.020 and 0.032 in. (0.50 and 0.81 mm).
11 Remove the brushes and solenoid as previously described. Unscrew and remove the two long bolts which secure the yoke to the front housing. Withdraw the yoke from the front housing, tapping it with a soft faced mallet if necessary to free it. Take great care not to damage the field coils of the yoke by catching them on the armature during removal.
12 Withdraw the armature with shift fork/pinion assembly attached.
13 Undercut the mica separators of the commutator using an old hacksaw blade ground to suit. The commutator may be polished with a piece of very fine glass paper - never use emery cloth as the carborundum particles will become embedded in the copper surfaces.
14 Refit the armature by reversing the removal procedure.
15 In the event of malfunction of pinion drive assembly, remove the armature as previously described in this Section. Prise the stop washer from the armature shaft using a screwdriver, detach the circlip from its groove and slide off the thrust washer, starter pinion and drive assembly.
16 Wash the components of the drive gear in paraffin and inspect for wear or damage, particularly to the pinion teeth and renew as appropriate. Refitting is a reversal of dismantling but stake a new stop washer in position and oil the sliding surfaces of

14.2A Disconnect these cables ...

14.2B ... and this earthing cable

14.3A Remove the mounting bolts ...

14.3B ... and lift the motor clear

the pinion assembly with a light oil, applied sparingly.
17 When the starter motor has been fully reassembled, actuate the solenoid which will throw the drive gear forward into its normal flywheel engagement position. Do this by connecting jumper leads between the battery negative terminal and the solenoid 'M' terminal and between the battery positive terminal end face of the drive pinion and the mating face of the thrust washer. This should be between 0.0118 and 0.0591 in. (0.30 and 1.49 mm) measured either with a vernier gauge or feeler gauge.

16 Starter motor bushes - inspection, removal and replacement

1 With the starter motor stripped down check the condition of the bushes. They should be renewed when they are sufficiently worn to allow visible side movement of the armature shaft.
2 The old bushes are simply driven out with a suitable drift and new bushes inserted by the same method.
3 As the bushes are of the phospher bronze type it is essential that they are allowed to stand in SAE 30 engine oil for at least 24 hours.

Fig. 10.18. Fusible links on some models only

1 Red fusible link for battery circuit
2 Green fusible link for left head lamp
3 Green fusible link for right head lamp

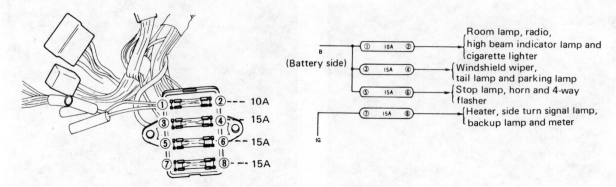

Fig. 10.19. Fuse distribution on some models

Note: Other models are fitted with an eight-way
fusebox and without any fusible links

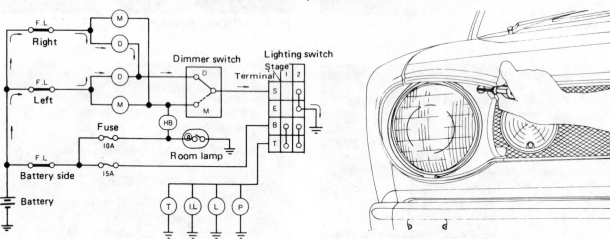

Fig. 10.20. Fusible link circuit details

Fig. 10.21. Adjusting the headlamps

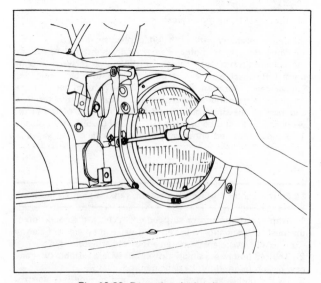

Fig. 10.22. Removing the headlamps

17 Fuses and fusible links

1   The main fusebox is located under the instrument panel. It
contains three 15 amp cartridge type fuses and one 10 amp. The
accessories and circuits protected by the individual fuses are
indicated on the fusebox cover and in Fig. 10.19.

2   Three fusible links are fitted: one in each headlamp circuit
and one in the starting, charging and ignition circuit. Each
headlamp circuit has a green link, while the starting circuit has a
red link. A melted fusible like can be detected by either a visual
inspection or carrying out a continuity test with a battery and
test lamp.

3   In the event of a fuse or fusible link blowing, always establish
the cause before fitting a new one. This is most likely to be due
to faulty insulation somewhere in the wiring circuit. Always
carry a spare fuse for each rating and never be tempted to
substitute a piece of wire or a nail for the correct fuse or a fire
may be caused or, at least, the electrical component ruined.

4   Some models are fitted with an eight-way fusebox and details
of circuit distribution are shown on the cover. When this type of
fusebox is fitted the fusible links are omitted.

18 Flasher circuit - fault diagnosis and rectification

1   The flasher unit is a small metal container located under the

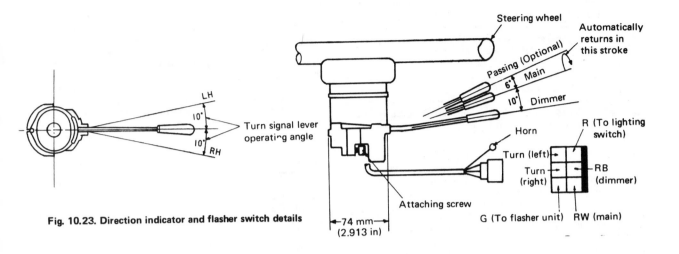

Fig. 10.23. Direction indicator and flasher switch details

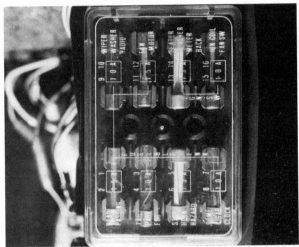

17.4 Fusebox found on some models

dashboard near to the fusebox. The unit is actuated by the direction indicator switch.

2   If the flasher unit fails to operate, or works very slowly or rapidly, check out the flasher indicator circuit as detailed below, before assuming that there is a fault in the unit:

a) Examine the direction indicator bulbs both front and rear for broken filaments.

b) If the external flashers are working but either of the internal flasher warning lights have ceased to function, check the filaments in the warning light bulbs and replace with a new bulb if necessary.

c) If a flasher bulb is sound but does not work check all the flasher circuit connections with the aid of the wiring diagram found at the end of this Chapter.

d) With the ignition switched on check that the current is reaching the flasher unit by connecting a voltmeter between the 'plus' terminal and earth. If it is found that current is reaching the unit connect the two flasher unit terminals together and operate the direction indicator switch. If one of the flasher warning lights comes on this proves that the flasher unit itself is at fault and must be replaced as it is not possible to dismantle and repair it.

19 Hazard warning lamp circuits - description

1   This system comprises a switch and independent flasher unit. When the switch is actuated, all the direction indicator flashers illuminate simultaneously as a warning to other drivers that the vehicle is stationary due to breakdown.

20 Headlamp flasher circuit - description

Irrespective of whether the headlamp switch is off or on, the headlamps may be flashed for signalling purposes by depressing the tapered knob on the end of the direction indicator switch.

21 Headlamp units - removal and refitting

1   Sealed beam, double filament units are fitted which in the event of failure must be renewed as units.
2   Remove the three headlamp moulding screws and take off the moulding (see Fig. 10.22). Take out four headlamp screws and remove the headlamp.
3   Pull the sealed beam unit forward far enough to detach the connecting plug and remove it.
4   Refitting is a reversal of removal but ensure that the word 'TOP' is correctly located.

22 Headlamps - adjustment

1   Although it is preferable to have the headlamps correctly set on modern optical setting equipment, the following procedure will provide a reasonable alternative, carried out in conditions of darkness.
2   Place the vehicle on level ground, (unloaded and with the tyres correctly inflated), square to and 33 ft (10 metres) from a wall or garage door.
3   Make two marks on the wall, each 22 inches (560 mm) either side of the vehicle centre-line and 26 inches (662 mm) above the ground.
4   Remove the rims from the headlamps to expose the lateral and vertical adjustment screws.
5   Switch the headlamps to full (main) beam and mask one of the lamps. Adjust the screws of the unmasked lamp until the maximum intensity of the light pattern is centred on the mark on the wall.
6   Mask the lamp which has been adjusted and repeat the operations on the other headlamp. Finally switch off and refit the rims.

23 Front indicator and parking lamps - bulb renewal

1 Remove the two screws which secure the lens and remove the bulbs which are of normal bayonet type.

24 Rear lamp cluster - bulb renewal

1 Tail, stop and flasher indicator bulbs are removed from the rear of the lamp cluster without the necessity of withdrawing the lens or lamp unit.

100A models
2 Remove the bulb holder by turning it in an anticlockwise direction and pulling it from the lamp housing. The bulb is fitted by the normal bayonet method.
3 The complete lamp assembly can be removed from inside the boot, if required, by removing the retaining nuts. Some later models are secured by three screws through the exterior fitment.

120A models
4 From inside the luggage compartment, remove the screws and nuts securing the protective cover of the relevant lamp cluster (photos). Remove the cover.
5 Remove the single screw securing the plastic bulb holder, to the car body (photo). Detach the bulb holder.
6 The two bulbs are now accessible (photo). Each can be removed using a push-and-twist action.

25 Side flasher and license plate lamp - bulb renewal

1 The bulbs of these two units are accessible after removal of the lens securing screws and lens.

26 Lighting switch - removal and refitting

1 Disconnect the cable from the battery negative terminal.
2 Working from behind the instrument panel, disconnect the connector from the lighting switch.
3 From the front of the instrument panel, depress the switch knob and turn the switch assembly anticlockwise to remove it.
4 Installation of a new switch is a reversal of removal.

27 Direction indicator and headlamp flasher switch - removal and refitting

1 Disconnect the cable from the battery negative terminal.
2 Disconnect the switch by uncoupling the connector on the wiring harness and disconnecting the flasher relay.

3 Remove the horn ring or bar and push-buttons, according to type, by unscrewing the retaining screws from the reverse side.
4 Unscrew the steering wheel retaining nut and remove the steering wheel. If it is tight on its splines, use a suitable puller but protect the plastic surfaces of the steering wheel hub.
5 Unscrew the retaining screws and remove the steering column shroud.
6 Unscrew and remove the switch retaining screws and remove the switch from the steering column.
7 Refitting is a reversal of removal but note the switch locating hole in the steering column.

28 Horns - description, fault diagnosis and adjustment

1 The single horn is mounted on the battery support. Normal maintenance consists of checking the security of the connecting leads to the horn and horn relay.
2 When horn does not operate (no sound is generated), inspect as follows:

A Battery
1) Check fuses (5) - (6) (15A).
2) See if current is applied to horn relay B-terminal.

B Horn
Disconnect green/white (GW) cable from horn, connect horn directly to positive (+) terminal of battery with a jumper lead and earth horn. If horn sounds, horn is normal.

C Horn relay
1) Disconnect black (B) cable from horn relay S-terminal.
2) Connect horn relay S-terminal to negative (−) terminal of battery with a jumper lead. If horn sounds, horn relay is normal.

Note: How to earth horn - Note that earth cable is connected to transmission selector lever installation bolt and steering gear clamp in this vehicle.
3 If the horns sound continuously then check the horn ring or push-button springs have not broken. If these are satisfactory, renew the relay.
4 Adjustment to the horn note can be made by loosening the locknut and turning the screw located on the back of the horn.

29 Combined ignition switch and steering column lock - removal and refitting

1 The unit is a combined lock and ignition switch, secured by a special clamp with shear-head bolts. A key-operated peg engages in a slot in the inner steering column. In the event of loss of keys without a record having been kept of the number or malfunction of the lock, then it should be removed as follows:

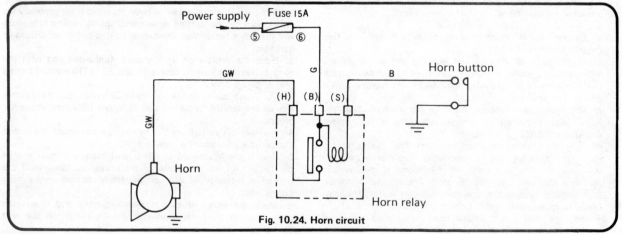

Fig. 10.24. Horn circuit

21.2A Remove the moulding ...

21.2B ... then the headlamp screws ...

21.2C ... then detach the connector

23.1 Removing the lens

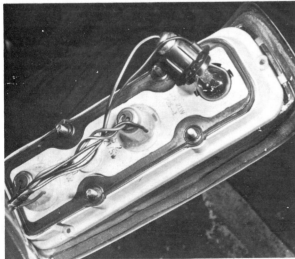
24.2 Rear lamp cluster bulb removal

24.3 Removing the complete lamp cluster

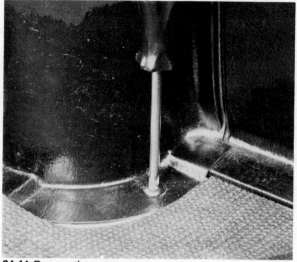

24.4A Remove the screws ...

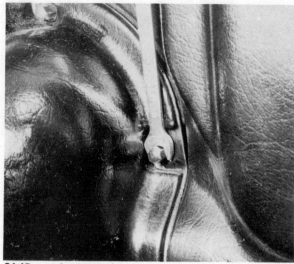

24.4B ... and nuts securing the protective cover

24.5 Unscrew the bulb holder retaining screw ...

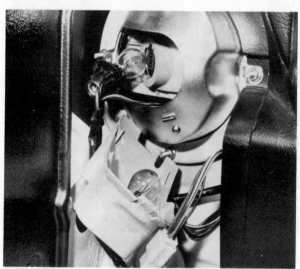

24.6 ... and detach the bulb holder. The two bulbs are now accessible

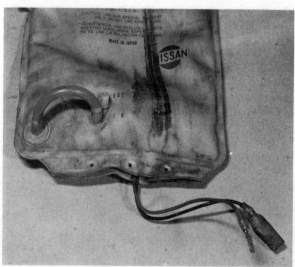

31.2A Windscreen washer bag and integral motor

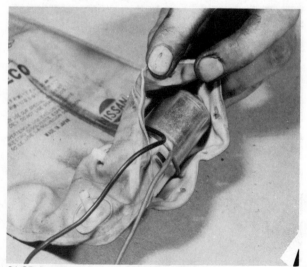

31.2B Access to the motor for replacement purposes

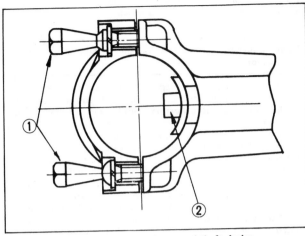

2 Disconnect the battery earth lead and steering column cowl.
3 Disconnect the ignition switch cables.
4 Centre punch each of the centre of the shear-head bolts. Do not remove the countersunk screws.
5 Drill out the centres of the shear-bolt heads.
6 Release the countersunk screws and remove the two halves of the unit.
7 Refitting is carried out by first setting the lock to the 'park' position so that the locking peg is disengaged.
8 Fit the new lock so that its locating tag engages correctly in the steering column hole and insert the shear-head bolts and countersunk screws finger-tight at this stage.
9 Check the operation of the lock for smoothness and engagement by inserting the key and if necessary, give the lock unit a slight twist in either direction. When satisfied that the unit is correctly positioned, fully tighten the countersunk screws and tighten the shear-head bolts sufficiently to shear their heads.
10 Reconnect the ignition cable, the battery earth lead and refit the steering column cowls.

Fig. 10.25. Steering column anti-theft device

1 Special screw   2 Locking spindle

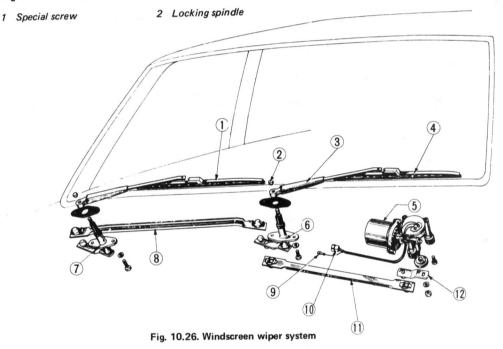

Fig. 10.26. Windscreen wiper system

1 Wiper blade (right	4 Wiper blade (left)	7 Pivot No. 2	10 Connector
2 Nut	5 Wiper motor	8 Connecting rod No. 2	11 Connecting rod No. 1
3 Wiper arm	6 Pivot No. 1	9 Ground	12 Motor arm

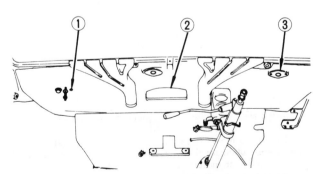

Fig. 10.27. Wiper motor and pivot installation holes

1 For wiper motor   3 For No. 2 pivot
2 For No. 1 pivot

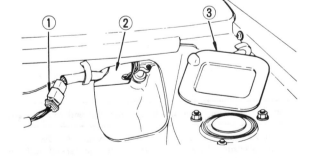

Fig. 10.28. Wiper motor access hole

1 Wiper motor harness connector   2 Wiper motor
3 Wiper motor cover

30 Anti-theft device - removal and refitting

1 This device may be fitted on some models in conjunction with the combined ignition/steering column lock. The circuit of this warning system is closed when the door is opened and the steering is in the unlocked state. A warning buzzer sounds to indicate unauthorized entry to the vehicle.
2 In the event of failure of components of the system, disconnect the two cables by pulling their connectors apart, remove the cap at the side of the steering lock, loosen the two switch securing screws and remove the switch.
3 The buzzer is located on the left hand side and at the rear of the facia panel. The door switch is a push fit in the hinge pillar.

31 Windscreen wiper and washer - description and maintenance

1 The wiper motor is of two speed type. It is mounted on the engine compartment rear bulkhead and drives the wiper arms through linkage located behind the facia panel.
2 The electrically operated windscreen washer unit (motor, bag and pump) is located to the left front of the engine compartment.
3 A combined wiper/washer switch is fitted. The switch operates the wipers by a two position push-pull action and the washer by twisting the switch knob clockwise. The washer knob is spring loaded and it should not be held in the 'ON' position for more than 30 seconds at a time.
4 At two yearly intervals or earlier if the screen is not being wiped effectively, renew the wiper blades.
5 Never operate the washer without liquid being in the bag.

parked position and tighten the arm securing nut.
4 Blade removal is shown in the associated photo.

33 Windscreen wiper mechanism - fault diagnosis and rectification

Should the windscreen wipers fail, or work very slowly then check the terminals for loose connections, and make sure the insulation of the external wiring is not broken or cracked. If this is in order then check the current the motor is taking by connecting a 1-20 volt ammeter in series in the circuit and turning on the wiper switch. Consumption should be less than 1.5 amps on low speed, and less than 2.0 amps on high.

If no current is flowing check that the fuse has not blown. The correct rating is 10 amps. If it has check the wiring of the motor and other electrical circuits serviced by this fuse for short circuits. If the fuse is in good condition check the wiper switch.

Should the motor take a very low current ensure that the battery is fully charged. If the motor takes a high current then it is an indication that there is an internal fault or partially seized linkage.

It is possible for the motor to be stripped and overhauled but the availability of spare parts could present a problem. Either take a faulty unit to the local automobile electricians or obtain a replacement unit.

34 Wiper motor and linkage - removal and replacement

1 Periodically check the wiper linkage for wear and renew as necessary.

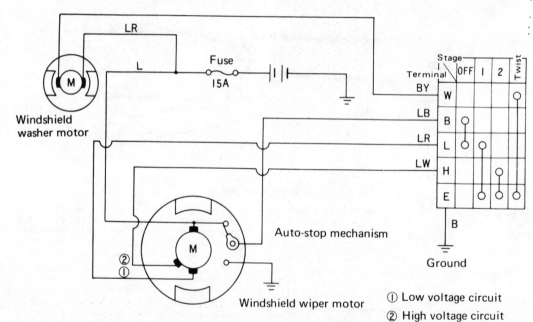

Fig. 10.29. Windscreen wiper and washer circuit

32 Windscreen wiper arm and blade - removal and replacement

1 Before removing a wiper arm, turn the windscreen switch on and off to ensure the arms are in their normal parked position parallel with the bottom of the screen and the outer tips 0.787 in. (20 mm) from the rubber.
2 To remove the arms, pivot the arm back, slacken the arm securing nut and detach the arm from the spindle.
3 When replacing an arm, place it so it is in its correct relative

2 In the event of failure of the wiper motor, check for a blown fuse and security of electrical leads.
3 To remove the motor, first remove the motor access panel on the engine bulkhead; then unscrew and remove the nut which secures the wiper motor arm to the linkage crank; this is located behind the facia inside the vehicle.
4 From outside the vehicle, unscrew and remove the wiper arm securing bolts and lift the wiper arms off their driving shafts.
5 The wiper motor may be removed by first detaching the

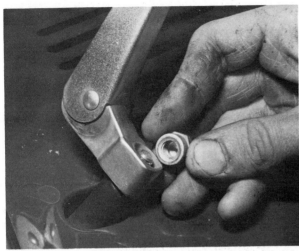
32.2 Removing a windscreen wiper arm

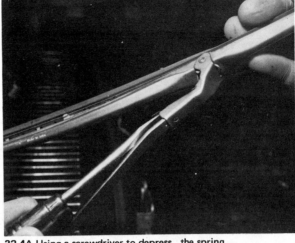
32.4A Using a screwdriver to depress the spring ...

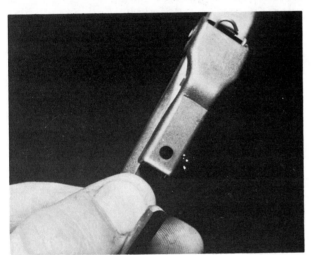
32.4B ... and then remove the blade

35.7 Instrument panel pulled forward for access to the gauges and lamp bulbs

electrical connector from it and unscrewing and removing the three mounting bolts. It is recommended that the wiper motor is exchanged for a factory reconditioned unit rather than attempt to repair a faulty assembly.

6 Refitting is a reversal of removal but when fitting the wiper arms ensure that they are positioned at the bottom when the motor is in the 'OFF' (parked position) before tightening the securing bolts.

35 Instrument panel - removal and refitting

1 This Section describes the removal of the instrument panel. Removal of the major facia panel assembly is described in Chapter 12.
2 Disconnect the cable from the battery negative terminal.
3 Push in and turn anticlockwise each of the following switches to remove them and their escutcheon discs: the windscreen wiper switch, the cigarette lighter (if fitted) and the choke knob.
4 Insert the hand into the rear of the instrument panel and disconnect the cigarette lighter cable and remove the lighter switch completely.
5 Remove the radio and heater control knobs which are secured to their shafts and levers by grub screws.

6 Unscrew and remove the screws which secure the instrument panel to the main facia.
7 Pull the instrument panel forward sufficiently to enable the speedometer cable to be disconnected from the speedometer head and the twelve pin electrical connecting plug and socket to be separated. Withdraw the instrument panel.
8 The instrumentation is secured to the rear of the panel by four screws and individual instruments may be removed from this sub assembly after unscrewing the small retaining screws.
9 Indicator/warning lamp holders are now accessible and may be withdrawn for bulb renewal simply by pulling them from their sockets.
10 Refitting the instruments and panel is a reversal of removal.

36 Front seat belt switches

1 On vehicles operating in certain territories, a contact switch is incorporated in each front seat. Its purpose is to prevent the starting of the engine by means of an inhibitor switch and to illuminate a warning sign in the vehicle interior unless with the weight of a passenger sitting in a seat the safety belt is securely fastened.

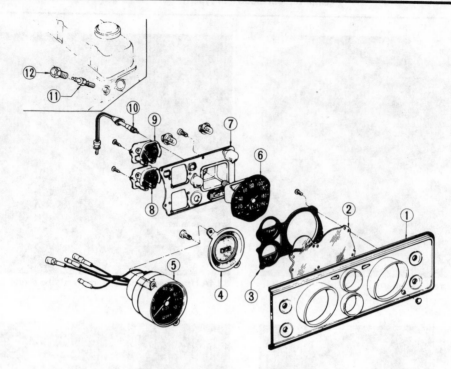

Fig. 10.30. Exploded view of instrument panel

1 *Meter cover*	7 *Meter case*
2 *Front cover*	8 *Fuel gauge*
3 *Shadow plate*	9 *Water temperature gauge*
4 *Tachometer cover*	10 *Speedometer cable*
5 *Tachometer (optional)*	11 *Thermal transmitter unit*
6 *Speedometer*	12 *Ground nut*

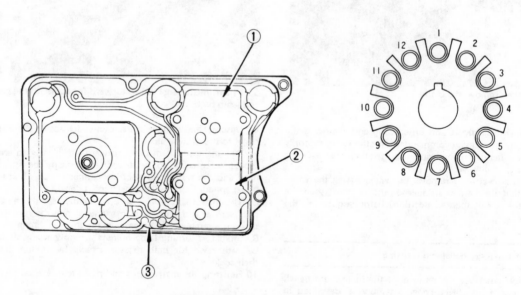

Fig. 10.31. Details of instrument panel rear

1 *Water temperature gauge*
2 *Fuel gauge*
3 *Meter connector pin layout*

CONNECTOR PIN DETAILS

No.	Printed circuit board side	Connector side (wire harness)	Cable colour
1	Meter illumination lamp	Lighting switch	R
2	Turn signal indicator lamp (right)	Turn signal switch	GB
3	Water temperature gauge	Thermal transmitter	YW
4	Ground	Ground	B
5	Power supply (Ignition circuit)	Fuse (8)	Y
6	Fuel gauge	Fuel gauge, fuel tank unit	YB
7	Turn signal indicator lamp (left)	Turn signal switch	GL
8	High beam indicator lamp	Turn signal switch, main beam	RW
9	Oil pressure warning lamp	Oil pressure switch	YL
10	———	———	———
11	High beam indicator lamp	Fuse (2)	RY
12	———	———	———

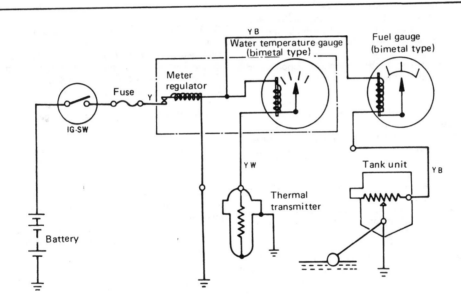

Fig. 10.33. Tachometer connections (if fitted)

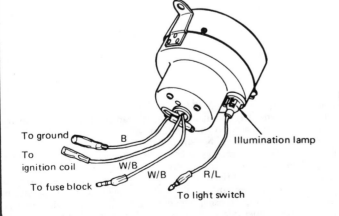

Fig. 10.32 Water temperature and fuel gauge wiring

2 The seat switches should be adjusted so that (using a test bulb) a weight of 24 lbs (10.88 kg) placed on a seat will close the switch contacts.

37 Heated rear window

1 Fitted as an option, the heater element is controlled by a switch and indicator lamp fitted under the left-hand edge of the facia panel. The system is wired in conjunction with the ignition switch to prevent the heater being left on when the vehicle is parked.
2 The electric supply cable is routed on the floor inside the vehicle and on the nearside. A break in the heating element can be repaired by your Datsun dealer using conductive silver composition (Dupont 4817) without the expense of a new rear window being incurred.

38 Clock - testing, removal and replacement

1 The clock is an optional fitting on early models but is basic on more recent versions.
2 If the clock fails to work, check the blue cable to verify the presence of 12 volts, using a test lamp or voltmeter. If this is satisfactory, check the black cable for a good earth connection. If the clock is not illuminated suspect the red/white cable connection.
3 If all the cables are satisfactory, and the power supplies and earth are present at the clock terminals, then the fault must lie in the clock.
4 Remove the clock by releasing the two screws that secure it to the instrument panel. No further breakdown is possible and a replacement unit should be obtained.
Note: If the fuse that supplies the clock is faulty, several other circuits will also be defective, including the interior light, the cigarette lighter and the beam indicator.

39 Radio - removal and adjustment

1 The radio is an optional fitting on early models but is basic on later versions.
2 To remove the radio, push the control knobs and turn anti-clockwise to remove. Remove the front-plate and disconnect the power supply, speaker and aerial cables from the radio. Remove the attachment screw from the bracket and withdraw the radio.
3 When radio is installed on the vehicle or when the aerial is replaced, adjust the aerial trimmer adjusting screw on the radio bottom in accordance with the following instructions:

   a) Fully extend aerial.
   b) Turn tuning dial and set frequency to or about 1,400 KC. (Noise may be received but it may be disregarded.)
   c) Do not tune completely to a station, but slightly off so that reception is not perfect.
   d) Turn aerial trimmer (indicated on aerial cable socket) slowly to both sides, and set it to a position where receiving sensitivity is highest.

4 If one is fitting an aerial for the first time, ensure that it is sited as far as possible from the distributor or other sources of interference, such as the alternator. Because of this, a position at the rear of the vehicle is recommended, providing that one can obtain the necessary protected run for the aerial lead to the radio. It will probably pay to take specialist advice on this point.

40 Speedometer head - removal and replacement

1 Refer to Section 35, and remove the instrument cluster lid.

2 If an odometer is fitted remove the 'trip' control knob.
3 Undo and remove the six screws and lift away the printed circuit housing together with the speedometer head, water temperature gauge and fuel gauge.
4 Undo and remove the two screws securing the speedometer head to the printed circuit housing. Lift away the speedometer head.
5 Refitting the speedometer head is the reverse sequence to removal.

41 Fuel and water temperature gauges - general description

1 The fuel gauge circuit comprises a tank sender unit located in the fuel tank (Chapter 3) and the fuel gauge. The sender unit has a float attached and this rides on the surface of the petrol in the tank. At the end of the float arm is a contact and rheostat which control current flowing to the fuel gauge.
2 The water temperature gauge circuit comprises a meter and thermal transmitter which is screwed into the side of the engine cylinder block. This is fitted with a thermistor element which converts any cooling system water temperature variation to a resistance. This therefore controls the current flowing to the meter.
3 The fuel gauge and water temperature gauge are provided with a bi-metal arm and heater coil. When the ignition is switched on, current flows so heating the coil. With this heat the bi-metal arm is distorted and therefore moves the pointer.
4 Because a slight tolerance may occur on the fuel or water temperature gauge due to a fluctuation in voltage a voltage regulator is used to supply a constant voltage resulting in more consistent readings. The output voltage to the meter circuits is 8 volts.
5 If it is found that both the fuel gauge and water temperature gauges operate inaccurately then the voltage regulator should be suspect.

42 Fuel and water temperature gauges - removal and replacement

1 Refer to Section 35, and remove the instrument cluster lid.
2 Undo and remove the screws securing the meter to the printed circuit housing. Lift away the meter.
3 Refitting the meter is the reverse sequence to removal.

43 Warning lights - general information

Oil pressure warning light

A switch is fitted to the engine lubrication system so that with the ignition switched on, a warning lamp will light when the engine is either stationary or the oil pressure has fallen below 5.7 - 8.5 lb in^2 (0.4 - 0.6 kg cm^2. When the engine is running normally and the oil pressure passes the minimum pressure mark so the pressure switch opens the circuit and the light is extinguished.

Handbrake warning light (LHD models)

Whenever the handbrake is applied and the ignition switched on, the warning lamp will light. When the handbrake is released so the light is extinguished.
On some models, this light is also used as a warning light to indicate that there is a leak in the brake hydraulic system. When a pressure difference between the front and rear brake line reaches a pre-set limit the switch in the brake line is operated by line pressure causing the contacts to close and the light to glow. For further information on the switch, refer to Chapter 9.

44 Fault diagnosis - electrical system

Symptom	Reason/s	Remedy
Starter motor fails to turn engine	Battery discharged	Charge battery.
	Battery defective internally	Fit new battery.
	Battery terminal leads loose or earth lead not securely attached to body	Check and tighten leads.
	Loose or broken connections in starter motor circuit	Check all connections and tighten any that are loose.
	Starter motor switch or solenoid faulty	Test and replace faulty components with new.
	Starter motor pinion jammed in mesh with flywheel gear ring	Disengage pinion by turning squared end of armature shaft.
	Starter brushes badly worn, sticking or brush wires loose	Examine brushes, replace as necessary, tighten down brush wires.
	Commutator dirty, worn or burnt	Clean commutator, recut if badly burnt.
	Starter motor armature faulty	Overhaul starter motor, fit new armature.
	Field coils earthed	Overhaul starter motor.
Starter motor turns engine very slowly	Battery in discharged condition	Charge battery.
	Starter brushes badly worn, sticking, or brush wires loose	Examine brushes, replace as necessary, tighten down brush wires.
	Loose wires in starter motor circuit	Check wiring and tighten as necessary.
Starter motor operates without turning engine	Starter motor pinion sticking on the screwed sleeve	Remove starter motor, clean starter motor drive.
	Pinion or flywheel gear teeth broken or worn	Fit new gear ring to flywheel, and new pinion to starter motor drive.
Starter motor noisy or excessively rough	Pinion or flywheel gear teeth broken or worn	Fit new gear teeth to flywheel, or new pinion to starter motor drive.
	Starter drive main spring broken	Dismantle and fit new main spring.
	Starter motor retaining bolts loose	Tighten starter motor securing bolts. Fit new spring washer if necessary.
Battery will not hold charge for more than a few days	Battery defective internally	Remove and fit new battery.
	Electrolyte level too low or electrolyte too weak due to leakage.	Top up electrolyte level to just above plates
	Plate separators no longer fully effective	Remove and fit new battery.
	Battery plates severely sulphated	Remove and fit new battery.
	Fan/alternator belt slipping	Check belt for wear, replace if necessary, and tighten.
	Battery terminal connections loose or corroded	Check terminals for tightness, and remove all corrosion.
	Alternator not charging properly	Take car to specialist.
	Short in lighting circuit causing continual battery drain	Trace and rectify.
	Regulator unit not working correctly	Take car to specialist.
Battery runs flat in a few days	Fan belt loose and slipping or broken	Check, replace and tighten as necessary.
	Alternator faulty	Take car to specialist.

Failure of individual electrical equipment to function correctly is dealt with alphabetically, item-by-item, under the headings listed below

Fuel gauge

Fuel gauge gives no reading	Fuel tank empty!	Fill fuel tank.
	Electric cable between tank sender unit and gauge earthed or loose	Check cable for earthing and joints for tightness.
	Fuel gauge case not earthed	Ensure case is well earthed.
	Fuel gauge supply cable interrupted	Check and replace cable if necessary.
	Fuel gauge unit broken	Replace fuel gauge.
Fuel gauge registers full all the time	Electric cable between tank unit and gauge broken or disconnected.	Check over cable and repair as necessary.

Horn

Horn operates all the time	Horn push either earthed or stuck down	Disconnect battery earth. Check and rectify source of trouble.
	Horn cable to horn push earthed	Disconnect battery earth. Check and rectify source of trouble.

Horn fails to operate	Blown fuse	Check and renew if broken. Ascertain cause.
	Cable or cable connection loose, broken or disconnected	Check all connections for tightness and cables for breaks.
	Horn has an internal fault	Remove and overhaul horn.
Horn emits intermittent or unsatisfactory noise	Cable connections loose	Check and tighten all connections
	Horn incorrectly adjusted	Adjust horn until best tone obtained.

Lights

Lights do not come on	If engine not running, battery discharged	Push-start car, charge battery.
	Light bulb filament burnt out or bulbs broken	Test bulbs in live bulb holder.
	Wire connections loose, disconnected or broken	Check all connections for tightness and wire cable for breaks.
	Light switch shorting or otherwise faulty	By-pass light switch to ascertain if fault is in switch and fit new switch as appropriate.
Lights come on but fade out	If engine not running battery discharged	Push-start car and charge battery (not automatics).
Lights give very poor illumination	Lamp glasses dirty	Clean glasses.
	Reflector tarnished or dirty	Fit new reflectors.
	Lamps badly out of adjustment	Adjust lamps correctly.
	Incorrect bulb with too low wattage fitted	Remove bulb and replace with correct grade
	Existing bulbs old and badly discoloured	Renew bulb units.
	Electrical wiring too thin not allowing full current to pass	Re-wire lighting system.
Lights work erratically - flashing on and off, especially over bumps	Battery terminals or earth connections loose	Tighten battery terminals and earth connection.
	Lights not earthing properly	Examine and rectify.
	Contacts in light switch faulty	By-pass light switch to ascertain if fault is in switch and fit new switch as appropriate.

Wiper motor

Wiper motor fails to work	Blown fuse	Check and replace fuse if necessary.
	Wire connections loose, disconnected or broken	Check wiper wiring. Tighten loose connections.
	Brushes badly worn	Remove and fit new brushes.
	Armature worn or faulty	If electricity at wiper motor remove and overhaul and fit replacement armature.
	Fuel coils faulty	Purchase reconditioned wiper motor.
Wiper motor works very slowly	Commutator dirty, greasy or burnt	Clean commutator thoroughly
	Drive to wheelboxes too bent or unlubricated	Examine drive and straighten out severe curvature. Lubricate.
	Wheelbox spindle binding or damaged	Remove, overhaul, or fit replacement.
	Armature bearing dry or unaligned	Replace with new bearings correctly aligned
	Armature badly worn or faulty	Remove, overhaul, or fit replacement armature.
Wiper motor works slowly and takes little current	Brushes badly worn	Remove and fit new brushes.
	Commutator dirty, greasy, or burnt	Clean commutator thoroughly
	Armature badly worn or faulty	Remove and overhaul armature or fit replacement.
Wiper motor works but wiper blades remain static	Driving cable rack disengaged or faulty	Examine and if faulty, replace.
	Wheelbox gear and spindle damaged or worn	Examine and if faulty, replace.
	Wiper motor gearbox parts badly worn	Ovehaul or fit new gearbox.

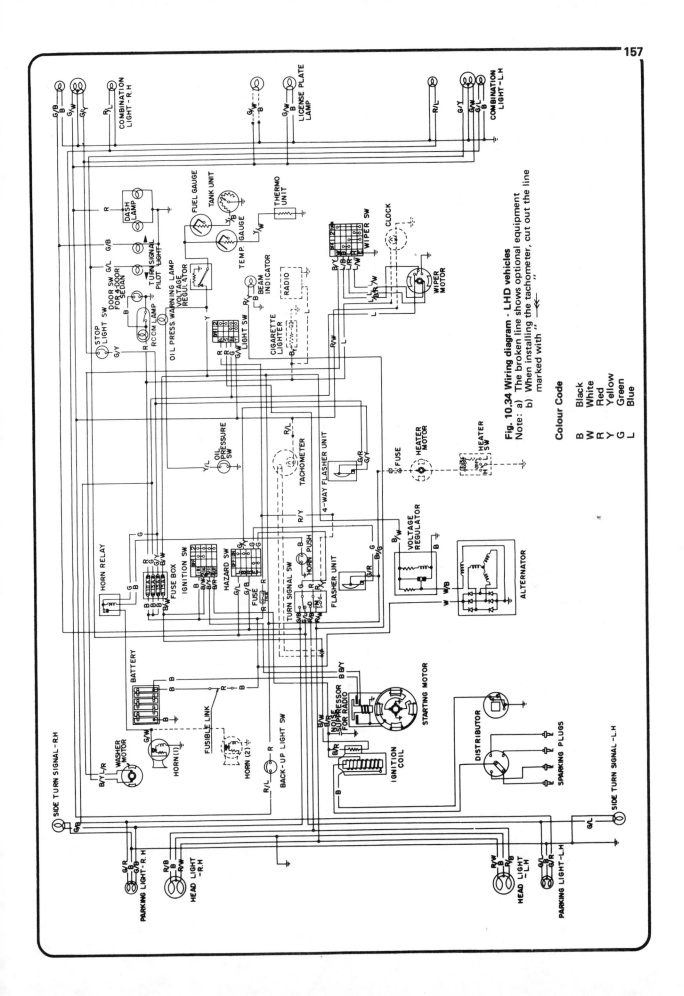

Fig. 10.34 Wiring diagram - LHD vehicles
Note: a) The broken line shows optional equipment
b) When installing the tachometer, cut out the line
marked with " "

Colour Code

B	Black
W	White
R	Red
Y	Yellow
G	Green
L	Blue

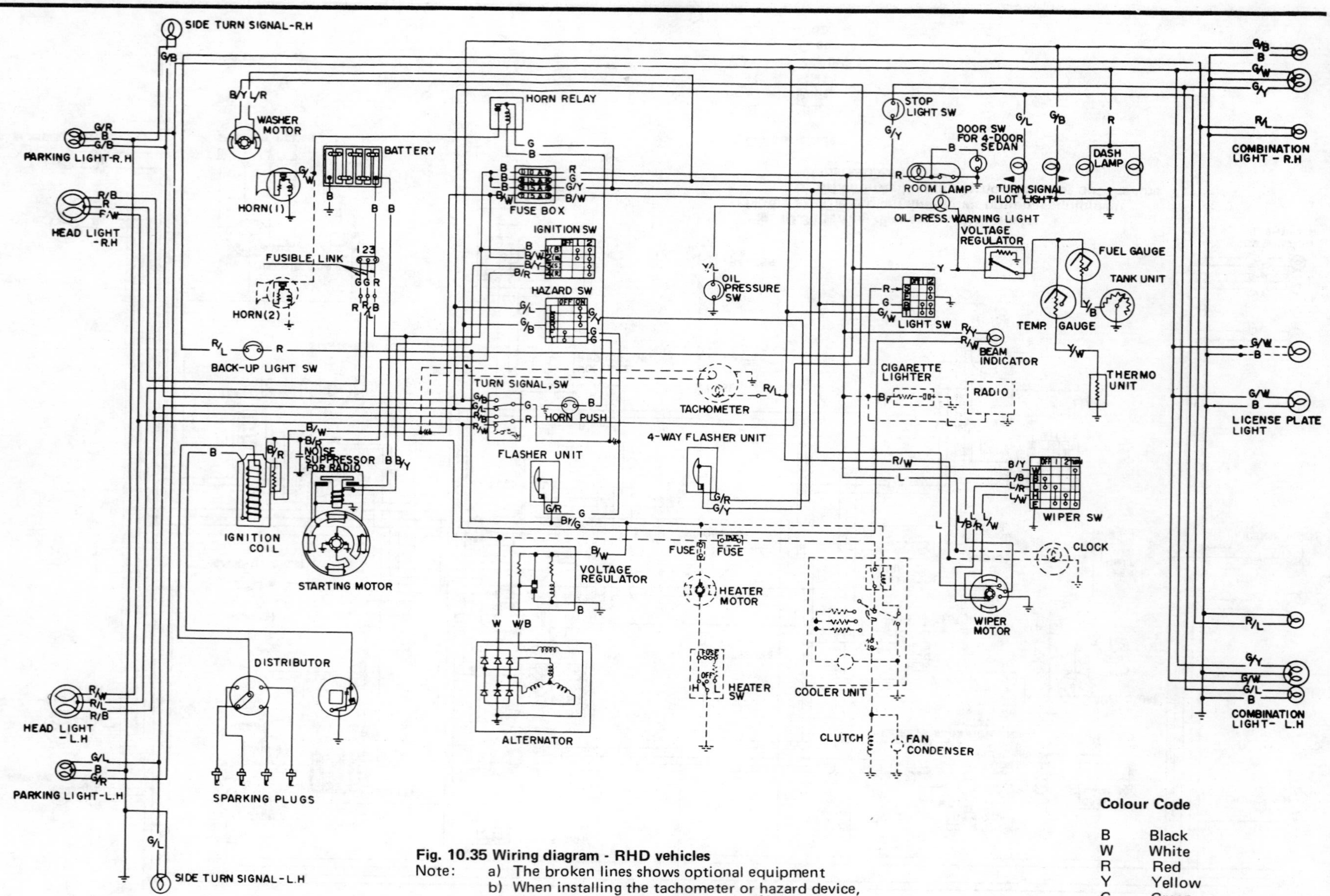

Colour Code

B	Black
W	White
R	Red
Y	Yellow
G	Green
L	Blue

COMBINATION LIGHT - R.H

LICENSE PLATE LIGHT

COMBINATION LIGHT - L.H

DASH LAMP

FUEL GAUGE

TANK UNIT

THERMO UNIT

TEMP. GAUGE

WIPER SW

CLOCK

WIPER MOTOR

STOP LIGHT SW

DOOR SW FOR 4-DOOR SEDAN

ROOM LAMP

TURN SIGNAL PILOT LIGHT

OIL PRESS. WARNING LIGHT

VOLTAGE REGULATOR

LIGHT SW

CIGARETTE LIGHTER

RADIO

BEAM INDICATOR

FAN CONDENSER

CLUTCH

COOLER UNIT

OIL PRESSURE SW

TACHOMETER

4-WAY FLASHER UNIT

HEATER MOTOR

HEATER SW

FUSE

HORN RELAY

FUSE BOX

IGNITION SW

HAZARD SW

TURN SIGNAL SW

HORN PUSH

FLASHER UNIT

VOLTAGE REGULATOR

ALTERNATOR

BATTERY

FUSIBLE LINK

WASHER MOTOR

HORN (1)

HORN (2)

BACK-UP LIGHT SW

NOISE SUPPRESSOR FOR RADIO

STARTING MOTOR

IGNITION COIL

DISTRIBUTOR

SPARKING PLUGS

SIDE TURN SIGNAL - R.H

SIDE TURN SIGNAL - L.H

PARKING LIGHT - R.H

HEAD LIGHT R.H

HEAD LIGHT L.H

PARKING LIGHT - L.H

Fig. 10.35 Wiring diagram - RHD vehicles

Note: a) The broken lines shows optional equipment
b) When installing the tachometer or hazard device, cut out the line marked with "——◁——".

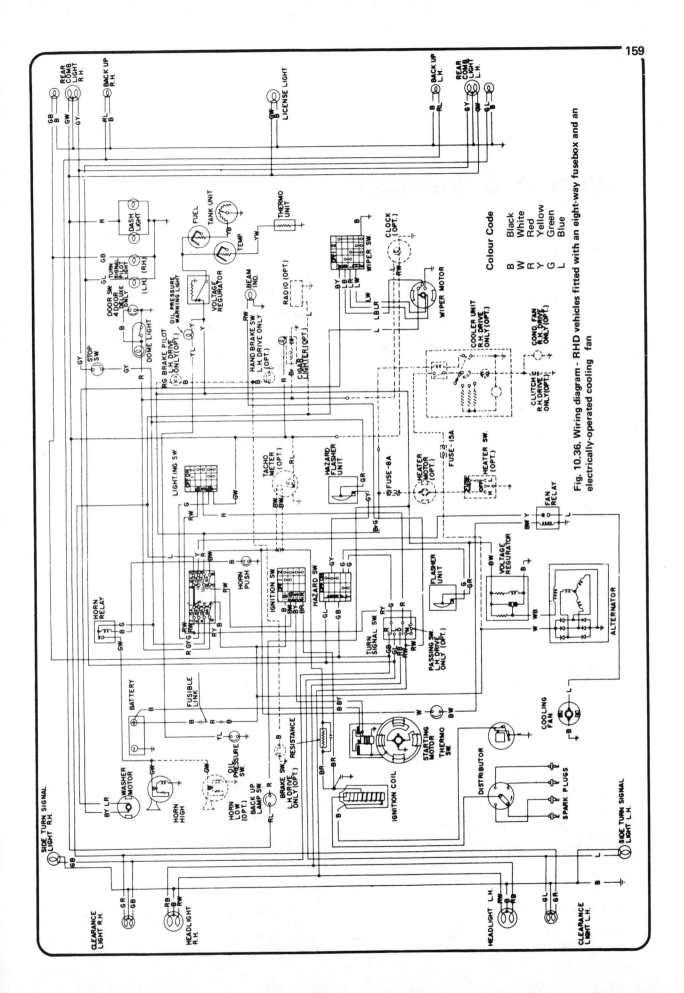

Fig. 10.36. Wiring diagram - RHD vehicles fitted with an eight-way fusebox and an electrically-operated cooling fan

Colour Code

B   Black
W   White
R   Red
Y   Yellow
G   Green
L   Blue

Chapter 11 Suspension

Contents

Specifications

Tyres

Sizes	600 x 12 or 155 SR 12

Pressures:

	Front	Rear
600 x 12	1.5 kgf/cm^2 (22 lbf/in^2)	1.5 kgf/cm^2 (22 lbf/in^2)
155 SR 12	1.7 kgf/cm^2 (24 lbf/in^2)	1.7 kgf/cm^2 (24 lbf/in^2)

Front Suspension

Wheel alignment (unladen)

	Saloon	Estate
Camber (non-adjustable)	1°40'	1°40'
Caster (non-adjustable)	1°15'	1°40'
Toe-in	5 to 7 mm (0.1968 to 0.2756 in.)	5 to 7 mm (0.1968 to 0.2756 in.)
King pin inclination (non-adjustable)	9°55'	9°55'
Steering angle:		
in	39°	39°
out	33°	33°

Coil spring

	Right side	Left side
(Color identification)	Yellow	Pink
Spring constance	2.09 kg/m (29 lb/in.)	1.89 kg/m (26 lb/in.)
Coil diameter	110 mm (4.33 in.)	110 mm (4.33 in.)
Free diameter	340 mm (13.4 in.)	339 mm (13.3 in.)
Length/Load (as-installed)	253.5/219 kg/mm (559/8.62 lb/in.)	228/219 kg/mm (508/8.62 lb/in.)

Strut assembly

Length of strut outer casing	328 mm (12.9 in.)	
Stroke	160 mm (6.30 in.)	
Piston rod outer diameter	18 mm (0.709 in.)	
Piston cylinder inner diameter	25 mm (0.984 in.)	
Damping force at piston speed of 0.3 m/sec:		
Expansion	48 kg (106 lb)	
Compression	22 kg (49 lb)	
Strut oil capacity	Approx. 210 cc (12.8 cu. in.)	
Guide bushing:		
Wear limit	0.05 mm (0.0020 in.)	
Piston rod	Atsugi	Kayaba
Outside diameter (standard)	17.975 to 17.945 mm (0.7077 to 0.706 in.)	17.981 to 17.935 mm (0.7079 to 0.7061 in.)
Wear limit	0.25 mm (0.0098 in.)	
Bending limit	0.1 mm (0.0039 in.)	

Maximum allowable clearance between piston rod and guide
bushing   ...   .   0.160 mm (0.0063 in.)   0.19 mm (0.0075 in.)
Cylinder:
   Standard dimension of inside diameter   ...   .   25.006 mm (0.9845 in.)
   Wear limit   ...   .   0.1 mm (0.0039 in.)
   Maximum allowable bending   ...   .   0.2 mm (0.0078 in.)
Ball joint stud swinging torque:
   Standard   ...   .   35 kg/cm (30 lb/in.)
   Limit   ...   .   10 kg/cm (8.7 lb/in.)

Maximum allowable tire unbalance   ...   .   165 gr/cm (2.3 in/oz)

Maximum allowable tire unbalance as measured at rim edge   10 gr. (0.4 oz)

Rear Suspension

Wheel bearing rotation starting force at hub bolt
When new bearing and oil seal are used (max)   ...   .   1.1 kg (2.4 lb)
When used bearing and oil seal are used (max)   ...   .   0.7 kg (1.5 lb)

Wheel bearing roation starting torque
When new bearing and oil seal are used.   ...   .   6.0 kg/m (43 ft/lb)
When used bearing and oil seal are used   ...   .   4.0 kg/m (29 ft/lb)

Wheel alignment
Camber angle:
   When empty   ...   .   50'
   When loaded   ...   .   30'

Torque wrench settings

Front suspension	lb f ft	kg f m
Wheel bearing locknut	72 to 87	10.0 to 12.0
Ball joint stud tightening nut	22 to 29	3.0 to 4.0
Strut to knuckle installation bolt	24 to 33	3.3 to 4.5
Strut to knuckle installation nut (through nut)	29 to 36	4.0 to 5.0
Gland packing	43 to 47	6.0 to 6.5
Piston rod tightening nut (to insulator)	46 to 53	6.3 to 7.3
Strut to hood ledge installation nut	10 to 13	1.4 to 1.8
Transverse link installation bolt (nut)	24 to 33	3.3 to 4.5
Transverse link to ball joint installation bolt	24 to 33	3.3 to 4.5
Steering side rod locknut	27 to 34	3.8 to 4.7
Side rod ball stud tightening nut	40 to 47	5.5 to 6.5
Ball nut	54 to 61	7.5 to 8.5
Subframe installation bolt (nut)	51 to 58	7.0 to 8.0
Rear Suspension		
Shock absorber (Saloon):		
Bolt (lower side)	11 to 17	1.5 to 2.4
Nut (upper side)	18 to 25	2.5 to 3.4
Shock absorber (Estate):		
Nut (upper and lower sides)	14 to 19	1.9 to 2.6
Rear arm bolt	35 to 43	4.8 to 6.0
'U' bolt	23 to 29	3.2 to 4.0
Shackle	6.5 to 10	0.9 to 1.4
Front pin	14 to 19	1.9 to 2.6
Bolt securing front pin	6.5 to 10	0.9 to 1.4

1   General description

1   The front suspension on the Datsun Cherry consists of independant struts with integral shock absorbers, and transverse links. The upper end of each strut is secured to the wing structure, while the lower end is retained by a knuckle fitting bolted to the rear of the wheel hub. Transverse links connect the lower end of each knuckle to the subframe via a balljoint and two rubber-bushed pivot points.

2   The rear suspension on the saloon version is a conventional trailing arm independant suspension utilizing coil springs and gas-filled shock absorbers.

3   The estate version rear suspension is different in that it consists of a rigid axle tube transversely secured to semi-eliptic leaf springs. Shock absorbers are provided and are secured, at the lower end, to the spring seat, and at the top to the body structure.

2   Springs and dampers - inspection

1   With the tyre pressures correct, fuel tank full and the car standing on level smooth ground, bounce it up and down a few times and let it settle. Check the height of the vehicle against the measurements detailed in Chapter 12. This will give you an approximate idea if any springs are broken or seriously weakened.

Make sure that any measurement outside specification is not affected by another before deciding how many springs may need renewal. This can be done by raising the car to the correct height on blocks at the faulty location and rechecking the remainder.

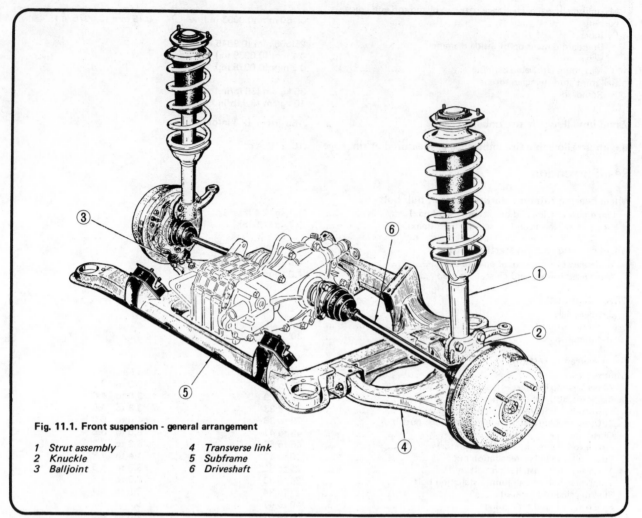

Fig. 11.1. Front suspension - general arrangement

1 *Strut assembly*   4 *Transverse link*
2 *Knuckle*   5 *Subframe*
3 *Balljoint*   6 *Driveshaft*

2 Dampers may be checked by bouncing the car at each corner. Generally speaking the body will return to its normal position and stop after being depressed. If it rises and returns on a rebound the damper should be suspect. Examine also the damper mounting bushes for any sign of looseness and the cylinders themselves for traces of hydraulic fluid leaks. (Rear dampers, however, are gas-filled). If there is any sign of leaks the unit must be renewed. Static tests of dampers are not entirely conclusive and further indications of damper failure are noticeable pitching; (bonnet going up and down when the car is braked and stopped sharply) excessive rolling on fast bends; and a definite feeling of insecurity on corners, particularly if the road surface is uneven. If you are in doubt it is a good idea to drive over a roughish road and have someone follow you to watch how the wheels behave. Excessive up and down 'patter' of any wheel is usually quite obvious, and denotes a defective damper.

3 Front wheel hubs, bearings and steering knuckle - removal, inspection and replacement

1 Jack-up the car and remove the roadwheel.
2 On drum brake models slacken off the brake adjusters, as described in Chapter 9. On disc brake models remove the brake caliper, as described in Chapter 9.
3 Remove the grease cap and the split pin locking the castellated hub nut.
4 Remove the castellated hub nut and the washer behind it.
5 Disconnect and remove the driveshaft as described in Chapter 7.

6 Using a suitable drift and hammer, drive out the hubs from inside. The drift must be the same diameter as the hubs or damage could result. Datsun have a special tool for the job which you might be able to borrow from a Datsun agent.
7 Cut the locking wire on the wheel bearing lock nuts and remove the nuts. A special tool is available for this, but since the nut is castellated, it should not be too difficult to make up a local tool. A piece of ½ inch (12.7 mm) square bar (mild steel) placed across the castellations and then knocked with a fairly heavy hammer should suffice. Take care not to damage the castellations, though.
8 Using a suitable drift, drive out the wheel bearings from the front of the wheel.
9 Lever out the outer oil seal; if using a screwdriver take care not to scratch the seal housing. The inner oil seal is integral with the bearing locknut and this can also be levered out.
10 Remove the bolts securing the backplate assembly and detach the brake assembly (drum brakes) or backplate alone (disc brakes).
11 Separate the balljoints from the knuckle using the technique(s) described in Section 7.
12 Remove the four bolts securing the knuckle to the lower end of the suspension strut and detach the knuckle.
13 Wash the bearings, cups and hub assembly in paraffin and wipe dry with a non-fluffy rag.
14 Inspect the bearing outer tracks and cones for signs of overheating, scoring, corrosion or other damage. Assemble each race and check for roughness of movement. If any of these signs are evident new races must be fitted.

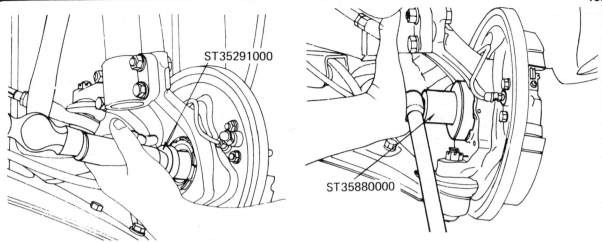

Fig. 11.2. Removing the front hub using Datsun special tool

Fig. 11.3. Removing the locknut using Datsun special tool

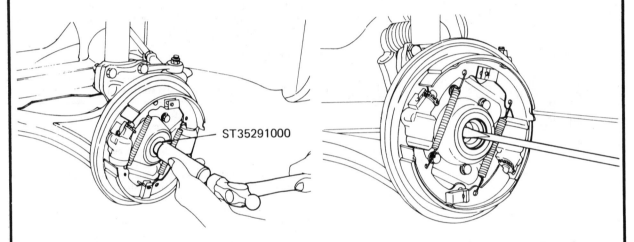

Fig. 11.4. Removing the wheel bearings using Datsun special tool

Fig. 11.5. Removing the wheel bearings using Datsun special tool

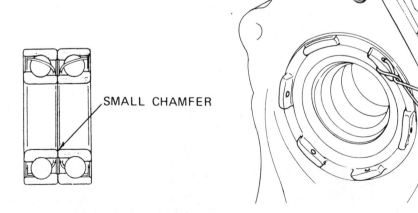

Fig. 11.6. Correct location of front wheel bearings

Fig. 11.7. Securing locknut with wire

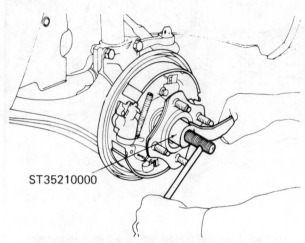

ST35210000

Fig. 11.8. Pressing hub using Datsun special tool

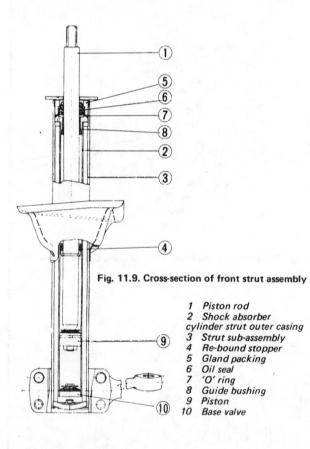

Fig. 11.9. Cross-section of front strut assembly

1   Piston rod
2   Shock absorber
cylinder strut outer casing
3   Strut sub-assembly
4   Re-bound stopper
5   Gland packing
6   Oil seal
7   'O' ring
8   Guide bushing
9   Piston
10 Base valve

15 Inspect the hub and knuckle for evidence of corrosion, cracks
or deformation. Replace if necessary.
16 Discard the old oil seals.
17 Before fitting the bearings, either new or old, ensure that
they are lubricated with the correct multi-purpose grease.
Correctly locate the bearings with the small chamfer, on each
bearing inner race, on the inside touching each other. Drive the
bearings back into the knuckle.
18 Replace the outer oil seal, with the lip innermost, gently
tapping into position until it is flush with the knuckle outer face.
19 Fit a new oil seal in the wheel bearing locknut, with the lip
innermost, pressing it in until it contacts the inside face of the
locknut.

20 Smear a little grease on the lips of both seals, before fitting,
to provide initial lubrication.
21 The remainder of the reassembly instructions is the reverse of
dismantling, remembering to replace the lockwire on the bearing
locknut and securing it to the nearest hole in the locknut, viewed
from an anticlockwise direction.

4 Front suspension spring and strut assembly - removal and replacement

1   Chock the rear wheels, apply the handbrake, jack-up the
front of the car and support on firmly based axle stands.
2   Remove the four bolts securing the strut to the knuckle and
separate the two components.
3   Detach the steering trackrod, as described in Chapter 8.
4   Working in the engine bay, remove the cap over the top of
the suspension strut and partially loosen the locknut securing the
piston rod.
5   Place a jack or suitable packing under the strut to support its
weight during the next operation.
6   Working under the bonnet undo and remove the three nuts
fastening the top of the strut to the inner wing panel.
7   Carefully lower the jack or remove the packing and lift away
the suspension strut assembly.
8   Refitting the suspension strut assembly is the reverse
sequence to removal.

5 Front suspension spring and strut assembly - overhaul

It is recommended that, if the strut assembly is in need of
overhaul or it is necessary for new coil springs to be fitted, this
job be left to the local Datsun garage. The reason for this is that
special tools are necessary to compress the spring, keep the
spring in a compressed state and to dismantle the strut assembly.

The following instructions are given for those who wish to
attempt the job. Before removing the strut assembly from the
car it is necessary to fit clips to the coil spring to keep it in the
compressed condition. These should be either borrowed from
the local Datsun garage or made up using some high tensile steel
rod at least 0.5 inch (12.70 mm) in diameter with the ends bent
over. The length should accommodate as many coils as possible.
Refer to Section 4, and follow the instructions given in
paragraph 1. Then place a jack under the strut and compress the
road spring by raising the jack. Fit the spring clips and tie firmly
in place with strong wire or cord. Now follow the instructions
given in paragraphs 2 to 9 inclusive.
To overhaul the strut assembly proceed as follows:
1   Thoroughly clean the unit by working in paraffin and then
wiping dry with a clean non-fluffy rag.
2   Fit the coil spring compressor to the suspension unit, make
sure that it is correctly positioned and then compress the spring.
This is not applicable if the spring clips are in position.
3   Carefully prise the snap-ring from the dust cover.
4   Undo and remove the self-locking nut. A new one will be
necessary on reassembly.
5   Lift off the strut insulator, and the rest of the top mounting
components. Note the order in which they are removed.
6   Remove the coil spring still in the compressed state.
7   Push the piston rod down until it reaches its fully retracted
position.
8   It is now necessary for the gland packing to be removed.
Ideally a special tool should be used but it may be improvised
using a wrench.
9   Remove the 'O' ring from the top of the piston rod guide.
10 Lift out the piston rod together with the cylinder.
Important: The piston and piston rod guide must never be
removed from the cylinder as these are set relative to each other.
11 Tilt the inner cylinder and allow the hydraulic fluid to drain
out into a container. Also drain out any fluid inside the outer
casing. Fresh fluid will be required during reassembly.
12 Wash all parts in petrol and wipe dry. Make quite sure no dirt

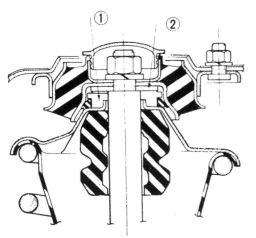

Fig. 11.10. Sectional view of front strut upper assembly

1   Thrust seat   2   Thrust plate

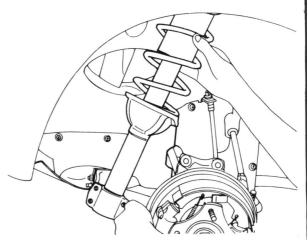

Fig. 11.11. Removing strut and spring assembly

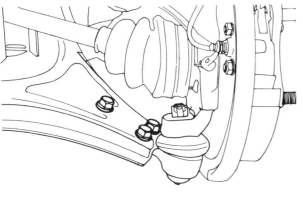

Fig. 11.12. Method of attaching transverse link to the balljoint

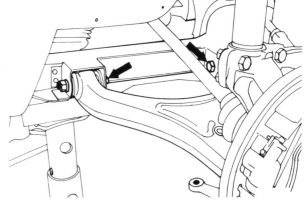

Fig. 11.13. Arrows indicate   transverse link inner mounting bolts

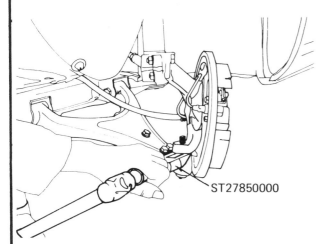

ST27850000

Fig. 11.14. Separating balljoint from knuckle

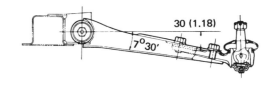

30 (1.18)

7°30'

Unit: mm (in)

Fig. 11.15. Correct position of transverse link   when fitted

is allowed to contact any internal parts.

13 Always renew the gland packing, and 'O' ring when the strut has been dismantled.

14 Inspect the outer casing for signs of distortion, cracking or accident damage and obtain new if any such condition is apparent.

15 Inspect the spindle for hair line cracks on the base or damaged threads. If evident the complete strut assembly should be renewed.

16 Inspect the rubber and metal joint for signs of damage or deterioration. Obtain new parts if evident.

17 If noise originated from the strut when driving over rough road surfaces the cause is probably due to the strut mounting bearing having worn. obtain a new bearing assembly.

18 Before reassembly commences make sure that every part is really clean and free from dust.

19 Fit the piston rod and cylinder into position in the outer casing.

20 Fill the assembly with the recommended grade of hydraulic fluid. For AMPCO (ATSUGI) units use 210 cc or KYB (KAYABA) units use 190 cc. Do not deviate from the quoted amounts otherwise the operating efficiency of the unit will be altered.

21 Place the rod guide on the top of the piston rod guide and refit the gland packing.

22 Lubricate the sealing lips with a little multi-purpose grease and tighten the gland packing to a torque wrench setting of 6.0 to 6.5 kg m (43 to 47 ft lb). This will have to be estimated if the special tool is not available. Note. When tightening the gland packing the piston rod must be extended approximately 4.724 in. (120 mm) from the end of the outer casing to expel most of the air out of the strut.

23 It is now necessary to bleed the shock absorber system by holding the strut with the spindle end down and pulling the piston rod out completely.

24 Now invert the strut so that the spindle end is uppermost and push the piston rod inward as far as it will go.

25 Repeat the procedure described in paragraph 23 several times, until an equal pressure is felt during both strokes.

26 Pull the piston rod out fully and fit the rebound rubber, to prevent the piston rod falling by its own weight.

27 Locate the spring on the lower spring seat with the end fitted into the recess and compress the spring with the special tool if spring clips are not fitted.

28 Refit the dust seal with the lip pointing downwards.

29 Lubricate the dust seals with a little multi-purpose grease. Fit the rest of the top mounting components as noted on removal and in accordance with Fig. 11.10.

30 Refit the piston rod self locking nut and tighten to a torque wrench setting of 43 - 47 lb ft (5.94 - 6.5 kg m).

31 With the spring correctly located release the spring compressor. If clips have been used leave in position until the strut has been reassembled to the car.

32 Raise the rebound rubber until it is seated under the upper spring seat.

33 The strut assembly is now ready for refitting to the car.

---

6 Transverse link - removal, overhaul and replacement

1 Remove the three bolts securing the transverse link to the balljoint.

2 Remove the two bolts securing the transverse link to the subframe and the transverse link from the vehicle.

3 Inspect the transverse link for evidence of cracks, corrosion or distortion. Check the bushes for ovality, cracks or other damage. Replace if necessary.

4 Renewal of the bushes calls for care as the transverse link must not be distorted during the course of removing and replacing the bushes. It is best to get the old ones out by cutting through them.

5 New bushes should be lubricated and drawn in using a long nut and bolt together with a tubular spacer (on the inside of the

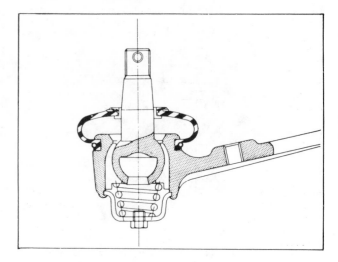

Fig. 11.16. Cross-section through balljoint

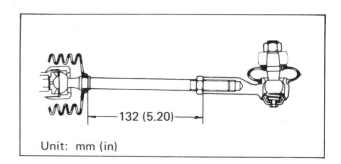

Unit: mm (in)

Fig. 11.17. Optimum length of side rod before toe in alignment

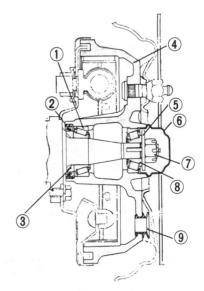

Fig. 11.18. Section through rear wheel hub

1	Taper roller bearing (inner)	
2	Oil seal	6 Hub cap
3	Oil seal spacer	7 Wheel bearing locknut
4	Drum	8 Taper roller bearing (outer)
5	Lock washer	9 Adjust hole plug

arm) and large washers to ensure the bushes are drawn in square. Do not attempt to drive the bushes in with a hammer. When installing the bushes should project equally either side of the link.

6 Replacement is the reverse of removal. Install the mounting bolts from inside the link.

7 With transverse link under standard load condition, (ie; the car weight off of the jack), tighten bolts so as not to deform bushing excessively.

7 Transverse link balljoint - removal and replacement

1 Although the normal technique for removing this particular balljoint involves removing the driveshaft beforehand, if great care is exercised it is possible to do it without this onerous task.

2 Remove the split pin and castellated locknut. Separate the joint from the knuckle. This can only be done with surety by using a claw clamp. However, it is possible to drive through but only if the knuckle is firmly supported. The joint will almost certainly be damaged in the process. Another method is to strike the side of the knuckle where the pin goes through whilst holding the head of another hammer on the opposite. This has a squeezing out effect on the tapered pin. If any difficulty arises that looks as though it might cause damage to the driveshaft, then you must remove the driveshaft.

3 Remove the bolts securing the balljoint to the transverse link and detach the balljoint.

4 Inspect the balljoint for end-play and damage. Check the dust cover for cracks and deterioration. Should there be end-play or damage to the balljoint a new one must be fitted. Generally a new balljoint assembly is supplied complete with a dust cover. Replenish the grease, if the old balljoint is being re-fitted, by removing the dust cover and using a grease gun.

5 Make sure that socket groove in which dust cover clamp fit securely is free from oil or grease. Wipe clean if necessary.

6 After a new dust cover is installed, move the stud until ball surface is coated with grease evenly. Make sure that stud swing torque is correctly obtained. (See Specifications).

7 After balljoint is installed on vehicle, replace plug with grease nipple. Apply grease to balljoint through this grease nipple until grease is forced out at grease vent hole.

Tightening torques:
Ball stud mounting nut − 22 to 29 ft lb (3 to 4 kg m)
Mounting bolt (link side) − 24 to 33 ft lb (3.3 to 4.5 kg m)

8 Rear hub - removal and refitting

1 Chock the front wheels. Remove the rear wheel trim, slacken the wheelnuts, jack-up the rear of the car and support on firmly based stands. Remove the roadwheel.

2 Knock off the cap from the end of the hub, remove the split pin and unscrew and remove the castellated nut and thrust washer.

3 Pull the hub assembly forward and extract the outer roller bearing then pull the unit from the stub axle.

4 To refit the hub, first clean out all traces of old grease and repack with fresh. To do this, carefully wipe clean the stub axle and seal track. Inspect the hub seal and axle threads for wear or damage. If there are any signs of leakage onto the brake back-plate fit a new seal.

5 Wipe away as much old grease as possible from the hub and then insert new grease into the bearings. Do not overfill the hub cavity. Remove any surplus grease other than that shown in Fig. 11.22.

6 Refit the hub assembly and plain washer to the stub axle. Screw on the castellated nut and tighten slowly using a torque wrench set to 14 to 17 lb ft (2.0 to 2.4 kg m).

7 Rotate the hub in both directions to settle the wheel bearings. Slacken the nut, then, with the socket *only* on the nut, tighten the nut as far as possible with finger and thumb. Insert a

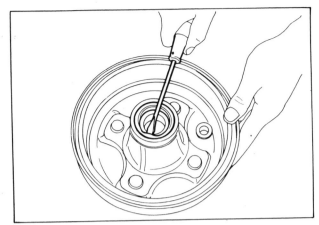

Fig. 11.19. Prising out oil seal

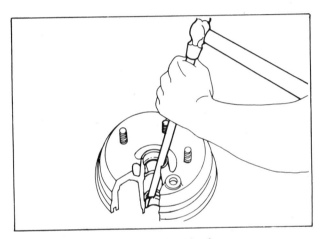

Fig. 11.20. Driving out   wheel bearing outer race

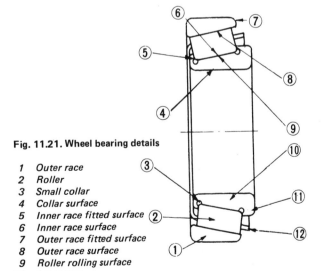

Fig. 11.21. Wheel bearing details

1   *Outer race*
2   *Roller*
3   *Small collar*
4   *Collar surface*
5   *Inner race fitted surface*
6   *Inner race surface*
7   *Outer race fitted surface*
8   *Outer race surface*
9   *Roller rolling surface*
10 *Inner race*
11 *Large collar*
12 *Supporter*

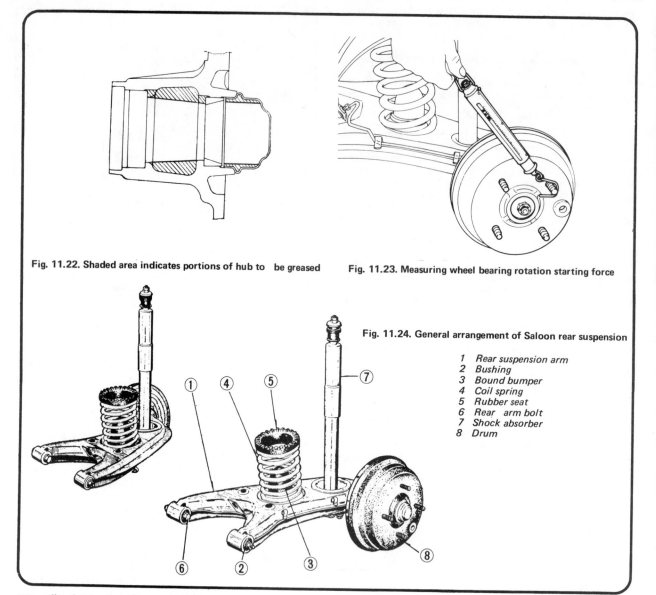

Fig. 11.22. Shaded area indicates portions of hub to be greased

Fig. 11.23. Measuring wheel bearing rotation starting force

Fig. 11.24. General arrangement of Saloon rear suspension

1 Rear suspension arm
2 Bushing
3 Bound bumper
4 Coil spring
5 Rubber seat
6 Rear arm bolt
7 Shock absorber
8 Drum

new split pin, turning the nut clockwise if necessary to align the holes, but do not bend it over at this stage.
8 If the adjustment is correct, there should be no hub endfloat and using a spring balance, the force required to rotate the hub should be: (i) new bearings 2.4 lbs; (ii) old bearings 1.5 lbs, with the spring balance connected to a wheel stud. This bearing preload should be checked periodically at the intervals specified in the Routine Maintenance section of this manual.
9 When adjustment is correct, bend over the ends of the split pin, fit the cap to the end of the hub, refit the roadwheel and lower the vehicle.

9 Rear hub - overhaul

1 Remove the rear hub as described in Section 8, paragraphs 1 to 3 inclusive.
2 Wash all internal grease from the hub using paraffin. If the bearings and seal are in good order, repack the interior of the hub and end cap with wheel bearing grease so that it occupies the area shown in Fig. 11.22.
3 If the bearings are worn or damaged, prise out the oil seal

from the inner end of the hub and extract the inner roller race. Drift out the inner and outer bearing tracks using a thin rod.
4 Fit the new bearing tracks using a piece of tubing as a drift. If both hubs are being dismantled at the same time, ensure that the bearings are kept as matched sets and do not mix up the races and tracks.
5 Press the new grease seal squarely into the inner end of the hub, with its lip towards the roller bearing.
6 Pack the hub with grease as described in paragraph 2.
7 Refitting is a reversal of removal, adjust the bearing preload, as described in the preceding Section.

10 Rear axle tube (estate) - removal and refitting

1 Jack-up the rear of the car and support on firmly based axle stands. Also support the weight of the rear suspension by placing a jack under the tubular beam axle.
2 Remove the rear wheels if access to their inner face is not good.
3 Disconnect the brake pipe from the wheel cylinder.
4 Disconnect the handbrake cable by removing the split pin from the clevis pin.

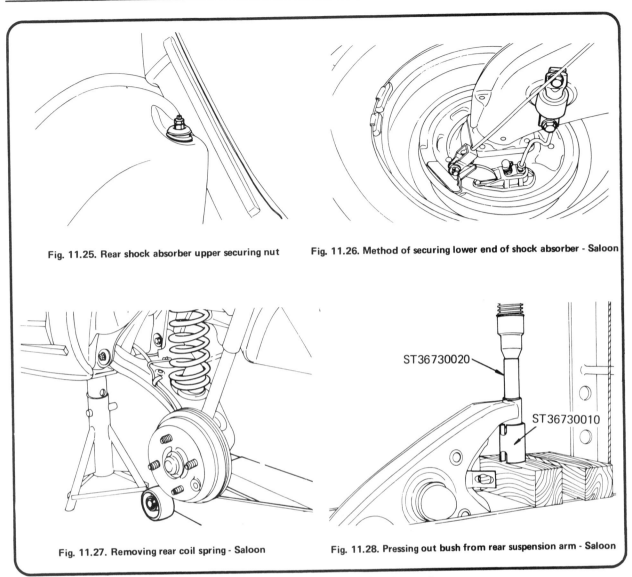

Fig. 11.25. Rear shock absorber upper securing nut

Fig. 11.26. Method of securing lower end of shock absorber - Saloon

Fig. 11.27. Removing rear coil spring - Saloon

Fig. 11.28. Pressing out bush from rear suspension arm - Saloon

5 Repeat operation 4 on the other wheel.
6 Remove the 3-way connector mounting bolt, then ease off the connector and the brake pipe assembly from the axle tube.
7 Remove the handbrake equalizer bracket, then lift away the complete handbrake cable assembly.
8 Remove the shock absorber nuts and U-bolts.
9 Undo and remove the bolts securing the rear end of the springs from the shackle. Detach the springs from the rear shackles.
10 Unbolt and remove the bolts holding the spring to the front pin.
11 Carefully lower the jack located under the tubular beam axle and wheel away the axle from the rear of the car.
12 Refitting is the reverse sequence to removal. It will be necessary to bleed the brake hydraulic system - details of this operation will be found in Chapter 9.

11 Rear shock absorber and coil spring (saloon) - removal, inspection and replacement

1 The rear dampers will need renewal if their mounting bushes are worn or if indications are that the unit is no longer performing properly. Similarly, replace the coil springs if they are weak or fractured.
2 Jack-up the rear of the vehicle and support with axle stands.
3 Remove the rear wheel.
4 Support the lower end of the suspension arm by means of a jack.
5 Remove the two upper nuts that secure the shock absorber, then the two bolts from the shock absorber lower mounting. If only the coil spring is being replaced, remove the upper mounting bolts only.
6 If the shock absorber only is being removed, it can be compressed and lifted out. Take care to collect the various washers and bushes that this will release from the top mounting. If the shock absorbers are definitely to be replaced, drill a hole on the lower portion of the tube to bleed high pressure gas out of it completely. This procedure makes it easy to remove the shock absorber.
7 Assuming both coil and shock absorber are to be removed, lower the jack under the suspension arm slowly to relieve the tension of the coil spring. Remove the spring, rubber seat and shock absorber.
8 Inspect the shock abosrber for evidence of leakage, reduced damping properties or deformed shaft. Replace any of the washers, bushes or shutters that are cracked, excessively worn or distorted.
9 Check the coil spring for cracks, corrosion or fatigue (ie; loss

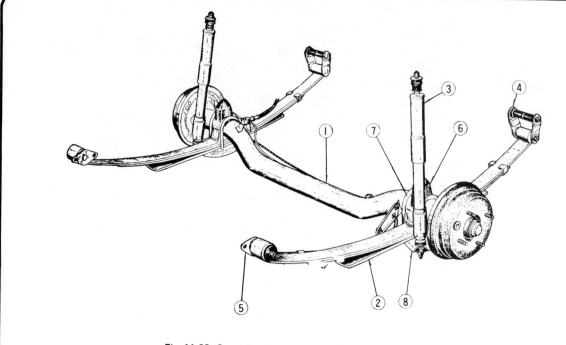

Fig. 11.29. General arrangement of Estate car rear suspension

1 Axle tube	3 Shock absorber	5 Front pin	7 'U' bolt
2 Leaf spring	4 Shackle	6 Bumper rubber	8 Spring seat

of resilience). The rubber seat should be free from splits, distortion or excessive wear.

10 Replacement is the reverse of the removal procedure, but note the following points:

a) When installing a shock absorber, if the shutter has been replaced then its periphery should be coated with a suitable adhesive before installing it.

b) To fit a coil spring, first position the upper (flattened) end of the coil spring in position with its rubber seat. Then attach the lower, open, end of the spring to the seating surface on the rear suspension arm. Gradually raise the jack to compress the spring.

12 Rear suspension arms (saloon) - removal, inspection and replacement

1 If the rubber mounting bushes on the arms are worn it will be necessary to remove the arms to replace them.

2 The initial operations to remove an arm are virtually identical with those given to remove a spring or shock absorber (Section 11): the only additions are that the brake pipe-to-brake hose joint must be disconnected, and the handbrake cable detached at the clevis pin on the wheel.

3 Having lowered the jack under the arm and removed the shock absorber and coil spring, next remove the two bolts that secure the arm to the body and detach the arm.

4 Inspect the arm for corrosion, distortion or cracks. Check the bushes for deterioration such as cracks or ovality; and check the rubber bump stop for damage.

5 If the arm is damaged it will have to be renewed.

6 Inspect the suspension arm bushes and if worn use a bolt, nut, washers and tubing to draw out the old bushes and fit new ones.

7 Refitting the rear suspension arm is the reverse sequence to removal. The following additional points should be noted:

a) Always use new self-locking washers.

b) Finally tighten all suspension attachments when the car is resting on the ground.

c) It will be necessary to bleed the brake hydraulic system, as described in Chapter 9.

13 Rear suspension shock absorber (estate) - removal and replacement

1 Chock the front wheels, jack-up the rear of the car and support on firmly based stands. Remove the roadwheel.

2 Undo and remove the nuts that secure the upper end of the shock absorber to the body after removing the shock absorber cover.

3 Undo and remove the nut and washer that secures the shock absorber to the spring plate attachment. Detach the shock absorber and lift away from the car.

4 Inspect the shock absorber for signs of leaks which, if evident, it must be discarded and a new one obtained. Since the shock absorbers are gas-filled, evidence of leakage is very difficult to detect.

5 Clean the exterior and wipe with a non fluffy rag. Inspect the shaft for signs of corrosion or distortion and the body for damage.

6 Check the action by expanding and contracting to ascertain if equal resistance is felt on both strokes. If the resistance is very uneven the unit must be renewed. It may be found that resistance is greater on the upward stroke than on the downward stroke and this is permissible.

7 Check the rubber bushes and washers for deterioration and obtain new if evident.

8 Refitting is the reverse sequence to removal.

14 Rear spring (estate) - removal and replacement

1 Chock the front wheels, jack-up the rear of the car and

support on firmly based stands. Remove the roadwheel.

2   Place the jack under the centre of the rear axle and raise until the strain is taken from the shock absorbers.

3   Undo and remove the nut and washer that secures the shock absorber to the spring plate attachment. Detach the shock absorber and contact until it is clear of the axle housing.

4   Undo and remove the 'U' bolt nuts and lift away the mounting plate. If tight tap with a hammer but take care not to damage the 'U' bolt threads.

5   Raise the jack until the weight of the axle has been taken from the spring.

6   Undo and remove the rear shackle nuts and washers.

7   Lift away the shackle plates noting the correct positioning of the shackle pins.

8   Rest the axle on wood blocks and lower the rear of the spring to the ground. Recover the two rubber bushes from the body spring shackle hanger.

9   Undo and remove the nut from the front pin bolt and tap out the bolt with a soft faced hammer.

10 The spring may now be removed from the car.

11 If any of the shackles or rubber bushes are worn they must be replaced together with the pins if they show signs of wear.

12 The bushes fitted to the rear road spring eyes are of the bonded tubber type. They may be removed and new ones fitted with the spring in position on the axle by using a threaded bolt, distance piece of similar diameter to the *outside* diameter of the bush and a washer. Tightening the nut will draw the old bush from the spring eye or draw the new one into position.

13 Where the road spring has been removed from the car, then the bushes may be drifted out or in by using a piece of tubing of appropriate outside diameter. Do not attempt to use the inner shackle pin locating hole of the bush as a means of removing the bush or the bonding will be destroyed.

14 If a spring is broken or has lost its resilience then it should be replaced: in this event the other spring should be replaced at the same time.

15 Replacement is a straightforward reversal of the dismantling process. Do not fully tighten the attachments until the car has been lowered to the ground and the spring is in its normal position. If this is not done the rubber bushes will require frequent replacement.

15 Steering geometry - checking and adjustment

1   Unless the front axle and suspension has been damaged the castor angle, camber angle and steering pivot angles will not alter, provided, of course, that the suspension balljoints and wishbone fulcrum pin bushes are not worn in any way.

2   The toe-in of the front wheels is a measurement which may vary more frequently and could pass unnoticed if, for example, a steering tie-rod was bent. When fitting new tie-rod balljoints, for example, it will always be necessary to reset the toe-in.

3   Indications of incorrect wheel alignment (toe-in) are uneven tyre wear on the front tyres and erratic steering particularly when turning. To check toe-in accutately needs optical aligning equipment, so get a garage to do it. Ensure that they examine the tie-rods for straightness and all balljoints and wheel bearings at the same time, if you have not done so yourself.

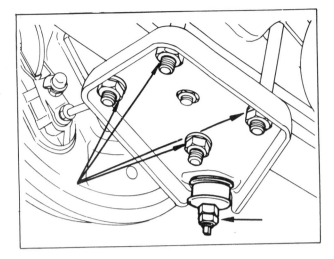

Fig. 11.30. Shock absorber and 'U' bolt retaining nuts - Estate

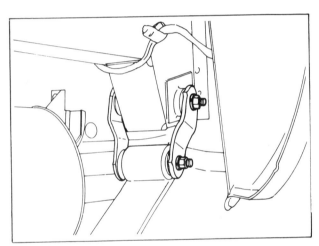

Fig. 11.31. Rear spring shackle attachment - Estate

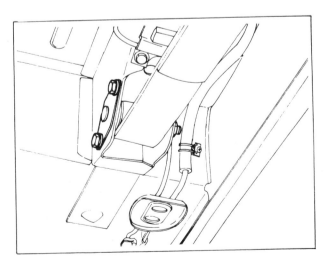

Fig. 11.32. Method of attaching the spring front pin - Estate

16 Fault diagnosis - suspension and steering

Symptom	Reason/s	Remedy

Front suspension and steering

Vibration, shock and shimmying of steering wheel

Steering wheel oscillation is often experienced when there exists an excessive free-play in steering linkage, improper backlash in steering gear, or oscillation of front wheels.
Steering shock or kickback can be felt at the steering wheel when the front wheels encounter obstructions in road. This condition can be due to improper backlash in steering gear or other associated units.
Shimmy is rapid oscillation of front syspension system and related parts and is often experienced when vehicle picks up a certain speed.

Reason/s	Remedy
Incorrect tyre pressures.	Adjust
Wheel out of balance or buckled.	Correct or replace.
Worn or loose tyre.	Renew or re-tighten.
Worn suspension ball joint or lack of preload.	Renew ball joint.
Steering gear out of adjustment.	Re-adjust.
Improper wheel alignment.	Re-adjust.
Worn rubber bushing in transverse link.	Renew.
Excessive free-play in steering linkage.	Check and correct.
Excessive play or wear on front wheel bearing.	Renew bearing, or adjust.
Loose steering gearbox.	Re-tighten.
Loose or inoperative shock absorber (in strut assembly).	Re-tighten or replace.

Car pulls to one side

This condition becomes evident when vehicle is running on a flat surface with your hands off steering wheel

Reason/s	Remedy
Incorrect tyre pressures, or loose wheelnuts.	Renew tyres. Tighten wheelnuts.
Difference in right and left tyre treads, or tyre type.	Renew tyres.
Defective front wheel bearing.	Renew.
Fatigued front spring, or use of incorrect spring.	Renew.
Improper wheel alignment.	Re-adjust.
Brake drag (out of adjustment).	Re-adjust.
Worn on rubber busing in transverse link.	Renew.
Deformed steering linkage or suspension link.	Renew.
Defective radial tyre.	Renew.

Vehicle wanders when steering wheel held stationary.	Incorrect tyre pressures.	Adjust.
	Improper wheel alignment.	Re-adjust.
	Excessive free-play or wear on steering linkage or suspension linkage.	Replace.
	Steering gear out of adjustment.	Re-adjust.
	Wheel buckled or out of balance.	Check and correct.
	Worn bushing in transverse link.	Renew.
Steering stiff.	*Check and correct in the following manner.* *Jack-up front portion of vehicle and support it on axle stands. Separate knuckle arm from side rod and manipulate steering wheel.* *a) If steering wheel operation is now light, check and locate cause of trouble in steering linkage, suspension system, or front axle.* *b) If steering wheel operation is now heavy, check and locate cause of trouble in steering gear or steering column.*	
	Incorrect tyre pressures.	Adjust.
	Incorrect lubrication in steering gear housing or dirt in oil (b)	Lubricate, service or renew.
	Improper lubrication in steering linkage, dirt in grease, or abnormal wear on steering linkage (a)	Lubricate or renew.
	Seized, damaged suspension ball joint. Lack of lubrication to ball joint (a)	Renew.
	Worn or seized wheel bearing (a)	Renew or adjust.
	Steering gear out of adjustment (b)	Re-adjust.
	Deformed steering linkage (a)	Renew.
	Improper wheel alignment (a)	Re-adjust.
	Damaged thrust seal on upper end of strut. (a)	Renew
	Seized or damaged piston or piston rod of shock absorber (in strut) (a)	Renew.
Excessive play at steering wheel.	Steering gear out of adjustment.	Re-adjust.
	Worn steering linkage.	Renew.
	Loose steering gearbox.	Re-tighten.
	Defective wheel bearing.	Renew.
	Worn bushing in transverse link.	Renew.
Unusual noises.	Incorrect tyre pressures.	Adjust.
	Damaged or worn suspension balljoint or steering linkage, or lack of lubrication.	Renew or lubricate.
	Loose steering gear linkage or suspension system.	Re-tighten.
	Defective shock absorber (in strut).	Renew.
	Defective wheel bearing.	Renew.
	Worn steering linkage or steering gear.	Renew.

	Worn bushing in transverse link.	Renew.
	Broken or fatigued coil spring.	Renew.
	Loose mounting nut on strut mounting insulator.	Re-tighten.
	Improper tightening of strut and gland packing.	Re-tighten.
	Loose bolt on subframe.	Re-tighten.
	Buckled wheel.	Renew.
Tyre squeal	Incorrect tyre pressures.	Adjust.
	Improper wheel alignment.	Re-adjust.
	Deformed knuckle, spindle or suspension.	Renew.
Abnormal or uneven tyre wear	Incorrect tyre pressures.	Adjust.
	Improper wheel alignment.	Re-adjust.
	Defective wheel bearing.	Renew.
	Brakes out of adjustment.	Re-adjust.

Rear suspension (Saloon models)

Unusual noises	Loose suspension linkages.	Tighten.
	Tyres out of balance or incorrectly inflated.	Adjust.
	Damaged rear arm bushing and shock abosrber thrust bushing.	Renew.
	Defective shock absorber.	Renew.
	Defective coil spring.	Renew.
	Defective wheel bearing.	Adjust or renew.
Unstable running	Loose wheelnuts.	Tighten
	Defective rear arm rubber bushing.	Renew.
	Defective shock absorber.	Renew.
	Defective coil spring.	Renew.
	Faulty wheel bearings.	Adjust or replace.
	Brakes out of adjustment (drag).	Adjust.
	Incorrect tyre pressures.	Adjust.

Rear suspension (estate models)

	Defective leaf spring.	Renew.
	Defective leaf spring bushing.	Renew.
	Defective rear wheel bearing.	Renew.
	Loose wheelnuts.	Tighten.

Loose or broken 'U' bolt.	Tighten or renew.
Loose shackle.	Tighten.
Defective shock absorber.	Renew.
Broken leaf spring	Renew.
Worn or damaged leaf spring bushing.	Renew.
Faulty wheel bearing.	Adjust or renew.
Brakes out of adjustment (drag)	Adjust.
Incorrect tyre pressures.	Adjust.

Chapter 12 Bodywork and fittings

Contents

1 General description

The body shells are of rigid sheet metal construction with the outer roof and body panels welded together to form an integral structure. The shells also incorporate a subframe, contributing to engine and transmission accessibility. Because of very rigid box section load-carrying members, exceptional shell rigidity is obtained. Use of the subframe keeps noise and vibration from being carried to the bodyshell.

The range comprises the 100A 2 and 4 door saloon, the 120A 2-door coupe and an estate version of the saloon.

The 120A coupe is one inch wider and three inches bigger than standard saloon models. It is also three inches lower.

The front wings are of bolt-on detachable type for economy of replacement in the event of accident damage.

The bonnet is locked from the vehicle interior as are the passenger rear doors. The front doors are locked externally by key.

A front towing bracket is fitted and the rear towing point is at a rear road spring shackle. Two jacking points are located at both sides of the vehicle for which a jack is supplied as standard equipment.

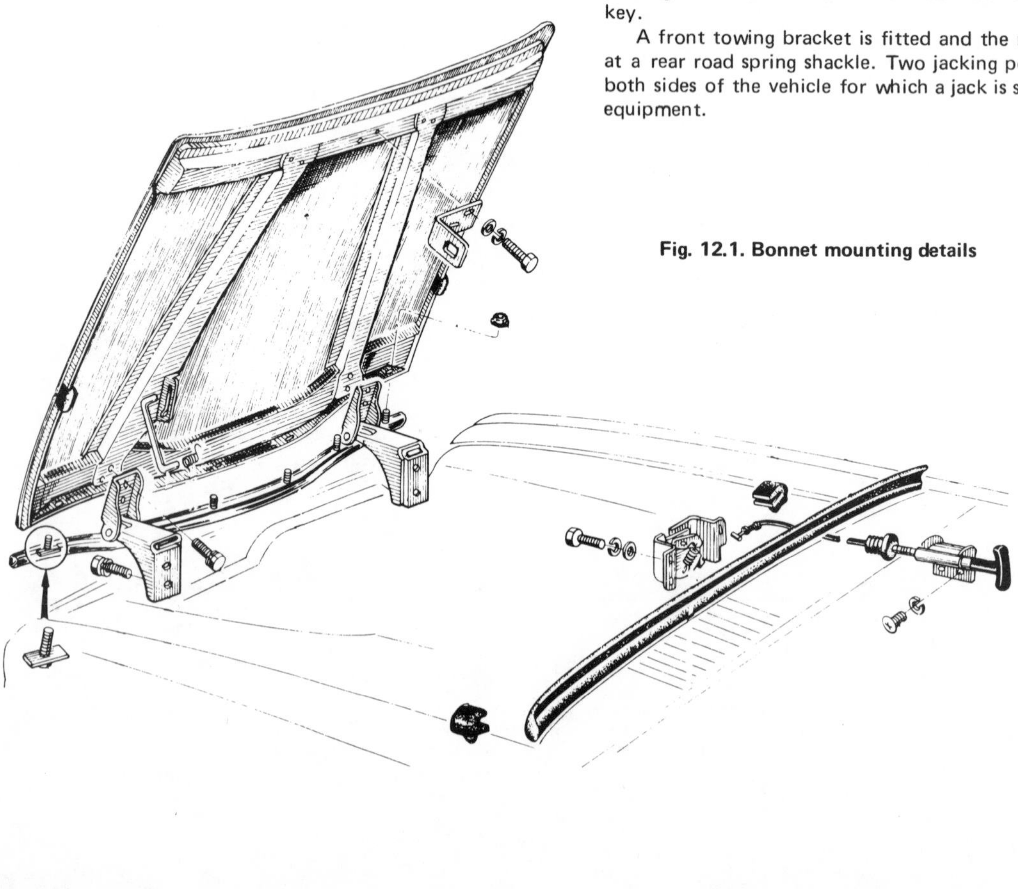

Fig. 12.1. Bonnet mounting details

2 Maintenance - bodywork and underframe

1   The general condition of a car's bodywork is the one thing that significantly affects its value. Maintenance is easy but needs to be regular and particular. Neglect, particularly after minor damage, can lead quickly to further deterioration and costly repair bills. It is important also to keep watch on those parts of the car not immediately visible, for instance the underside, inside all the wheel arches and the lower part of the engine compartment.

2   The basic maintenance routine for the bodywork is washing - preferably with a lot of water, from a hose. This will remove all the loose solids which may have stuck to the car. It is important to flush these off in such a way as to prevent grit from scratching the finish.

The wheels arches and underbody need washing in the same way to remove any accumulated mud which will retain moisture and tend to encourage rust. Paradoxically enough, the best time to clean the underbody and wheel arches is in wet weather when the mud is thoroughly wet and soft. In very wet weather the underbody is usually cleaned of large accumulations automatically and this is a good time for inspection.

3   Periodically it is a good idea to have the whole of the underside of the car steam cleaned, engine compartment included, so that a thorough inspection can be carried out to see what minor repairs and renovations are necessary. Steam cleaning is available at many garages and is necessary for removal of accumulation of oily grime which sometimes is allowed to cake thick in certain areas near the engine, gearbox and back axle. If steam facilities are not available, there are one or two excellent grease solvents available which can be brush applied. The dirt can then be simply hosed off.

4   After washing paintwork, wipe off with a chamois leather to give an unspotted clear finish. A coat of clear protective wax polish will give added protection against chemical pollutants in the air. If the paintwork sheen has dulled or oxidised, use a cleaner/polish combination to restore the brilliance of the shine. This requires a little effort, but is usually caused because regular washing has been neglected. Always check that the door and ventilator opening drain holes and pipes are completely clear so that water can drain out. Bright work should be treated the same way as paintwork. Windscreens and windows can be kept clear of the smeary film which often appears if a little ammonia is added to the water. If they are scratched, a good rub with a proprietary metal polish will often clear them. Never use any form of wax or other body or chromium polish on glass.

3 Maintenance - upholstery and carpets

1   Mats and carpets should be brushed or vacuum cleaned regularly to keep them free of grit. If they are badly stained remove them from the car for scrubbing or sponging and make quite sure they are dry before replacement. Seats and interior trim panels can be kept clean by a wipe over with a damp cloth. If they do become stained (which can be more apparent on light coloured upholstery) use a little liquid detergent and a soft nail brush to scour the grime out of the grain of the material. Do not forget to keep the head lining clean in the same way as the upholstery. When using liquid cleaners inside the car do not over-wet the surfaces being cleaned. Excessive damp could get into the seams and padded interior causing stains, offensive odours or even rot. If the inside of the car gets wet accidentally it is worthwhile taking some trouble to dry it out properly, particularly where carpets are involved. **Do not** leave oil or electrical heaters inside the car for this purpose.

4 Minor body repairs

See colour sequence on pages 182 and 183.
Repair of minor scratches in the car's bodywork
If the scratch is very superficial, and does not penetrate to

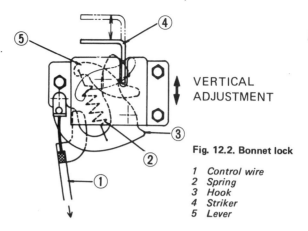

VERTICAL
ADJUSTMENT

Fig. 12.2. Bonnet lock

1   *Control wire*
2   *Spring*
3   *Hook*
4   *Striker*
5   *Lever*

the metal of the bodywork, repair is very simple. Lightly rub the area of the scratch with a paintwork renovator (eg; T-Cut), or a very fine cutting paste, to remove loose paint from the scratch and to clear the surrounding bodywork of wax polish. Rinse the area with clean water.

Apply touch-up paint to the scratch using a thin paint brush, continue to apply thin layers of paint until the surface of the paint in the scratch is level with the surrounding paintwork. Allow the new paint at least two weeks to harden; then, blend it into the surrounding paintwork by rubbing the paintwork, in the scratch area with a paintwork renovator (eg; T-Cut), or a very fine cutting paste. Finally apply wax polish.

An alternative to painting over the scratch is to use Holts "Scratch-Patch". Use the same preparation for the affected area; then simply pick a patch of a suitable size to cover the scratch completely. Hold the patch against the scratch and burnish its backing paper; the patch will adhere to the paintwork, freeing itself from the backing paper at the same time. Polish the affected area to blend the patch into the surrounding paintwork. Where the scratch has penetrated right through to the metal of the bodywork, causing the metal to rust, a different repair technique is required. Remove any loose rust from the bottom of the scratch with a penknife, then apply rust inhibiting paint (eg; Kurust) to prevent the formation of rust in the future. Using a rubber or nylon applicator fill the scratch with bodystopper paste. If required, this paste can be mixed with cellulose thinners to provide a very thin paste which is ideal for filling narrow scratches. Before the stopper-paste in the scratch hardens, wrap a piece of smooth cotton rag around the top of a finger. Dip the finger in cellulose thinners and then quickly sweep it across the surface of the stopper-paste in the scratch; this will ensure that the surface of the stopper-paste is slightly hollowed. The scratch can now be painted over as described earlier in this Section.

Repair of dents in the car's bodywork

When deep denting of the car's bodywork has taken place, the first task is to pull the dent out, until the affected bodywork almost attains its original shape. There is little point in trying to restore the original shape completely, as the metal in the damaged area will have stretched on impact and cannot be reshaped fully to its original contour. It is better to bring the level of the dent up to a point which is about 1/8 inch (3 mm) below the level of the surrounding bodywork. In cases where the dent is very shallow anyway, it is not worth trying to pull it out at all.

If the underside of the dent is accessible, it can be hammered out gently from behind, using a mallet with a wooden or plastic head. Whilst doing this, hold a suitable block of wood firmly against the impact from the hammer blows and thus prevent a large area of bodywork from being 'belled-out'.

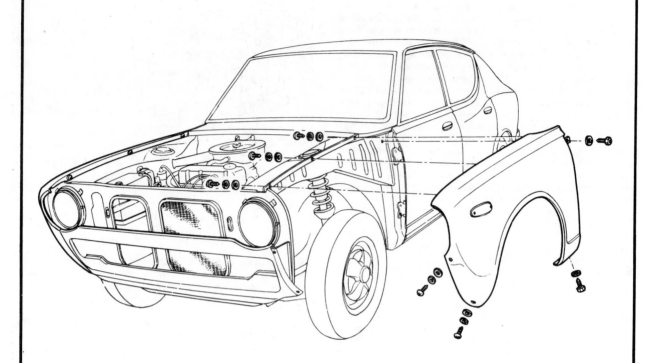

Fig. 12.3. Wing attachment points

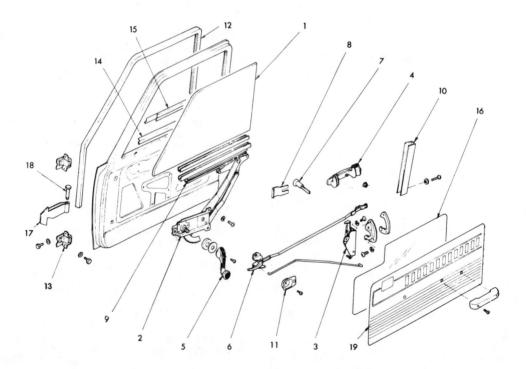

Fig. 12.4. Front door components

1	Door window glass	5 Regulator handle	10 Rear door sash	15 Outside weatherstrip
2	Door window regulator assembly	6 Inside handle	11 Inside remote cover	16 Door screen
3	Door lock assembly	7 Key cylinder	12 Sealing rubber	17 Door stopper
4	Door outside handle	8 Clip	13 Door hinge	18 Stopper pin
		9 Glass holder	14 Inside weatherstrip	

Should the dent be in a section of the bodywork which has a double skin or some other factor making it inaccessible from behind, a different technique is called for. Drill several small holes through the metal inside the dent area - particularly in the deeper sections. Then screw long self-tapping screws into the holes just sufficiently for them to gain a good purchase in the metal. Now the dent can be pulled out by pulling on the protruding heads of the screws with a pair of pliers.

The next stage of the repair is the removal of the paint from the damaged area, and from an inch or so of the surrounding 'sound' bodywork. This is accomplished most easily by using a wire brush or abrasive pad on a power drill, although it can be done just as effectively by hand using sheets of abrasive paper. To complete the preparations for filling, score the surface of the bare metal with a screwdriver or the tang of a file, or alternatively, drill small holes in the affected area. This will provide a really good 'key' for the filler paste.

To complete the repair see the Section on filling and respraying.

Repair of rust holes or gashes in the car's bodywork

Remove all paint from the affected area and from an inch or so of the surrounding 'sound' bodywork, using an abrasive pad or a wire brush on a power drill. If these are not available a few sheets of abrasive paper will do the job just as effectively. With the paint removed you will be able to gauge the severity of the corrosion and therefore decide whether to replace the whole panel (if this is possible) or to repair the affected area. Replacement body panels are not as expensive as most people think and it is often quicker and more satisfactory to fit a new panel than to attempt to repair large areas of corrosion.

Remove all fittings from the affected area except those which will act as a guide to the original shape of the damaged bodywork (eg; headlamp shells etc.,). Then, using tin snips or a hacksaw blade, remove all loose metal and any other metal badly affected by corrosion. Hammer the edges of the hole inwards in order to create a slight depression for the filler paste.

Wire brush the affected area to remove the powdery rust from the surface of the remaining metal. Paint the affected area with rust inhibiting paint (eg; Kurust); if the back of the rusted area is accessible treat this also.

Before filling can take place it will be necessary to block the hole in some way. This can be achieved by the use of one of the following materials: Zinc gauze, Aluminium tape or Polyurethane foam.

Zinc gauze is probably the best material to use for a large hole. Cut a piece to the approximate size and shape of the hole to be filled, then position it in the hole so that its edges are below the level of the surrounding bodywork. It can be retained in position by several blobs of filler paste around its periphery.

Aluminium tape should be used for small or very narrow holes. Pull a piece off the roll and trim it to the approximate size and shape required, then pull off the backing paper (if used) and stick the tape over the hole; it can be overlapped if the thickness of one piece is insufficient. Burnish down the edges of the tape with the handle of a screwdriver or similar, to ensure that the tape is securely attached to the metal underneath.

Polyurethane foam is best used where the hole is situated in a section of bodywork of complex shape, backed by a small box section (eg; where the sill panel meets the rear wheel arch - most cars). The unusual mixing procedure for this foam is as follows: Put equal amounts of fluid from each of the two cans provided in the kit, into one container. Stir until the mixture begins to thicken, then quickly pour this mixture into the hole, and hold a piece of cardboard over the larger apertures. Almost immediately the polyurethane will begin to expand, gushing out of any small holes left unblocked. When the foam hardens it can be cut back to just below the level of the surrounding bodywork with a hacksaw blade.

Bodywork repairs - filling and re-spraying

Before using this Section, see the Sections on dent, deep scratch, rust hole, and gash repairs.

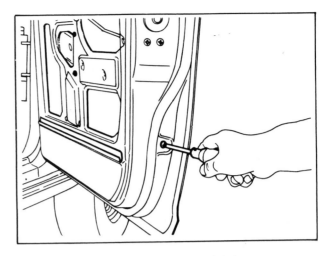

Fig. 12.5. Removing lower sash bolts

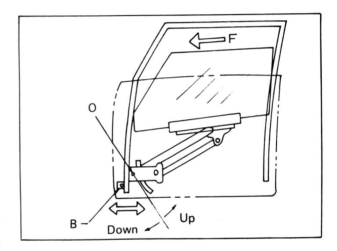

Fig. 12.6. Adjusting the door glass position

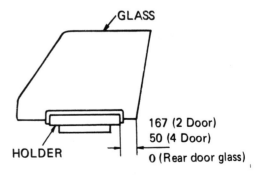

GLASS

HOLDER

167 (2 Door)
50 (4 Door)
0 (Rear door glass)

Fig. 12.7. Correct position of glass holder

Many types of bodyfiller are available, but generally speaking those proprietary kits which contain a tin of filler paste and a tube of resin hardener (eg; Holts Cataloy) are best for this type of repair. A wide, flexible plastic or nylon applicator will be found invaluable for imparting a smooth and well contoured finish to the surface of the filler.

Mix up a little filler on a clean piece of card or board - use the hardener sparingly (follow the maker's instructions on the packet) otherwise the filler will set very rapidly.

Using the applicator, apply the filler paste to the prepared area; draw the applicator across the surface of the filler to achieve the correct contour and to level the filler surface. As soon as a contour that approximates the correct one is achieved, stop working the paste - if you carry on too long the paste will become sticky and begin to 'pick-up' on the applicator. Continue to add thin layers of filler paste at twenty-minute intervals until the level of the filler is just 'proud' of the surrounding body-work.

Once the filler has hardened, excess can be removed using a Surform plane or Dreadnought file. From then on, progressively finer grades of abrasive paper should be used, starting with a 40 grade production paper and finishing with 400 grade 'wet-and-dry' paper. Always wrap the abrasive paper around a flat rubber, cork, or wooden block - otherwise the surface of the filler will not be completely flat. During the smoothing of the filler surface the 'wet-and-dry' paper should be periodically rinsed in water. This will ensure that a very smooth finish is imparted to the filler at the final stage.

At this stage the 'dent' should be surrounded by a ring of bare metal, which in turn should be encircled by the finely 'feathered' edge of the good paintwork. Rinse the repair area with clean water, until all of the dust produced by the rubbing-down operation is gone.

Spray the whole repair area with a light coat of grey primer - this will show up any imperfections in the surface of the filler. Repair these imperfections with fresh filler paste or bodystopper, and once more smooth the surface with abrasive paper. If bodystopper is used, it can be mixed with cellulose thinners to form a really thin paste which is ideal for filling small holes. Repeat this spray and repair procedure until you are satisfied that the surface of the filler, and the feathered edge of the paintwork are perfect. Clean the repair area with clean water and allow to dry fully.

The repair area is now ready for spraying. Paint spraying must be carried out in a warm, dry, windless and dust free atmosphere. This condition can be created artificially if you have access to a large indoor working area, but if you are forced to work in the open, you will have to pick your day very carefully. If you are working indoors, dousing the floor in the work area with water will 'lay' the dust which would otherwise be in the atmosphere. If the repair area is confined to one body panel, mask off the surrounding panels; this will help to minimise the effects of a slight mis-match in paint colours. Bodywork fittings (eg; chrome strips, door handles etc.,) will also need to be masked off. Use genuine masking tape and several thicknesses of newspaper for the masking operation.

Before commencing to spray, agitate the aerosol can thoroughly, then spray a test area (an old tin, or similar) until the technique is mastered. Cover the repair area with a thick coat of primer; the thickness should be built up using several thin layers of paint rather than one thick one. Using 400 grade 'wet-and-dry' paper, rub down the surface of the primer until it is really smooth. While doing this the work area should be thoroughly doused with water, and the 'wet-and-dry' paper periodically rinsed in water. Allow to dry before spraying on more paint.

Spray on the top coat, again building up the thickness by using several thin layers of paint. Start spraying in the centre of the repair area and then, using a circular motion, work outwards until the whole repair area and about 2 inches of the surrounding original paintwork is covered. Remove all masking material 10 to 15 minutes after spraying on the final coat of paint.

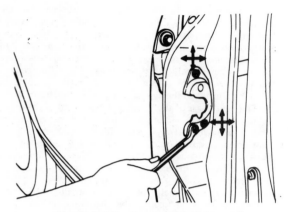

Fig. 12.8. Adjusting position of door striker

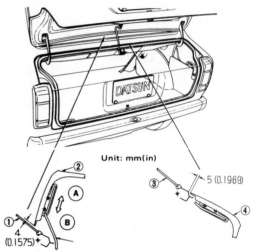

Unit: mm(in)

Fig. 12.9. Boot clearance details - Saloon

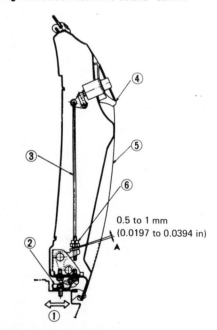

0.5 to 1 mm
(0.0197 to 0.0394 in)

Fig. 12.10. Rear door lock - Estate

1   Fore-aft adjustment   4   Handle
2   Striker   5   Back door outer panel
3   Rod   6   Nylon nut

Allow the new paint at least 2 weeks to harden fully; then, using a paintwork renovator (eg; T-Cut) or a very fine cutting paste, blend the edges of the new paint into the existing paintwork. Finally, apply wax polish.

5 Major body repairs

Where serious damage has occurred or large areas need renewal due to neglect, it means certainly that completely new sections or panels will need welding in and this is best left to professionals. If the damage is due to impact it will also be necessary to completely check the alignment of the bodyshell structure. Due to the principle of construction the strength the shape of the whole can be affected by damage to a part. In such instances the services of a Datsun agent with specialist checking jigs are essential. If a body is left misaligned it is first of all dangerous as the car will not handle properly and secondly uneven stresses will be imposed on the steering, engine and transmission, causing abnormal wear or complete failure. Tyre wear may also be excessive.

6 Maintenance - hinges and locks

1 Oil the hinges of the bonnet, boot and doors with a drop or two of light oil periodically. A good time is after the car has been washed.
2 Oil the bonnet release catch pivot pin and the safety catch pivot pin periodically.
3 Do not over lubricate door latches and strikers. Normally a little oil on the rotary cam spindle alone is sufficient.

7 Doors - tracing rattles and their rectification

1 Check first that the door is not loose at the hinges and that the latch is holding the door firmly in position. Check also that the door lines up with the aperture in the body.
2 If the hinges are loose or the door is out of alignment it will be necessary to reset the hinge positions, as described in Section 13.
3 If the latch is holding the door properly it should hold the door tightly when fully latched and the door should line up with the body. If it is out of alignment is needs adjustment as described in Section 13. If loose, some part of the lock mechanism must be worn out and requiring renewal.
4 Other rattles from the door would be caused by wear or looseness in the window winder, the glass channels and sill strips or the door buttons and interior latch release mechanism. All these are dealt with in Sections 12 and 13.

8 Front wing - removal and replacement

1 Jack-up the front of the vehicle and secure with stands or blocks placed under the bodyframe sidemembers. Remove the roadwheel.
2 Disconnect the cable from the battery negative terminal.
3 Disconnect the headlamp electrical connections and the side direction indicator repeaters.
4 Remove the front bumper, the radiator grille and the headlamp embellisher.
5 Prise off the side moulding from its body clip holes.
6 Unscrew and remove the wing securing nuts from inside the engine compartment the front and rear edges of the wing, and the front pillar.
7 Break the sealant at the wing joints using a sharp knife if necessary.
8 Clean the wing mating joints on the body and apply a bead of fresh sealant. Refit in the reverse manner to removal.
9 Apply an underbody protective coating to the surface under the wing and have the outer surface re-sprayed to match the vehicle's original colour.

9 Windscreen glass - removal and replacement

1 Where a windscreen is to be replaced then if it is due to shattering, the facia air vents should be covered before attempting removal. Adhesive sheeting is useful to stick to the outside of the glass to enable large areas of crystallised glass to be removed.
2 Where the screen is to be removed intact then an assistant will be required. First release the rubber surround from the bodywork by running a blunt, small screwdriver around and under the rubber weatherstrip both inside and outside the car. This operation will break the adhesive of the sealer originally used. Take care not to damage the paintwork or cut the rubber surround with the screwdriver. Remove the windscreen wiper arms and interior mirror and place a protective cover on the bonnet.
3 Have your assistant push the inner lip of the rubber surround off the flange of the windscreen body aperture. Once the rubber surround starts to peel off the flange, the screen may be forced gently outwards by careful hand pressure. The second person should support and remove the screen complete with rubber surround and metal beading as it comes out.
4 Remove the beading from the rubber surround.
5 Before fitting a windscreen, ensure that the rubber surround is completely free from old sealant, glass fragments and has not hardened or cracked. Fit the rubber surround to the glass and apply a bead of suitable sealant between the glass outer edge and the rubber.
6 Refit the bright moulding to the rubber surround.
7 Cut a piece of strong cord greater in length than the periphery of the glass and insert it into the body flange locating channel of the rubber surround.
8 Apply a thin bead of sealant to the face of the rubber channel which will eventually mate with the body.
9 Offer the windscreen to the body aperture and pass the ends of the cord, previously fitted and located at bottom centre into the vehicle interior.
10 Press the windscreen into place, at the same time have an assistant pulling the cords to engage the lip of the rubber channel over the body flange.
11 Remove any excess sealant with a paraffin soaked rag.

10 Front door lock - removal, refitting and adjustment

1 Wind the window to the fully closed position and remove the retaining screw from the window regulator. Remove the regulator handle.
2 Remove the single screw that secures the interior lock handle escutcheon.
3 Unscrew and remove the door pull retaining screws and detach the door pull.
4 Insert a broad bladed screwdriver under one corner of the door trim panel and prise the trim retaining clip from the door frame. Now insert the fingers between the trim and the door frame and working round the panel pull all the retaining clips out of engagement. Remove the trim panel sideways so that the interior lock handle passes through the aperture in the escutcheon plate. Remove the sealing panel taking care not to tear it excessively.
5 Remove the screw that retains the lower sash and remove the nun channel from the sash.
6 Remove the two screws from the interior lock handle and the two screws which secure the lock assembly to the door edge and withdraw the lock mechanism complete with remote control rod through the door aperture. The exterior door lock cylinder may be removed after releasing the retaining clip from within the door cavity and the exterior door release handle after removal of the securing screws and clips.
7 If the lock mechanism is worn, do not attempt to dismantle or repair it but renew the assembly complete.

This sequence of photographs deals with the repair of the dent and paintwork damage shown in this photo. The procedure will be similar for the repair of a hole. It should be noted that the procedures given here are simplified — more explicit instructions will be found in the text

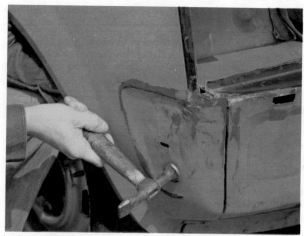

In the case of a dent the first job — after removing surrounding trim — is to hammer out the dent where access is possible. This will minimise filling. Here, the large dent having been hammered out, the damaged area is being made slightly concave

Now all paint must be removed from the damaged area, by rubbing with coarse abrasive paper. Alternatively, a wire brush or abrasive pad can be used in a power drill. Where the repair area meets good paintwork, the edge of the paintwork should be 'feathered', using a finer grade of abrasive paper

In the case of a hole caused by rusting, all damaged sheet-metal should be cut away before proceeding to this stage. Here, the damaged area is being treated with rust remover and inhibitor before being filled

Mix the body filler according to its manufacturer's instructions. In the case of corrosion damage, it will be necessary to block off any large holes before filling — this can be done with aluminium or plastic mesh, or aluminium tape. Make sure the area is absolutely clean before ...

... applying the filler. Filler should be applied with a flexible applicator, as shown, for best results; the wooden spatula being used for confined areas. Apply thin layers of filler at 20-minute intervals, until the surface of the filler is slightly proud of the surrounding bodywork

Initial shaping can be done with a Surform plane or Dreadnought file. Then, using progressively finer grades of wet-and-dry paper, wrapped around a sanding block, and copious amounts of clean water, rub down the filler until really smooth and flat. Again, feather the edges of adjoining paintwork

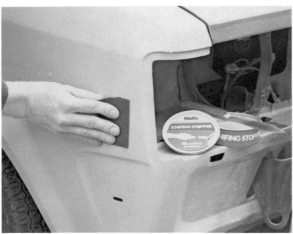

Again, using plenty of water, rub down the primer with a fine grade wet-and-dry paper (400 grade is probably best) until it is really smooth and well blended into the surrounding paintwork. Any remaining imperfections can now be filled by carefully applied knifing stopper paste

The top coat can now be applied. When working out of doors, pick a dry, warm and wind-free day. Ensure surrounding areas are protected from over-spray. Agitate the aerosol thoroughly, then spray the centre of the repair area, working outwards with a circular motion. Apply the paint as several thin coats

The whole repair area can now be sprayed or brush-painted with primer. If spraying, ensure adjoining areas are protected from over-spray. Note that at least one inch of the surrounding sound paintwork should be coated with primer. Primer has a 'thick' consistency, so will find small imperfections

When the stopper has hardened, rub down the repair area again before applying the final coat of primer. Before rubbing down this last coat of primer, ensure the repair area is blemish-free – use more stopper if necessary. To ensure that the surface of the primer is really smooth use some finishing compound

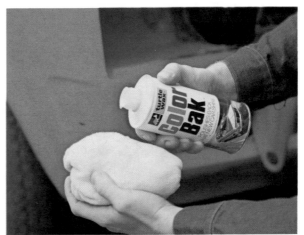

After a period of about two weeks, which the paint needs to harden fully, the surface of the repaired area can be 'cut' with a mild cutting compound prior to wax polishing. When carrying out bodywork repairs, remember that the quality of the finished job is proportional to the time and effort expended

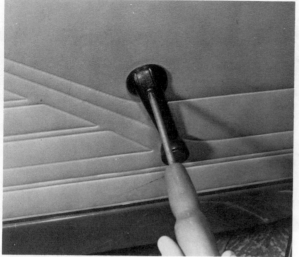
10.1 Removing the regulator handle

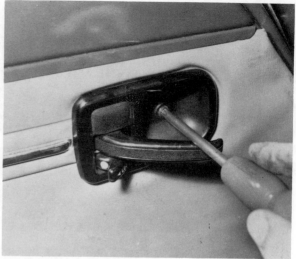
10.2 Removing the interior handle cover

10.3 Removing the door pull screws

10.6 Interior lock handle

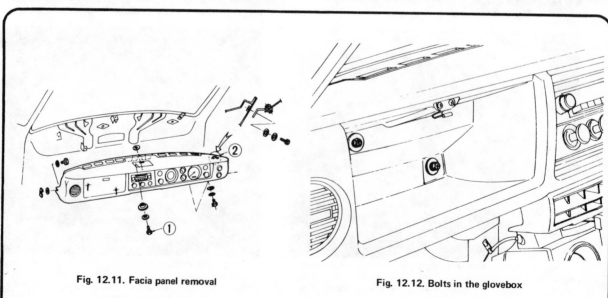

Fig. 12.11. Facia panel removal

Fig. 12.12. Bolts in the glovebox

8 Refitting is a reversal of removal but, with the door fully locked, bring the remote control rod into contact with the locking knob.

11 Rear door lock - removal, refitting and adjustment

1 The procedure for the removal of the front door lock described in the preceding Section will generally apply except that no exterior cylinder lock is fitted.
2 A door sash is not fitted on the rear door; therefore this instruction in the preceding Section can also be ignored.
3 Armrests are secured by two self-tapping screws located at their base.
4 Refitting is similar to that described for front door locks.

12 Winding windows - removal and refitting

1 Remove the interior door trim and controls as described in Section 10.
2 Remove the glass stop and bracket from the bottom of the door cavity and by temporarily refitting the window regulator handle, wind the glass down to its fullest extent so that the roller on the end of the winder arm is detached from the window channel.
3 Pull the window glass up and out of the door cavity.
4 Unscrew and remove the three screws which secure the window regulator assembly to the door and remove it through the door aperture.
5 Refitting is a reversal of removal but adjust the lower ends of the window side channels so that the glass slides easily without any sideways movement. This is most easily done by adjusting screw 'B' in Fig. 12.6, so that play is held within 0.039 to 0.118 in. (1.0 to 3.0 mm).

13 Doors - removal, refitting and adjustment

1 Although the doors may be removed by unscrewing the hinge plates from their edges, it is recommended that the doors are removed complete with hinges by unbolting the hinges from the bodypillars.
2 Whichever method is used, first mark round the hinges for ease of refitting.
3 Remove the metal guard on the door step and peel off the side trim from inside the vehicle where it covers the access to the hinge bolts.
4 Remove the pin from the door stop then support the bottom of the door on jacks or blocks and unscrew and remove the hinge bolts from the door pillars and lift the doors away.
5 If the original doors and hinges are refitted, locate them in previously marked positions. If new hinges or doors are used, then do not fully tighten the hinge bolts until the correct hanging of the door has been checked. Ensure that the gap all round the door is even and of consistent width, otherwise adjust the hinge plate position on either the door edge or pillar. Finally tighten the hinge bolts to a torque of 12 lb/ft (1.65 kg/m).
hinge bolts to a torque of 12 lb/ft (1.65 kg/m).
6 Check the closure of the door and adjust the pillar striker plate if necessary, by loosening the three securing screws. Replace the door stopper pin.

14 Bonnet and boot lid - hinge and lock adjustment

1 The bonnet lid is hinged at the front and may be adjusted if necessary by loosening the retaining bolts and utilising the movement provided by the elongated hinge bolt holes. Vertical adjustment is by the body hinge holes and fore-and-aft by the bonnet hinge holes. An assistant will be required to remove the bonnet lid for major engine overhaul.
2 The bonnet lock is controlled by a lever and cable located

12.1 Ready to remove the window regulator

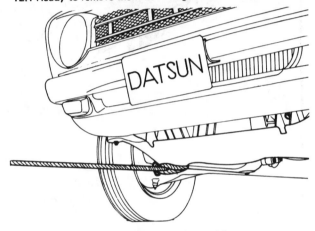

Fig. 12.13. Front towing position

within the vehicle.
3 Adjustment of the lock is correct when the bonnet lid striker engages centrally with the female section of the lock. Sideways adjustment of both units is made by slackening the lock securing bolts.
4 The bonnet lid should lock positively without excessive pressure being required and at the same time prevent rattle when closed.
5 The boot lid can be adjusted in the same manner as the bonnet. The important thing is to check the clearances detailed in Figure 12.9 and adjust the hinge and stay rail positions if necessary.
6 The boot lid or tailgate used on estate car versions are all counterbalanced with torsion rods. If the boot lid or tailgate is to be removed, first mark the position of the hinges and release the tension of the torsion rods using a lever or adjustable wrench as the hinge bolts are withdrawn.
7 The striker plate of the lock mechanism is adjustable after loosening the securing screws. Estate car versions should be adjusted in accordance with Figure 12.10 if the lock mechanism is not working correctly.

15 Facia panel - removal and refitting

1 The instrument panel may be removed from the facia panel as described in Chapter 10 or the facia panel removed complete with instrument panel as described in this Section.
2 Disconnect the lead from the battery negative terminal.
3 Disconnect all the multi-pin connectors at the rear of the

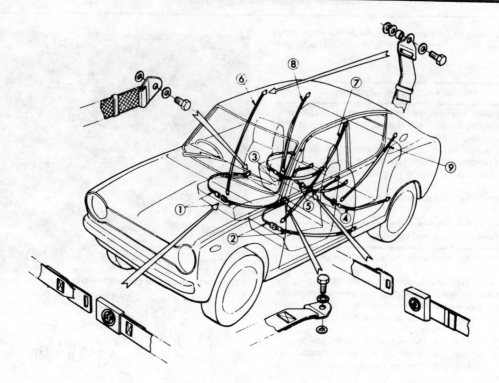

Fig. 12.14. Seat belt attachments

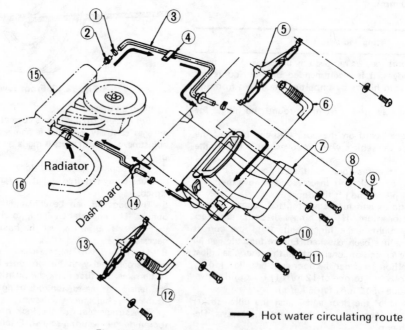

→ Hot water circulating route

Fig. 12.15. Heater installation details

Radiator

Dash board

1 Heater hose clip (4 clips)
2 Heater hose connector
3 Heater hose
4 Heater hose clamp
5 Defroster nozzle (right)
6 Defroster hose (right)
7 Heater unit
8 Washer (4 washers)

9   Nozzle attaching screw (4 screws)
10 Washer (4 washers)
11 Heater unit attaching screw (4 screws)
12 Defroster hose (left)
13 Defroster nozzle (left)
14 Grommet (2 each)
15 Engine
16 Heater inlet tube. Plugged with cover when heater
    is not fitted

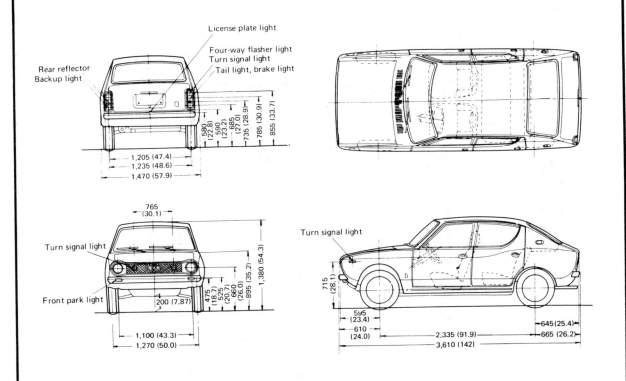

Fig. 12.16. Body dimensions - 100A 4-door Saloon

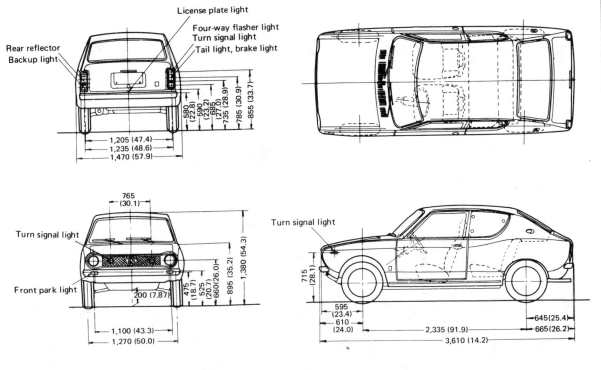

Fig. 12.17. Body dimensions - 100A 2-door Saloon

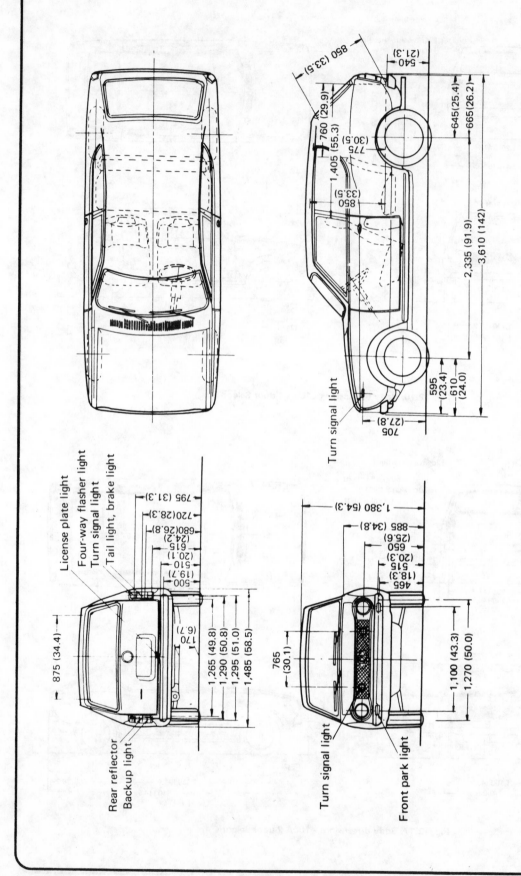

License plate light
Four-way flasher light
Turn signal light
Tail light, brake light

Rear reflector
Backup light

Turn signal light

Front park light

Turn signal light

Fig. 12.18. Body dimensions - 100A Estate car

facia panel, also the speedometer cable from the speedometer head and the heater control cable. Disconnect the choke cable.

4 Take out the ash tray and remove bolts (1) and (2) indicated in Fig. 12.11.

5 Remove the steering column clamp bolts and the remaining facia panel bolts, including those inside the glovebox. The bolts at the sides of the facia panel only need be loosened enough to prise out the edge of the panel. (Fig. 12.12).

6 Withdraw the facia panel forward and remove towards the passenger side to clear the steering wheel, ensuring that all electrical leads and control cables are disconnected.

7 Refitting is a reversal of removal.

16 The safety belts

1 Arrangement of the front seat safety belts and their locating points are shown in Fig. 12.14. No alteration should be made to the fixing point positions as the original anchorages are especially strengthened.

2 The belts which are made from synthetic fibre should be cleaned in a warm detergent solution only.

3 Periodically inspect the belts for wear or chafing and renew if necessary. The belts should also be renewed when they have been subjected to accident impact shock of severe proportions.

4 When fitting new belts, ensure that the fixing point attachment bolt assembly is correctly made.

17 Heater and ventilation system - general description

1 The heater system delivers fresh air to the windscreen for demisting purposes and to the car interior. The flow to each may be varied in respect of volume and temperature by the two facia mounted controls. A flow-through fresh air ventilation system is fitted which delivers unheated air through the two facia mounted controllable ducts and exhausts the stale air through the flap valves at the rear of the rear side windows.

2 The heater assembly comprises a matrix heated by water from the engine cooling system and a booster fan controlled by a two-position switch. During normal forward motion of the car, air is forced through the air intake just forward of the windscreen and passes through the heater matrix absorbing heat and carrying it to the car interior. When the car is stationary or travelling at low speed then the booster fan may be actuated.

18 Heater removal and refitting

1 Drain the cooling system (Chapter 2) ensuring that the heater controls are set to the full heat (H) position.

2 Disconnect the two heater hoses at the engine rear bulkhead.

3 Remove the facia panel. (Section 15).

4 Disconnect all electrical leads from the heater motor and control switch and the rods which connect the control levers to the heater assembly.

5 Pull off the two windscreen demister hoses and then remove the four heater securing screws and withdraw the heater unit, taking care not to damage the matrix or to spill coolant in the vehicle interior.

6 If required, the demister nozzles, the heater control lever assembly and the scuttle grille may be removed after withdrawal of their retaining screws.

7 Refitting is a reversal of removal. Always refill the cooling system slowly with the heater controls full on.

19 Heater - inspection and servicing

1 The heater unit is simple and provided the electrical switches and wiring are securely connected, any fault must lie in the matrix or the booster motor.

2 If the heater fails to warm up, check the setting of the control levers and the control valve and ensure that the latter is passing coolant by pulling off the heater connecting hose for a moment with the engine running.

3 Reverse flush the heater matrix with a cold water hose (the heater need not be removed from vehicle) but if the unit is clogged do not use chemical cleaners but renew it.

4 If the heater matrix is leaking, do not attempt to repair it yourself but renew the unit.

5 Failure of the booster motor may be due to faulty brushes, or even a fuse blown, and these should be checked, otherwise remove the heater unit from the vehicle, dismantle the motor and refit a new one.

6 It should be remembered that the efficiency of the heater is largely dependent upon the engine cooling system and failure of the heater may be due to a defective thermostat or water pump or to air trapped in the heater pipes or matrix.

20 Body leaks and their rectification

1 The nuisance of water entering the interior of the car or the luggage boot can usually be overcome by proper attention to the windscreen seal and the rubber sealing of doors. A suitable sealant may be squeezed between the glass of the screen and the rubber surround and between the rubber and the body. The windscreen may be left in position during the operation and should be bright moulding become detached, it can be refitted with the use of a small screweriver.Seelastik (black) is suitable for the sealing process and where a pressure gun is not available, then the small tubes available from most shops can have the nozzles pressed into a flattened spout to facilitate entry behind the rubber screen seal. Paraffin or white spirit, generously applied will clean off any surplus sealant and impart a smooth finish to the seal.

2 Inspection of rubber grommets used in floor holes and to seal cables and controls entering from the engine compartment, should be regularly carried out and renewal implemented where necessary.

Index

Printed by
J H Haynes & Co Ltd
Sparkford Nr Yeovil
Somerset BA22 7JJ England